INTO THE MAIN STREAM

RACE RELATIONS DIVISION
AMERICAN MISSIONARY ASSOCIATION

Into the Main Stream

A SURVEY OF BEST PRACTICES IN RACE RELATIONS IN THE SOUTH

by

CHARLES S. JOHNSON

and Associates

ELIZABETH L. ALLEN, HORACE M. BOND, MARGARET McCULLOCH,

ALMA FORREST POLK

THE UNIVERSITY OF NORTH CAROLINA PRESS

Chapel Hill · 1947

INTRODUCTION

WHEN MARGOT ASQUITH, a keen-witted British woman and wife of a Premier, visited the United States for the first time several years ago, she was asked the premature question which is often put by reporters to celebrities, but which can seldom be intelligently answered: "What do you think about America?" She had an answer that was not lacking in incisive wit, even if it did not tell the whole story. She said, in substance, that America's progress is ahead of its civilization.

With perhaps an equal measure of generalization, it might be said with respect to race relations that the civilization of the South is still somewhat ahead of its progress. For the American creed and the Christian ethic, which would normally be a sufficient basis for all our human relations, are, at least as philosophies, a vital part of the southern tradition. The problem is that there have not yet been found sufficient ways of implementing these common convictions.

It will be said immediately that if these are real convictions they will express themselves in action and that there is no need for programs and sermons to help in the task of building understanding. The truth is that the general character and persistence of the concern for improved relations are the best possible indications that race and race relations are on the minds and consciences of the people of the region and that no one is yet satisfied that a final formula has been found.

Over the years the South has progressively recognized an obligation in the field of education and has moved to the point where it has conceded the ideal of equalization of educational facilities. This was exemplified in the agreement of eleven southern governors that the number-one objective of southern states should be the "equalization of educational opportunities for all citizens of the South." One southern state and many cities have actually equalized salaries for white and Negro teachers and have put the problem aspect of adjusting an old discrepancy behind them. The *principle* of equalization has also been extended at points to include health, welfare, transportation, and recreation facilities; and a substantial number of forward-looking white Southerners acknowledge the right of Negroes to equality of employment opportunities on the basis of ability, to equal treatment by police and in the courts, and to suffrage. In *practice* this process of equalization makes only slow headway; but the recognition of the *principle* is a great advance over the situation twenty years ago when inequality, if not defended, was certainly not very strongly disavowed.

An important issue has grown up more or less parallel with that of improved facilities. It is the increasing insistence on the principle of separation. The line of demarcation has been drawn with growing rigidity by the white majority both in law and in practice; correspondingly, it has at times been somewhat intensified by Negroes who, more and more, as education has made them less able to fit into the superior-inferior pattern, have drawn the line as a means of spiritual and physical protection. In a world being drawn closer and becoming more interdependent it is obviously impossible to achieve any such ideal except perhaps in limited areas of one's personal or social life. "No one," to paraphrase John Donne's classic phrase, "can be an island unto himself."

This is, however, a disposition to rationalize the principle of segregation as something necessary and sacred, and to insist upon its full acceptance by Negroes as a condition to the execution of even the smallest social services. Mr. David Cohn has stated this policy very emphatically in an article in the *Atlantic Monthly:*

"No notable improvement of race relations can be achieved, in my opinion, unless the ground is cleared by a recognition on the part of both whites and Negroes that (a) the problem is incapable of solution, and (b) the issue of segregation must not be called into question. . . ."[1]

Strangely enough, it can be observed that, provided the ritual of

[1] *Atlantic Monthly,* January, 1944, p. 50.

public homage to the principle of segregation is performed, white Southerners seem less disturbed by incidental violations of it in practice. This can be seen in many working relationships throughout the South. What seems to be considered absolutely essential is that Negroes should join in the ritual too, by publicly and in so many words accepting separation of the races as a final solution of the problems of race relations in a democratic society. But this is the very thing that Negroes cannot do if they are to retain either their own self-respect or the respect of other Negroes; and without these they would have neither influence nor effectiveness. For the Negro to accept segregation and all of its implications as an ultimate solution would be to accept for all time a definition of himself as something less than his fellow man. This would be the case even if Negroes believed that it is possible to establish actual, practical equality of opportunity on the basis of segregation.

It may also be observed, however, that southern Negro leaders have shown themselves willing to work for the improvement of conditions within the framework of segregation, and that they have not on the whole pushed the issue embarrassingly, even in ways that are obviously possible. They have fought for the equalization of teachers' salaries and other educational expenditures, but they have not seriously pushed demands for the admission of Negroes into southern colleges which offer educational facilities, graduate and professional, not available at Negro institutions. They have worked instead to improve the Negro institutions. They have not brought more than casual pressure on the churches to fit their practices to the principles they profess, even though it is always difficult for the church to give moral reasons for excluding Negro Christians from a common fellowship. They have not embarrassed southern states and municipalities by continual suits in matters affecting transportation facilities, although it is clear that present conditions and daily occurrences afford a basis for prosecution of carriers and other agencies which, after all, receive public support in various forms and are clearly affected with a public interest. The suggestion of one Virginia editor that the present laws requiring separation of the races on all vehicles of public transportation in Virginia be abolished, and the actual passage of a bill to repeal such laws by one chamber of the Maryland legislature, arose less from Negro pressure than from the conviction that the present confusion was hampering transportation without effectively separating anyone. The kind of situations arising out of these laws and the problems which they present to drivers and passengers are illustrated by a paragraph from instructions issued by the vice-president of a southern bus company to all of the company's drivers:

"Look over your passengers before you start to load, in order to get some idea of the amount of space which will be needed for each race. Remember that most of the white passengers will usually board ahead of the colored, therefore it is up to you to make your space allocation before the bus becomes overloaded with white passengers.

"We realize that during war-time this business of segregation is a problem to you, but if you will carefully follow the above instructions, it should assist in accommodating the greatest number with the least friction."

Out of this sort of situation, incidents arise daily which afford a basis for Negroes to bring pressure which could be embarrassing, but they have shown considerable restraint about doing so. They have brought no pressure for admission to public recreational facilities available to whites, although they have only to look around them to see such situations as that in Atlanta, for example, where Negroes comprise 33 per cent of the population, but have access to only one per cent of the park space. They have not seriously asked for violation of the principle of separation, but they *have* seriously attacked inequalities such as these and are willing to work with all who wish to see them reduced. Yet progress appears to be more or less retarded because they will not and cannot say that they will never disturb the present policy of segregation. The result is a stalemate which must somehow be broken if we are to move forward together in the South— a forward movement which, incidentally, is just as important for the welfare of the white part of the population as for the Negro.

It appears, therefore, that a new basis of accommodation must be reached; that both groups should cease to demand what is for the present impossible, but undertake together programs of action in those areas where there *is* agreement—programs which offer Negroes better facilities, more equal opportunities, and a fuller participation in the obligations and privileges of citizenship.

There can be an honest recognition on the part of the white majority that they are compromising with democratic and Christian principles, and less shutting of the eyes on the part of the minority to actual social and cultural lags in the Negro population. Negroes in the South have shown that they can work constructively on many levels of cooperation without insisting first upon the total abandonment by their white collaborators of all the symbols which they revere—holding these to be personal for the whites, but not necessarily universal. Similarly it is true that numbers of white leaders who hold firm general views about segregation have actually relaxed the principle in their preoccupation with goals and values more important and vital than keeping people apart.

It has been felt by many observers that race relations in the South became a great deal worse during the recent war. This observation has been supported by the undeniable fact that racial tensions and incidents growing out of them increased greatly over the war period. It has been said, too, that Negroes have developed a "new belligerency," and this attitude has been attributed variously to the influence of northern Negroes, outside agitators, the New Deal, Communists, and various other unpopular symbols.

Actually, however, it is possible to view this undeniable increase in tension and in the expression by Negroes of protest against inequalities and discriminations as a symptom of social changes which may in the long run prove wholesome for the entire South. If the absence of tensions and protest is to be the only index of good race relations, then such relations are certainly not as good as they were. But such quiescence may also be a sign of immobility and unhealthy social stagnation. War conditions did not really make any fundamental change in the attitude of Negroes toward inadequate schools, denial of civil rights, and other forms of discrimination. That they should protest against these things became inevitable when the South first recognized its obligation to educate the Negro population. As education increasingly familiarized them with the American creed of democracy and equal opportunity and with the constitutional rights of citizens, they were bound to look about them and compare the theory with the practice, as far as they themselves were concerned. The only new elements that the war period introduced into this situation were to speed up the impact of new ideas upon the old, to make certain changes not only possible but necessary, and to create a climate of public opinion in which protest, long felt, could be more safely expressed. The fact that we fought a war in the name of democracy against enemies who glorify racial prejudice has of course sharpened the issue at home and disturbed the consciences of many Americans. War did not so much change the fundamental dilemmas of American race relations, or the respective viewpoints of the persons involved, as it brought them out into the open. And it is possible to regard this as an essentially wholesome development.

It has been suggested that the present tensions may be symptoms of social changes in process which may likewise prove wholesome in the long run. It was entirely natural that all kinds of tensions should be created by the movement of masses of people from isolated rural areas to centers of production and population, by the military training of thousands of Negro soldiers from the North in the neighborhood of southern communities, by the exodus of Negro domestics from southern households, and by their entrance into new industrial occupations. But there are indications of constructive forces at work in the total situation.

In spite of the tensions, threats, abuses, and limitations of the racial system, large-scale racial violence seldom occurred, although the frictions and antagonisms threaten to continue indefinitely. As a matter of fact, recent months have shown a decline in the number of incidents sufficiently important to be reported nationally. Situations arising out of the congestion on public modes of transportation, police handling of Negro suspects, and conflicts involving Negro soldiers and white civilians or soldiers were the principal causes of open violence.

Some of the favorable elements in the situation are the following:

1. The pressure of population over the long run was relaxed by the migration of both whites and Negroes to the North and West.

2. Constant advances in education are changing the character of race relations by gradually improving the conditions of both groups.

3. The increased industrialization and unionization of the region has been augmenting the number and character of natural contacts between whites and Negroes in the most numerous population class. The necessities for labor and class solidarity have shown themselves vital enough to overcome many racial customs and traditions.

4. As has already been said, many white Southerners, while struggling with a dilemma for which there appears to be no solution both acceptable and consistent with American democratic beliefs, have shown themselves ready to work with Negro Southerners for the removal of particular discriminations or for the establishment of better facilities, and these instances of cooperation have brought better understanding in certain areas.

5. The more forward-looking southern political leaders and statesmen are increasingly aware that many of the problems of the South are not racial but economic, geographical, and social. They are showing a new willingness to work for the general improvement of conditions in the area which includes whites and Negroes alike. They are recognizing that change is inevitable, and they are going forward to meet it. An outstanding example is the action of the Georgia legislature, under the leadership of Governor Arnall, in repealing the poll tax with almost startling suddenness. But there are many other examples.

6. Southern colleges and universities are contributing to a more objective approach to race relations, as well as to the general problems of the southern region, by establishing course programs and study projects in these fields; and as a result of this and related factors, more southern people are showing a disposition to question old traditions and to try out new approaches.

At the present moment the whole question of race relations is intimately linked up with the problems of postwar adjustment and the course of American and world development. We can chart the constructive and disruptive forces now at work, but we cannot know which will prevail without knowing whether postwar America will be able to provide a reasonably adequate number of jobs and a reasonable standard of living for the whole population. Predictions as to the effect on race relations of the return of white and Negro southern servicemen varied from gloomy mutterings that "blood will flow" to the statement by a retiring governor of North Carolina that "men who come back from the war, white and colored, are going to have an even better desire to work these things out." There is at least a recognition on the part of southern leaders that demobilization, reconversion, and their attendant problems require careful planning and prompt, constructive action.

This survey of better practices in race relations is intended to serve a very practical purpose. It is limited to the South, where both custom and law make social changes difficult even in practices regarded as undesirable and outmoded. The fear of disturbing the controls of the racial system frequently places restraints upon progressive action in racial matters of any sort. Always there are in every locality a few well-meaning humanitarians willing to do something, but action carries a responsibility that only the stoutest hearts can sustain for long. For if such persons have little influence in the community, their efforts are likely to be of little avail, and they are soon overcome by their own frustrations. If they are persons of influence, there are limits beyond which they cannot go without jeopardizing this influence, at least with their local public. If they persist, they are likely to be held responsible for any disturbance in the racial scene, whether actual, fancied, or feared. That is undoubtedly why it so often happens that the intellectual liberals who know what should be done are torn between their private convictions and their public caution, and the most forthright declarations of the need for change are made by persons who are estimated by the community to have so little weight as to be innocuous.

There are at least two notable exceptions to this general observation. There are a few white leaders of prestige and influence who have the courage to propose and support bold, forward-looking democratic programs, and who are secure enough in the esteem of moral leaders throughout the nation to be indifferent to local criticisms and fears of going too far. There are also some who, by virtue of their persistent and uninhibited humanitarianism, are regarded as merely eccentric on the question of race. Indeed, there is some evidence that these eccentric spokesmen for the moral values are tolerated locally as undisturbing "conscience vents" on matters on which it is not regarded as expedient for the community generally to have forceful moral views. They are tolerated as long as they are estimated to be harmless.

In spite of these various limitations on leadership, many encouraging things are actually happening in the South that are little known because constructive incidents and programs are usually less dramatic and newsworthy than conflict situations or noisy racist demagoguery. They are not all happening in the same community or always in the same way in different communities. In most instances the incidents or programs that are in operation in one locality are elsewhere assumed to be impossible or untimely or inexpedient for the South. They are so regarded because it is simply not known that they have been demonstrated as possible and actually beneficial in the region.

The experiences recorded here provide evidence of these patterns and values and help to define good practice in race relations on the best level demonstrated as attainable. If common practice can thus be raised to these moderate goals, there will be measurable gains for the fundamental democracy that the southern region, along with the rest of the nation, respects.

This survey represents the work of many persons. Some seven hundred or more individuals over the South, recognized as responsible and informed, cooperated with the project by providing special material, by developing reports, by interviewing in certain communities, and by calling to the attention of the Race Relations staff notable programs and individuals whose work should be further studied. Field trips were made by three staff members between March and December, 1943. The responsibility for following up hundreds of the items drawn in, as well as for collecting, abstracting, and collating a large part of the material, fell to Miss Margaret McCulloch, whose careful work provides the main structure of this volume.

These reports are given when possible in the actual words of the reporters, and when that is not possible, as close to them as could be managed with necessary condensations. In view of the responsible and authoritative nature of the persons reporting, most of the documents are thus used practically as received. Only in a few cases, where some inaccuracy of observation or interpretation seemed apparent, was it felt necessary to check or to modify the statements made. It is thus the South itself, rather than a commentator, that speaks through the book.

In evidence of the dynamic character of the situation, it can be noted that there have been further changes in practically every field since the closing of the field visits and the compilation of the text. These changes continue both in number and in significance, but an arbitrary period had to be set beyond which no further general coverage would be attempted.

Even a casual reading of this volume will reveal the fact that all the items are set on the credit side of the ledger. Such is one of the fundamental purposes of the book; namely, to present a selected number of activities, events, and programs which are not intended to give a complete picture of race relations in the South, but to show some of the "better practices." The totality of these incidents and programs undoubtedly suggests progress and a will to change, both of which have been accelerated by the war. It is by no means as yet an ideal situation, but also it clearly is not static. "If you know well the beginning," says an African proverb, "the end will not trouble you much."

CHARLES S. JOHNSON, *Director*
Race Relations Division
American Missionary Association

CONTENTS

INTO THE MAIN STREAM

CHAPTER I

CITIZENSHIP

CITIZENS AND THE COMMUNITY

WISE MEN AND WOMEN in every country in recent years have called upon their fellow men to recognize that this has become "one world"; that what happens to any of us is important to all of us, and that the "white peoples" and the "colored peoples" are fellow citizens in the world community. Our alliance with China, the full citizenship of all races in our allied nation, the Soviet Union, the rise of strong and able leadership in India are all contributing to this same recognition. More and more we are realizing that in world community, in national community, or in local community we shall build soundly only when all citizens participate.

This world-wide recognition is reflected in the national scene. Fresh interest is being shown in all our minority groups, Negro, Indian, Mexican, and Oriental, for the better protection of their rights and for their fuller participation in the responsibilities of citizenship. The Department of Justice is increasingly energetic in prosecuting violations of Federal law directed against members of minority groups, and the Supreme Court in its recent decisions has continued its tradition of upholding the constitutional rights of citizens irrespective of race.

Private citizens, too, are expressing their reawakened concern for the rights and interests of all American citizens through many organizations, local and national. Some of these organizations have long been in the field, but are extending and intensifying their efforts. Others have been newly established, in part in response to the need to strengthen and renew democracy at home while fighting for it abroad, in part to meet the problems of increased racial tensions caused by war conditions.

During the period April, 1943, to July, 1944, there were organized no less than 224 committees dealing with the problems of racial minorities.[1] Actually the number of committees and subcommittees working on problems of race relations far exceeds this count, since it is limited to committees reported in the press or through other channels and excludes the innumerable subcommittees of social agencies, individual churches, labor, and civic groups. Of the committees listed by the *Monthly Summary,* thirteen are national, two regional, sixteen state, and one hundred and thirty-five local. Although many of these organizations are interested in the full citizenship of all minority groups, the majority are chiefly concerned with Negro-white relations. The very fact that in the country as a whole these committees are so numerous and so widely distributed is one indication that Negroes are moving into the main stream of American life, and that their place in our democracy is a matter of national concern, not a peculiar problem of the southern region.

This has had a healthy effect upon the outlook of citizens of both races, North and South. The Northerners have lost a little of their self-righteousness, the Southerners are less on the defensive. Not only do white and Negro Southerners serve along with representatives from other sections in organizations which are interested in race relations as a national problem, but requests come to strictly southern organizations and agencies for experts of both races to give advice on northern local problems. This has brought the South into a new relationship to the country as a whole in the matter of race relations, and is increasing cooperation and understanding among believers in democracy in all parts of the nation.

Twenty-seven of the committees in the *Monthly Summary* list are located in southern or borderline cities. Again this count falls short of reflecting the amount of activity which is actually going on in this field. Most of these committees, formed for the betterment of race relations, necessarily undertake activities in special fields, such as housing, health, education, and similar fields, so that the scope of their activities far outruns a narrow interpretation of "citizenship." In

[1] *A Monthly Summary of Events and Trends in Race Relations,* August-September, 1944.

these other connections we shall come upon them frequently in the various chapters of this volume. For lack of a better classification, however, we present in this section a general discussion of southern organizations working in the field of race relations, with special emphasis on citizen participation in community and governmental planning.

The biggest single development in the field of citizenship and race relations in the South within recent years has been the organization of the Southern Regional Council. Its story is best told in its own words, quoted from a 1944 publication.

"The Southern Regional Council . . . is primarily the outgrowth of two parent movements. One of these was the Commission on Interracial Cooperation. The other was the Durham-Atlanta-Richmond series of conferences.

"In 1919, during the dark days of racial conflict and Ku Kluxism which followed World War I, the Commission on Interracial Cooperation was born. It represented a new idea in race relations—the idea that white people and Negroes should come together and strive to reach a 'meeting of minds' on their mutual problems. This idea spread until there were scores of interracial committees operating in the South and elsewhere.

" . . . In its 25 years of operation, the Commission has made interracial conferences respectable almost everywhere in the South, has marshalled thousands of the church women of the South in opposition to lynching and other injustices, has sponsored significant researches on race relations, has issued two million copies of pamphlets and leaflets, and has symbolized the faith of the Southern white people and Negro people in the processes of understanding and cooperation.

"In 1939 the Commission's leaders, feeling that the educational program which it started out to do had become thoroughly established, and recognizing the need for new blood and new ideas, began to explore the possibility of broadening the scope of the organization and improving its techniques. In October, 1940, the Commission

instructed its executive Committee to 'take whatever steps are necessary to carry out the plans for the formation of a council on Southern
regional development,' which would include in its program 'the work
of the Commission and other activities connected with the economic,
educational, and social development of the South.' "[2]

While a committee of the Commission was working on plans for
this new approach, the younger parent of the Southern Regional
Council, the Atlanta-Durham-Richmond series of conferences, was
maturing a similar purpose.

"The first chapter in the story of these conferences began with the
meeting of a group of Southern Negro leaders at Durham in October,
1942. This conference was an outstanding event in the history of the
South. It was a product of the rising tide of racial friction, and it
was also in a sense a product of both the successes and the failures
of the Commission on Interracial Cooperation. These Negro leaders
expressed their purpose as follows: 'We are proposing to set forth
in certain "Articles of Cooperation" just what the Negro wants and
is expecting of the postwar South and nation. Instead of letting the
demagogues guess what we want, we are proposing to make our wants
and aspirations a matter of record, so clear that he who runs may
read. We are hoping in this way to challenge the constructive cooperation of that element of the white South who express themselves
as desirous of a New Deal for the Negroes of the South.' "

The conference appointed a committee to draw up the statement
of "wants and aspirations," and in December, 1942, it was issued under
the title "A Basis for Interracial Cooperation and Development in the
South—A statement by Southern Negroes." On April 8, 1943, a "Conference of White Southerners on Race Relations" was held in Atlanta,
Georgia, to reply to the Durham statement. These white leaders said,
among other things, "Their statement is so frank and courageous, so
free from any suggestion of threat and ultimatum, and at the same
time shows such good will, that we gladly agree to cooperate." Accordingly on June 16, 1943, a third conference was held at Richmond,
Virginia, composed of delegates from both the Atlanta and Durham
conferences. This conference appointed twenty-two whites and nineteen

[2] *The Southern Regional Council, Its Origin and Purpose,* June, 1944.

Negroes to serve as a kind of continuing committee to decide next steps to be taken. The outgrowth of their work was the formal establishment in February, 1944, of the Southern Regional Council, which at the same time absorbed and rededicated the program of the Commission on Interracial Cooperation. The Council's area was defined as the states of Alabama, Arkansas, Florida, Georgia, Kentucky, Louisiana, Mississippi, North Carolina, Oklahoma, South Carolina, Tennessee, Texas, and Virginia. Charter membership was offered to all who had participated in the preliminary conferences and to all members of the Commission on Interracial Cooperation residing in the Council's area. Of approximately 270 persons thus designated, over 90 per cent accepted charter membership. The first officers were: Dr. Howard Odum of the University of North Carolina, president; P. B. Young of Norfolk, Virginia; Homer P. Rainey of Austin, Texas; and Carter Wesley of Houston, Texas, vice-presidents; Miss Emily H. Clay, secretary-treasurer. The executive director is Dr. Guy B. Johnson of the University of North Carolina.

What is it that these leading white and Negro Southerners are seeking to do? What was it that southern Negroes said about citizenship at Durham? And for what purpose was the Southern Regional Council organized?

The statement issued by the Durham Conference is the best interpretation of the thinking of the Negro leaders who drew it up:

"1. Our Nation is engaged in a world-wide struggle, the success of which, both in arms and ideals, is paramount and demands our first loyalty.

"2. Our loyalty does not, in our view, preclude consideration now of problems and situations that handicap the working out of internal improvements in race relations essential to our full contribution to the war effort, and of the inevitable problems of postwar reconstruction, especially in the South where we reside.

"3. The South, with its twenty-five million people, one-third of whom are Negroes, presents a unique situation, not only because of the size of the Negro population but because of the legal and customary patterns of race relations which are invariably and universally associated with racial discriminations. We recognize the strength and age of these patterns.

"We are fundamentally opposed to the principle and practice of compulsory segregation in our American society, whether of races or classes or creeds; however, we regard it as both sensible and timely to address ourselves now to the current problems of racial discrimination and neglect, and to ways in which we may cooperate in the advancement of progress aimed at the sound improvement of race relations within the democratic framework.

"4. We regard it as unfortunate that the simple efforts to correct obvious social and economic injustices continue, with such considerable popular support, to be interpreted as the predatory ambition of irresponsible Negroes to invade the privacy of family life.

"5. We have the courage and faith to believe, however, that it is possible to evolve in the South a way of life, consistent with the principles for which we as a nation are fighting throughout the world, that will free us all, white and Negro alike, from want, and from throttling fears."

Following this introduction, the statement outlines the specific steps that need to be taken to implement Negro citizenship in the fields of civil and political rights, industry and labor, service occupations, agriculture, military service, social welfare and health. In closing, the statement says:

"It is a wicked notion that the struggle of the Negro for citizenship is a struggle against the best interests of the Nation. To urge such a doctrine, as many are doing, is to preach disunity and to deny the most elementary principles of American life and government.

"The effect of the war has been to make the Negro, in a sense, the symbol and protagonist of every other minority in America and in the world at large. Local issues in the South, while admittedly holding many practical difficulties, must be met wisely and courageously if this Nation is to become a significant political entity in a new international world. The correction of these problems is not only a moral matter, but a practical necessity in winning the war and in winning the peace. Herein rests the chance to reveal our greatest weakness or our greatest strength."

The entire statement deserves to be read in detail, but we can only summarize here those points in the proposed program which most directly affect the exercise of the rights and responsibilities of citizenship.

In the field of political and civil rights, the statement urged: abolition of the poll-tax as a prerequisite to voting, abolition of the white primary; abolition of all forms of discriminatory practices, evasions of the law, and intimidation of citizens seeking to exercise their right of franchise; the end of exclusion of Negroes from jury duty; personal security against abuses of police power by white police, and employment of Negro police to control the lawless elements among Negroes; really equal accommodations in public carriers and terminals where segregation is now required by law; state law enforcement, and if it fails, federal legislation against lynching; Negro participation in emergency rationing, wage and rent control programs. With regard to military service, the conference asked an end of the unnecessary racial problems in transportation, recreation and leave areas, and of mistreatment at the hands of local police, which confront the Negro soldier in the South. In the field of social welfare and health they asked that, as minimum health measures for Negroes, there be (a) laws requiring that "a proportion of the facilities in all public hospitals be available for Negro patients"; (b) use of Negro nurses and doctors on the staff of such hospitals or on the same basis as other doctors in the community; (c) more extensive use of Negro public health nurses as social workers; (d) further slum clearance and low-cost housing projects. In the field of education the statement asked, among other things, for equalization of school facilities and equitable distribution of educational appropriations.

Point by point, there can be found in this book examples of almost all of these things actually being done in the South today, in individual cases. The theory of this survey and record is that these individual cases can and will within a reasonable period broaden into general practice.

But there is another point about the Durham statement that is important. It is in itself a good practice. The Negro Southerners who in the face of problems of the gravest importance put forth a statement at once so frank and so reasonable, so comprehensive and so practical, were exercising a degree of responsible citizenship which could only be met by an equally fundamental and responsible reply. The white Southerners who met in Atlanta a few months later to consider the statement were deeply conscious of this responsibility. In regard to political and civil rights they said:

"These Negro leaders rightly placed emphasis on discrimination in the administration of our laws on purely racial grounds. We are sensitive to this charge and admit that it is essentially just. From the Potomac to the Rio Grande, there are some ten million Negroes. While all citizens are governed by the same laws it is recognized that Negroes have little voice in the making and enforcement of the laws under which they must live. They are largely dependent upon the majority group for the safety of life and property, education and health, and their general economic condition. This is a violation of the spirit of democracy. No Southerner can logically dispute the fact that the Negro as an American citizen is entitled to his civil rights and economic opportunities."

In terms of action: "This means correcting the discrimination in the administration of these laws . . . in the allocation of school funds, in the number and quality of schools, and in the salaries of teachers . . ." in transportation facilities and in "public utilities and public benefits, such as sewers, housing, street and side-walk paving, playgrounds, public health and hospital facilities." Discrimination in the courts, "false arrest and brutal beatings" are listed among other existing evils to be eliminated.

Both groups recognized that civil and political rights cannot maintain themselves without economic opportunity and economic justice. "In the economic field," the white Southerners said, "procedures should be undertaken to establish fully the right to receive equal pay for equal work . . . if we cannot plan for a well-trained, well-employed and prosperous Negro population, the economic future of the South is hopeless."

The program of the Southern Regional Council, then, comprehends action in all of these fields where these white and Negro leaders agreed that action was needed. To quote from its own statement of programs and methods, issued in June, 1944, the Council "represents the combined efforts of liberal and progressive people of both races to give democracy a chance in the South. Its long-time goal is the improvement of social, civic, economic, and racial conditions in the South."

"The Council's functions may be summarized as follows: (1) clearing house and coordinating work with numerous agencies working on Southern problems; (2) research and survey to determine the facts and the state of public opinion as a basis for sound social action; (3) educational activities through a monthly paper, *The Southern Frontier,* and through pamphlets, press, radio, conferences, and personal contacts; (4) consultative services to private or official agencies; (5) constructive action at every possible point on the social, economic, political, and racial problems of the South."

As a basis for carrying out these functions, the Council is now engaged in developing its staff and facilities for effective work, and in renewing its contacts in order to conserve and revitalize the work of existing state and local interracial groups. Later parts of this chapter will give evidence of this renewed vitality.

Other immediate projects on which the Council is working are the promotion of a strategy conference of the major agencies working on social problems in the South, and the initiation of studies and conferences in the areas of police administration, postwar employment, and household service.

The Council's board of directors is composed of 64 persons, 27 Negro members and 37 white members. Their occupational distribution is as follows: education and related interests, 23; business, law and medicine, 14; religion, 8; public office and civic work, 9; journalism, 4; labor, 4; miscellaneous, 2. A national advisory committee will coordinate the work of the Council with the work of similar organizations in other parts of the country; and there will also be one hundred Honorary Fellows of the Council, drawn from the ranks of young Southerners who show promise of progressive leadership, whose function will be to assist the Council as observers, correspondents, and special investigators.

STATE AND CITY INTERRACIAL COMMITTEES

With all the good will in the world a southern regional council alone could not accomplish much; it needs to be sustained by smaller councils of citizens in southern states and cities, working out its ideals in terms of local practices. We shall attempt here to show to what extent such committees are already at work in southern communities, and what they are doing.

We have reports of state or local committees working for better race relations in all of the states, with the exception of Oklahoma, which fall within the area of the Southern Regional Council. In some states and cities, former local and state-wide affiliates of the Commission on Interracial Cooperation are being revived and reorganized for effective cooperation in the program of the Council. In other communities, new committees have sprung up in response to some situation which required immediate action, or have been formed because of the recognition of a need for a long term program. In two states, Maryland and Kentucky, the Governors have appointed committees, and the Mayors of Baltimore, St. Louis, Dallas, and Louisville have appointed official committees to deal with interracial problems.

In general the citizens' committees follow a common pattern. They are made up of about equal numbers of both races, with a similar division of office-holding. Drawn from a wider panel of interested, representative citizens, they work through an executive committee of not less than five nor more than fifty persons. They are made up as a rule of moderate and liberal citizens known for their interest and dependability. Church, college, and professional people representing civic groups or social agencies often take the lead, but in communities where organized labor is strong its representatives are frequently active, and representatives of chambers of commerce and industry have sometimes taken the initiative. The ideal is to secure as wide a cross-section of the community as possible, without defeating the fundamental purpose of the committee, which is to make progress.

These committee members usually meet together in a church, a Y.M.C.A., or some public hall to plan a program of action. Often subcommittees are appointed to work out plans in some special field such as recreation, housing, law enforcement, or public education.

Most of the groups work along similar lines and with similar methods, although some are naturally more active and effective than others, and they differ in emphasis and scope. Basically, the technique is educational, beginning with rather careful fact-finding either about minority problems in general or in regard to some special local situation. If action is decided upon, it is carried out by conferences with public officials or influential private citizens, by putting the matter before the public through meetings and forums, or by some other means of peaceful persuasion. Probably the most important single thing about these groups is that they afford a means of bringing people together, of educating them to respect each other's judgment, to learn each other's accomplishments, and to work for common purposes by common effort.

This plan and practice have been made familiar to the South through the work of the Commission on Interracial Cooperation. When the first such committees were organized through the efforts of the Commission following the last world war, the pattern was quite new. It called for a great deal of courage for the members of both races to venture forth to meet each other on this basis. Twenty years ago many southern white people had never met any educated Negroes and were embarrassed at shaking hands with them or saying "Mr." and "Mrs." At that time only a few Negroes had had the educational background, or the business and professional experience, to meet leading white people on a common ground and take their part of the responsibilities easily and naturally. Today it is rare for an educated person to suffer any embarrassment in meeting citizens— although of another race—with similar interests and culture. Also today there is a large group of able business and professional Negroes in every large southern city qualified to serve competently on such committees; and in the ranks of organized labor there are increasing numbers of men and women of both races accustomed to working out their common problems together.

Because many people are still unaware of the small but rapidly growing body of able and civic-minded Negro Southerners who devote much of their time to volunteer community services, it may not be amiss to cite here the record of two such women, not for personal publicity, but as typical of this group of public spirited citizens.

Mrs. Marcella Dumas Huggins is president of the Louisiana Congress of Colored Parents and Teachers. She is a native of Natchez, Mississippi, and received her education at Straight College, New Orleans, and Howard University. She was instrumental in the establishment of a project in Baton Rouge to give employment in white-collar fields to Negro college graduates, and, with the aid of a staff of five, she conducted one of the most successful vocational surveys of that region. Working through the Louisiana Congress of Colored Parents and Teachers, Mrs. Huggins secured over 5,000 signatures on a petition for a home for delinquent Negro youth. At the same time she has found time to bring up a family of three children and be an active church member.

Mrs. Fredericka Douglass Sprague Perry, founder of the Missouri State Association of Colored Girls, served as its state supervisor for eighteen years and as chairman of the National Association of Colored Girls. Through her efforts, the Big Sister Home in Kansas City, Missouri, has carried on for nine years work for the rehabilitation of under-privileged girls. She is organizer of the Women's Auxiliary of the Wheatley Provident Hospital, which has netted the institution more than $30,000 during the past twenty-five years. The site for a nurses' home was purchased by the Wheatley Hospital Beacon Club, also founded by Mrs. Perry. She served as president of the Kansas City Civic Association which supplied lawyers for the defense of any persecuted Negro. A graduate of Mechanics Art Institute, Rochester, New York, she established the Home Economics Department at Lincoln University, Missouri, and Lincoln High School, Kansas City, Missouri. Mrs. Perry, who is the granddaughter of Frederick Douglass, was recently elected to the Board of Trustees of the Frederick Douglass Memorial Historical Association.[3]

It is in large degree the presence, in a community, of Negro citizens such as these that is at once improving the quality and broadening the

[3] *Crisis*, June. 1943, p. 175.

basis of sound Negro citizenship and making possible civic cooperation between the races.

The different local problems, emergencies, or points of interest which call these cooperative groups into being, the various ways in which they work, and some of the things they are doing will be illustrated in the following state-by-state survey.

Alabama

Alabama has for years had a State Committee of the Commission on Interracial Cooperation which has recently revived its activities. Under the chairmanship of an Episcopal minister, the Committee is carrying out a program to "educate the public to an awareness of conditions which result in injustice to many citizens, with special emphasis on education, health, economic opportunity, law enforcement, and social security; it is also developing a program of local activities through the state directed to the improvement of these conditions." There are four subcommittees: (1) a committee to get as many speakers before civic and religious groups as possible; (2) a committee to promote study of race relations in colleges; (3) a committee on forums, which is planning public forums in all the cities of the state, four of which had been arranged at the time of the report; (4) a speakers' committee to secure qualified speakers for all these engagements, to analyze propaganda, and to serve as a clearing house of information.

Local communities in Alabama too have active interracial committees. A committee in Birmingham holds bi-monthly forums on minority problems, brings occasional guest speakers to the community, and between meetings investigates reported cases of injustice, police brutality, transportation difficulties, and the like.[4] In Montgomery, war-time tensions stimulated the white and colored Ministerial Associations to take the lead in forming an interracial committee of local leaders, representing the Y.M.C.A., the Y.W.C.A., the USO, colleges, parent-teacher and school groups, and other civic agencies. Three subcommittees are studying local conditions with respect to health, education, and recreation, and the committee has been active in several local cases of civil rights.[5]

[4] *Southern Frontier*, September, 1943.
[5] The Reverend D. C. Whitsett, letter, June, 1944.

In Birmingham, Negro citizens are also taking the initiative and assuming responsibility for their special problems as citizens. A newly organized group of social workers discussed at length in its first meeting what could be done to meet intelligently the postwar problems of Negroes. A steering committee was set up to study any laws enacted or bills proposed in the state or national legislature affecting social welfare, and to cooperate with other agencies. Cooperating in this planning were representatives of a local community center, the National Negro Youth Congress, the City Federation Day Nursery, the local chapter of the National Association for the Advancement of Colored People, Alpha Kappa Alpha Sorority, and the City Federation of Colored Women's Clubs.[6]

Arkansas

In Arkansas, several specific accomplishments can be credited to the Urban League of Greater Little Rock. The Little Rock League was permanently organized in 1937 as an affiliate of the National Urban League by a group of leading white and Negro citizens, and is one of twenty-five community chest agencies. The presidents of its interracial governing board have been successively a local attorney, a former Y. W. C. A. executive secretary who was also secretary of the Arkansas Department of the American Legion's Auxiliary, and a Labor Relations Specialist of the Farm Security Administration. The League employs a full time Negro executive secretary, and conducts a vigorous local program. For example, in 1941, it was active in the following fields:

1. Employment—As an employment agency it aided placement of Negro workers in defense jobs, in NYA, WPA, and domestic service. It helped to open up jobs to Negroes in housing construction. It organized a workers' council to discuss matters of common concern and welfare. It stimulated Negroes to take civil service examinations, conducted a vocational opportunity campaign, and aided in securing additional CCC camps.

2. Recreation—It surveyed and reported on recreational needs of Negroes in the community, especially parks. It organized a softball league and cooperated with other agencies in scouting, war recreation,

---

[6] Field Report, October, 1943.

improving picnic grounds, and in efforts to secure establishment of a Negro Y.M.C.A.

3. Education—In addition to the vocational work indicated, it aided in the educational program of civilian defense and in adult education, and brought nationally known speakers to the city.

4. Health—It sponsored a Negro Health Week program.

In 1942, in addition to these same general activities, the Little Rock League negotiated with the Arkansas Ordnance Plant for use of Negro employees, with the result that first one hundred and twenty-five Negro women, then fifty more, were employed in the plant. It also organized the Negro division of the Pulaski County Defense Council which conducted classes in first aid, home nursing, and other subjects, and made appointments for Negro blood donors.[7]

With this background of solid achievement, the Urban League was well-equipped to cooperate effectively with other Little Rock agencies when a need for prompt and decisive action arose. Such an emergency did come when a Negro sergeant stationed at nearby Camp Robinson was shot and killed by a civilian policeman. An investigation by a federal grand jury (on which, by the way, some Negroes were serving) cleared the policeman, and as a temporary measure all Negro troops were removed from Camp Robinson. Before the camp was reopened to Negro troops, the Urban League, the City Council, the USO, and a bi-racial Committee for Racial Service appointed by the Governor cooperated to remedy some of the conditions that had led to violence. There had already been Negro M. P.'s in Little Rock; now the City Council added to the civil police force eight Negroes who were trained for special duties by a Sergeant who was a graduate of a Federal Bureau of Investigation school. The United Service Organization enlarged its center for Negroes and recommended a special bus service between the camp and the center for the use of Negro soldiers. A service club was built at the camp itself to house a library, reading and writing room, a cafeteria and game room; a guest house for soldiers' relatives and a theater were also provided. A special post exchange was opened for the use of the 5,000 Negro troops.

[7] Reports of Greater Little Rock Urban League, 1941, 1942.

Florida

Florida has a state Council of the Commission on Interracial Co-operation which works largely through eleven active local committees to do an educational job of making the public aware of discriminations and necessary remedial action. The local committees also work on community projects such as getting additional playgrounds for children, securing the appointment of Negro police, securing better health facilities and so forth.

In Miami, a new interracial committee was formed in August, 1944. Six white public officials, including two city commissioners, the director of public safety and the sheriff, joined with six Negro citizens to form a committee dedicated to action and results. "We don't want to sit around and talk," one city commissioner said, "we want action and results." Immediately the Commission set to work on problems of housing, health, transportation facilities, bathing beaches and schools. By September, at least one "result" was reported. Five Negro police officers were appointed, and within a few weeks the number had been increased.[8]

Georgia

All the world knows that Georgia has its race relations problems, but the good things that are going on in Georgia, especially in Atlanta, are less widely publicized. Yet Atlanta is proud of the group of institutions which recently merged to form Atlanta University, with its colleges and graduate school, and with the only accredited graduate school of social work for Negroes in the South. Here, too, is the headquarters of the Southern Regional Council and here was organized the Association of Southern Women Against Lynching, which became the focus of the protest of decent southern women against being used as an alibi for the continuation of this regional disgrace. In Atlanta, also, an active Urban League is functioning to bring together the civic purposes of whites and Negroes.

The services which such an active and responsible interracial group can perform may be illustrated by a series of events in Atlanta. In January, 1943, the Atlanta Chamber of Commerce distributed a questionnaire to approximately 3,500 people in the city of Atlanta and

[8] Associated Negro Press report, September, 1944.

throughout the state of Georgia in an effort to determine what the people considered to be the three most important needs of the city and the state, the results to be used by the Chamber of Commerce in developing its program of postwar planning. At first the questionnaires were distributed to whites only. However, in response to an inquiry from the secretary of the Urban League, the Chamber of Commerce at once requested the names of three hundred Negro citizens representing a cross-section of the community, and sent questionnaires to all of these, with assurances to the Urban League that the replies would be incorporated in the findings.[9]

The summary of the returns showed that the citizens thought that the most urgent problems were: (1) better government, especially consolidation of city and county functions; (2) education; (3) traffic; (4) race relations; (5) health; (6) business and industry; (7) agriculture; (8) parks; (9) housing and construction; (10) transportation. With reference to race relations, the report noted that 35 per cent of Atlanta's population is Negro and that the following needs of the Negro community should be met: (1) adequate park facilities; (2) adequate schools with curriculum fitted to needs; (3) equal justice in the courts; (4) encouragement to Negroes to train as doctors, dentists, nurses, and lawyers in sufficient numbers to meet the needs of Negroes; (5) an increase in the earning level through better wage standards for domestic service and unskilled labor. A few citizens pointed out the need for more economic opportunities for Negroes, Negro personnel in hospitals and clinics, and Negro police.

The Chamber of Commerce has appointed a special committee which is now studying these needs.

The creation of an atmosphere in which the Chamber of Commerce begins to plan for the needs of Negro citizens as a normal aspect of planning for the community as a whole is never the result of a single influence. The Interracial Commission operating in Atlanta through the years had undoubtedly had an educational effect. Another factor was a valuable series of conferences which took place during the summer of 1943. During that hot summer, which was also the summer of the Detroit riots, Atlanta had been alarmed by rumors

[9] Grace Towns Hamilton, Field Report, 1943.

of impending race riots. The conferences grew out of the desire of responsible white and Negro citizens to meet this situation constructively. They started in part on the initiative of Dr. Ira De A. Reid in his capacity as an associate on the race relations program of the American Missionary Association. Among the first persons he consulted were Mr. Alonzo C. Moron, manager of University Homes Housing Project, Mr. Philip Weltner, a lawyer, former president of the State Board of Regents and former chairman of the Atlanta Housing Authority, Mr. Forrester Washington, director of the Atlanta University School of Social Work, and Mr. W. Y. Bell, Jr., associate regional director of the USO. The names are not important to the story, but the type of person selected is.

When this group began to explore the situation, they found that a desire for action was already stirring among the white and Negro ministers, the Atlanta branch of the N.A.A.C.P., and the Interracial Committee. These groups decided to join forces and to send two delegates to the mayor to present the common desire of Atlanta's white and Negro citizens for better understanding and peaceful relationships.

Out of this grew a small but vital conference with the mayor, the chairman of the Board of Commissioners of Fulton County, the chairman of the Atlanta Housing Authority, the managing editor of the *Atlanta Journal,* Mr. Weltner, Mr. Moron, Mr. Bell, and Dr. Reid. There was very frank discussion of the police force, of efforts to trace and eradicate the rumors, and of such obstacles to mutual understanding as the lack of Negro participation in civic affairs, the absence of normal Negro news in the white press, and the playing up of race tensions in the Negro press, as well as the suppression of news by both press and radio. The problems of civil liberties, police beatings, homicides and transportation were discussed. No "solutions" were arrived at; no specific actions were outlined to be taken, though there appeared to be some sentiment in favor of a "Mayor's Committee on Public Morale in War Times." Nevertheless, among the forces which led to the inclusion of problems of race relations in Atlanta's planning for the future, this conference must be reckoned.

Georgia also has a state-wide Committee of the Commission on Interracial Cooperation which has stated as its objectives: (1) equalization of teachers' salaries; (2) Negroes on the board of parks and playgrounds; (4) equity for Negroes in the courts of law; (5) better labor conditions; (6) support for the home for delinquent girls at Macon, Georgia; (7) the end of the abuse of Negroes by the police and on the busses.

Kentucky

Kentucky is a border state, and as a consequence there is less hesitation in giving official recognition to the need for common action in the field of race relations. The appointment of committees and commissions on race relations by mayors of cities and governors of states has become quite a common practice in the North as a method of dealing with war-time tensions, but in the South it is much more likely to be an unofficial citizens' group which tries to formulate a state or local program. In Kentucky, however, committees of white and Negro citizens have been appointed by the Governor and by the Mayor of Louisville to study problems in this field.

In October, 1944, Governor Simeon Willis appointed six white and six Negro leaders to a Commission on the Needs of Negro Citizens which was directed to determine all the facts and conditions relating to the economic, educational, housing, health and other needs for the betterment of the Negro citizens of Kentucky and to report on needed legislative action ninety days before the 1946 session of the Kentucky legislature.[10] The Negro members included a minister, a state representative, a woman well known in community activities, and other civic leaders; the white members included a newspaper editor, and various leaders in educational and social fields. As in the case of some but not all of the northern commissions, no appropriation was made for the work of the Kentucky Commission. It is clear that this not only limits the effectiveness of any studies or projects which the Commission may undertake unless private support is obtained, but it also detracts somewhat from the authority of the Commission as an agency of the state, since the state does not pay its expenses. It is worth noting that the most effective state official commissions have been those for which regular appropriations were made from state funds sufficient to maintain an office to give continuity to the work

[10] Associated Negro Press report, October, 1944.

and to direct such programs and studies as may be undertaken. Nevertheless, the appointment of such a commission by the governor of a southern state is a significant recognition of governmental responsibility and of the importance of Negro participation in planning for the needs of Negroes.

Incidentally, a state citizens' committee, the Kentucky Council on Interracial Cooperation, had been functioning for years before the Governor appointed his official commission. It is safe to say that without the educational groundwork laid by the citizens' group, no official body would ever have come into existence.

Similarly, in Louisville, an active interracial committee prepared the way for the appointment of a mayor's committee. In June, 1944, the citizens' group held an interracial conference which made recommendation for (1) discontinuance of Red Cross blood segregation in Louisville; (2) election of a Negro to the Board of Education; (3) more favorable attitudes toward Negro women shoppers in downtown stores; (4) appointment of more Negroes to the Louisville Area Development Association and provision of more war housing units for Negroes; (5) employment of Negro operators by the Louisville Railway Company. It was about this time that Mayor Wilson Wyatt appointed a Mayor's Interracial Council to study the problems of the Negro citizens of Louisville; and Mrs. Louise Young, one of the Negro members of the Mayor's Council, became a candidate for the Board of Education.[11]

Louisiana

The history of the recently established New Orleans Citizens' Committee on Race Relations illustrates some of the difficulties that may beset such groups in the early stages—difficulties which can be overcome by the common effort of just and determined citizens of both races.

In 1943 the Chamber of Commerce of New Orleans appointed a race relations committee. While this appears on its face to be a good move, the committee actually was composed only of white persons, who expressed a desire not to have any meetings with Negroes. Sub-

[11] Associated Negro Press report. Mrs. Young was defeated in the election by a very narrow margin.

sequently the committee was reorganized and invited a few Negroes to one of its meetings. No Negroes however, could be members of the committee, since the Association of Commerce took the position that only its members could sit on an Association Committee. One of the responsible Negro citizens who were consulted stated frankly to the Association Committee members that they did not feel that much good could come of a white committee on which Negroes were asked to serve in a purely advisory capacity; and they declined to serve unless the technicality of formal membership could be overlooked and Negroes could be invited to participate in the deliberations on an equal basis.

In the meantime a number of smaller interracial committees were active in New Orleans, but none was strong enough to speak for the community as a whole. Some of the most responsible Negroes therefore took up in the Council of Community Agencies the possibility of establishing an over-all coordinating interracial committee composed of influential Negro and white citizens. The executive director of the Council of Social Agencies, a Jewish rabbi, and the superintendent of Flint Goodridge Hospital, a Negro, were appointed to secure a chairman for this overall committee, and in the summer of 1944 the Citizens' Committee on Race Relations held its first meeting. While its program is still in the organization stage, the plan is to bring in members from all of the smaller groups, asking each to limit itself in its activities to a certain area. Thus it is hoped that the Chamber of Commerce Committee will work in the field of employer-employee relations, while other agencies will work on equalization of educational facilities, voting rights, and so on.[12]

Maryland

Under Governor O'Connor, Maryland has taken some very constructive steps towards the improvement of race relations. From 1938 to 1942 there had been increasing tensions in Baltimore over the treatment of Negroes by white police officers. Since September 21, 1938, when a new police commissioner had been installed, nine Negroes had been killed in Baltimore by police officers. There were additional reports of widespread and needless police violence in making arrests

[12] A. W. Dent, Field Reports, January, 1944, and subsequent months.

of Negroes. Yet in every case the policemen involved had been exonerated and not one had been brought to trial. The final incident that touched off action was the killing of a Negro private of the United States Army on February 1, 1942, by a white policeman.

Stirred by these events, Negroes held mass meetings in their churches, and finally some two thousand persons met on April 24, 1942, in Annapolis in an organized meeting of protest. Those present represented some 150 Negro organizations, including church, labor, civic, business, and fraternal groups. "This delegation presented a brief to the Governor, which included the following recommendations:

"1. Investigation of the police administration in the Negro areas of Baltimore.

"2. Appointment of Negro police officers in uniform.

"3. Negro representation on all state institutions operated for Negroes.

"4. Official support for President Roosevelt's Executive Order No. 8802 forbidding discrimination in war work based on race, creed, or color."

On May 18 the Governor appointed a Commission to study problems affecting Maryland's Negro population. There were 18 members on the Commission, 13 white and 5 Negro, 16 men and 2 women. This Commission on May 27 recommended the setting up of six committees, Housing, Police and Liquor License, Health, Education, Employment, and Problems in Counties. The committees were organized and began work at once, and by the fall of 1942 most of their reports were in. In addition to their specific recommendations for action, they recommended continuing study of the whole problem.

Among their specific recommendations were:

Police: 1. That a copy of the Commission's report on questions affecting the police be sent to the state's attorney with the request that the Bender case (police officer who killed army private) be sent again to the Grand Jury.

2. That a copy also be sent to the Commissioner of Police with request for appropriate action.

3. That the Commissioner of Police appoint a colored police-woman at an early date.

4. That one or more of the Negro policemen on the force be assigned to the duty of patrolmen in uniforms.

5. That qualified young Negroes be encouraged to prepare themselves to pass the examination and to secure places on the eligible lists.

6. That an amendment of the law relating to the Board of Police Examiners be sought, so as to secure the appointment of non-partisan examiners with long terms in office.

Education. This committee made extensive, detailed recommendations too long to report in full but covering such points as Negro representation on the Board of School Commissioners, improvements in the facilities for preparing Negro elementary teachers, extension of vocational education in the colored day schools, training of Negro war production workers.

Health. This committee found effort in every field to meet the health problems of the whole community, but recommended especially increased beds for Negro tubercular cases and the training of more young Negro mid-wives for the rural regions.

Employment. This was found to be a major problem. Recommendations were made first to employers in war industry for all-out utilization of all man power; second, to the Governor and to the Mayor of Baltimore that they see to it that institution boards and department heads "reexamine their policies and canvass the possibility of more Negro employment . . . skilled, unskilled, and semi-skilled," especially in Negro institutions, on their staffs and boards; third, to the white leaders of Baltimore to include serious consideration of Negro employment in all long-range planning and give Negroes greater participation in all community activities which affect their race; fourth, to Negro leaders to recognize the new opportunities and challenge their people to train for and make good in them and to share in an all-out effort to win the war; fifth, to the Governor to set up a Commission to cooperate with the War Manpower Commission, not coercively, but bringing to bear "the practical viewpoint of industry itself."

Housing. Recommendations: (1) Improvement of existing facilities by enforcement of health and rent rules and by repair and conversion of dwellings; (2) use of large buildings and suitable churches as emergency dormitories for single men or single women; (3) emergency regulation of migration; (4) voluntary evacuation of non-defense Negro families living near defense work; (5) requiring industry to forecast its labor needs "defining the proportion that will be Negro" to enable housing authorities to make necessary preparation for Negroes; (6) new housing in undeveloped areas, in existing developed areas, and in land now used as parks. In addition to this emergency program, a long-term program includes plans for postwar housing and for raising the income level of Negroes. A minority report stressed government housing as the only solution possible with adequate size, speed, and justice.

The Committee on the Counties found the task of three persons assigned to study all the racial problems of twenty-five counties a bit too large, and, under the current extremely unstable conditions, insoluble.[13]

By March, 1944, four Negro police officers had been put in uniform and had been doing well, one in particular being outstanding. The police commissioner was at work on securing fifteen more through careful procedures. A Negro was added to the school board. In the state institutions Negroes have been added to the boards, and in one case it was decided to change from a white to a Negro superintendent. There is evidence of increased employment of Negroes, and labor unions in their public stand have taken a more liberal attitude than before. The Commission does not claim any of these developments as due exclusively to its own activities.[14] Many other forces and agencies are at work. But it can hardly be doubted that the Commission has been at least one important contributory factor in these developments.

In Baltimore, also, several Negroes serve as members of postwar planning groups. For instance, the president of Morgan State College is a member of the Mayor's Post-War Planning Committee; the in-

[13] Taken from the report of the Governor's Commission on Problems Affecting the Negro Population, March, 1943. Recommendations are summarized on pp. 137-45.
[14] Joseph P. Healy, letter, March 24, 1944.

dustrial secretary of the Baltimore Urban League is a member of the Post-War Planning Committee of the Citizens' Planning and Housing Association; a Negro serves as member of the Baltimore Housing Authority; and another is a member of the City Plan Commission.[15]

So that Negro women in Baltimore might become more familiar with their local government and with community services, and be better prepared to share in the responsibility for these services as well as to benefit from them, the Woman's Auxiliary of the Baltimore Urban League recently launched a series of trips to various social agencies, city departments, and institutions. Through these contacts, the women who participate will be able to serve as interpreters of the different agencies and their functions to other Negro citizens.

In Elkton, Maryland, an Interracial Committee was organized early in 1944 through the efforts of Mr. Charles C. Jacobs, director of race relations for Triumph Explosives, Incorporated. Its membership of about twenty-four persons represents the professions, civic organizations, and industry. It has decided to work for (1) more amicable relations between the races; (2) separate as well as integrated recreation for both groups; (3) lecture series; (4) panel discussions; (5) easing or eradicating unnecessary controls which breed racial tensions.[16] This committee in the summer of 1944 paid the expenses of one of its members to attend the American Missionary Association Institute of Race Relations held at Fisk University in Nashville.

Mississippi

From Mississippi come a number of reports showing growth at the grass roots. The State Department of Education is receiving numerous requests to send representatives to speak before various civic and religious organizations in the state to give facts about the status of the Negro in Mississippi, especially with reference to school opportunities. Among the organizations making such requests are the Delta Council, Rotary Clubs, Kiwanis Clubs, church societies, and P.-T.A. organizations.[17] But more than fact-finding is desired. Groups are at work on programs to better the conditions found. At a joint meeting of the

[15] J. Harvey Kearnes, Field Report, October, 1943.
[16] *A Monthly Summary of Events and Trends in Race Relations,* April, 1944.
[17] P. H. Eason, letter, March, 1943.

Executive Committee of the Delta Council and Delta Farm Bureau representatives in Greenville, Mississippi, March, 1943, a discussion was held of the problem of bettering racial relationships in the Delta. This group recommended: (1) better schools for Negro children; (2) attempting a uniform wage scale in agriculture; (3) justice in the courts; (4) impartial observance and enforcement of segregation laws in transportation; (5) prohibition of intermingling of races at establishments selling liquor; (6) enlarged and adequate hospitalization, medical clinics, and health workers; (7) a uniform policy among the planters of the Delta as to wage scale, interest, land breaking, ditching, clearing costs, etc., with a County Grievance Committee to hear complaints; (8) more courteous treatment of Negroes in retail establishments; (9) a coordinating organization to work with the Delta Council in promoting good will and mutual organization.[18] Here on a small regional scale we see the same type of practical cooperative approach to realization of genuine citizenship by all citizens that we saw on a south-wide scale in the establishment of the Southern Regional Council.

There is in Mississippi also a Mississippi Council on Interracial Cooperation, F. C. Wilcox of Vicksburg being chairman. This committee organized in the summer of 1943 two special committees, one on research in "the fields of education, health, civil rights, etc," and one on education, "to prepare materials for use in newspapers, forums, church groups, and other groups in the state." It is also organizing county units wherever possible and hopes to have fifteen or twenty of these going in 1944, and to "continue until we have organized practically all of the counties of Mississippi."[19]

The Jackson, Mississippi, Chamber of Commerce on November 28, 1944, announced the formation of an advisory committee on interracial problems, the first of its kind in the state, to work with a like group from the Jackson Negro Chamber of Commerce in studying methods to improve race relations in the city. The committee, which includes in its membership the Mayor-elect of Jackson, is headed by a well-known lawyer and civic leader. The letter sent to those who

[18] G. A. Sanford, letter, April, 1943.
[19] *Southern Frontier*, September, 1943.

were asked to serve on the committee by the president of the Chamber of Commerce said: "Three representatives of the Negro Chamber of Commerce met with the executive committee of the Jackson Chamber of Commerce regarding important problems affecting Jackson Negroes on which they desired help and advice of our organization. In the belief that a committee of interested and able representatives of the chamber of commerce could fill a real need, the executive committee recommended to the board of directors that an advisory committee be authorized to meet with representatives of the Negro Chamber when important interracial problems developed. Your committee has a very real responsibility as well as a very real opportunity to promote better racial relations between the two races and I know you can render a real service as a member of this committee."[20]

It is too early to say whether such an advisory committee will prove effective, but as an evidence of willingness on the part of leading white citizens in a Deep South community to confer seriously with leading Negroes on community problems, this development is clearly a good practice.

Missouri

In both Kansas City and St. Louis there are official race relations committees. The St. Louis committee started as an unofficial citizens' group. Shortly after the Detroit race riot a number of St. Louis citizens, Negro and white, formed an interracial committee. "The present mayor, Aloys Kaufman, deeply interested in any move to forestall interracial troubles in St. Louis, proposed that the committee be enlarged, divided into subcommittees, each one charged with some specific phase of Negro welfare, and given official standing as the St. Louis Race Relations Commission."[21]

The subcommittees deal with housing, employment, education, public relations, health and recreation, finance and coordination. The city makes no appropriation for the work of the Commission, but enough has been raised in contributions from citizens and corporations to pay the expenses of a full-time secretary.

The subcommittee on health and recreation has taken the lead in

[20] Associated Negro Press release, December, 1944.
[21] *Survey Graphic*, May, 1944, p. 267.

the conversion of vacant lots owned by the city in Negro slum areas into small parks and playgrounds, several of which were equipped and in use in the summer of 1944. In general, the chairman of the commission reports: "Race relations problems in our community are being submitted to the Commission, and fortunately we have been able to iron out many of these problems by bringing about a better understanding of the difficulties presented."[22]

A somewhat similar development took place in Kansas City. An interracial committee originally set up by the Council of Social Agencies to deal primarily with health and welfare problems was reorganized under the sponsorship of the Council and with the endorsement of Mayor Gage. The president of the Chamber of Commerce also endorsed the committee and promised the cooperation of the Chamber. Five subcommittees are working on law enforcement, management and labor, research, education and public relations, and health, welfare and recreation. Fifty-three distinguished white and Negro Kansas City citizens are members of the committee, and a smaller executive committee of nine directs the program. There is a full-time executive secretary. The general purposes of the committee are to prevent race disturbances and to improve conditions of minority groups in the community.[23]

Although Missouri has segregation laws relating to schools and inter-marriage which tend to classify it as a southern state, its geographical location and its history have opened it to influences which result in patterns very different from those found in most parts of the South. For instance, there is in Kansas City a "Committee for the Practice of Democracy" organized in January, 1942, by a group of whites and Negroes for the following purposes: (1) to investigate and publicize undemocratic practices embodying racial discrimination; (2) to correct such practices whenever possible; (3) to restore and perpetuate those democratic ideals upon which our nation was founded."

This group has held interracial picnics to break down the tradition of separate parks; its members have gone together to concerts at the

[22] Edwin B. Meisner, letter, November, 1944.
[23] Owen Davison, letter, June, 1944.

Municipal Auditorium; it has sponsored similar procedures in theatres and public eating-places to break down the tradition of segregated seating; it has worked to gain the admission of Negro teachers to the state teachers' organization; and it is working for the omission of all segregation laws in the new Missouri Constitution which is now being framed. Incidentally, the St. Louis Race Relations Commission has also asked that the law requiring the segregation of public schools on a racial basis be omitted from the new constitution.[24]

North Carolina

North Carolina deserves a more leisurely treatment than can be given here because it has in so many ways, over a long period of time, been in the lead among southern states in good citizenship. It has been progressive not alone in regard to race relations but also in regard to roads, schools, penal and welfare institutions, and the development of a state university recognized over the nation for its distinguished work as in many respects the leading university in the South. One North Carolinian writes: "The state has done more, I believe, in consideration of the welfare of its colored people than any other southern state and today, in spite of all increased strains—and they are dangerously increasing—I believe that the relationship between the races in North Carolina is more just and friendlier than in any other state with a large proportion of Negroes in its population."[25]

Over a nation-wide hook-up on December 16, 1944, Governor Broughton of North Carolina participated with three other leading citizens of the state in a broadcast of the People's Platform, a Columbia Broadcasting feature. The subject of the discussion, led by Columbia's educational director, Mr. Lyman Bryson, was "Is the South Solving the Race Problem?" The other participants were the presidents of two Negro colleges, both Negroes, and the white publisher of the Asheville *Citizen-Times*. From the point of view of cooperative citizenship, the important things about this broadcast were: (1) the repeated emphasizing by all four North Carolina participants that the progress and prosperity of the South as a whole depended on the progress and prosperity of its Negro citizens; (2) the acknowledge-

[24] G. T. Bryant, letter, December, 1944.
[25] Jonathan Daniels, letter, March 26, 1943.

ment by the white participants that Negroes were entitled to equal facilities and opportunities with respect to health, housing, employment, transportation, and education; (3) the general agreement that progress toward all these goals is accelerating and that the public generally favors moves to this end; (4) the general agreement that in nearly every community in North Carolina and probably in most southern communities there are now established interracial groups used to meeting together and talking over common problems and to working together for common ends; (5) the fact of the broadcast itself. The Governor stated that he thought that Negro soldiers returning from the war would be justifiably more insistent on the recognition of their full rights and full participation in responsibilities as citizens, and he also thought that white soldiers who had seen Negro soldiers working, fighting and dying for a common cause would more readily accept the justice of this claim.[26]

The North Carolina Interracial Commission has been functioning steadily for nearly a generation, and did not need to be dug out of a tomb, dusted off, and resurrected when the present war crisis came. Here is its story, told by a member:

"In 1921 it was suggested by the Southern Interracial Commission in Atlanta that we organize in North Carolina a Commission on Interracial Cooperation. A member of the Y.M.C.A. in one of our largest cities came to Raleigh for that purpose. A small group of men, including the State Superintendent of Public Instruction, the secretary of the State Board of Health, the President of Wake Forest College, and several other important individuals met together. The director of Negro Education was also a member of the group. It was proposed at that time that the group present organize a state commission and begin functioning at once. One member of the group raised the question as to what authority would be behind such a group and pointed out that it might be desirable to ask Governor Cameron Morrison to appoint members of this group and any others that might be desired to form a North Carolina Commission on Interracial Cooperation. After much discussion this suggestion was accepted. A list of names was presented to Governor Morrison and he was glad

[26] Field Report of "People's Platform" Broadcast, December 16, 1944.

to send an official Commission bearing the great seal of the state and all of the usual formal insignia of such commissions to these persons, and by that act the Commission was officially born in North Carolina."

The small committee set to work at once; other prominent people were gradually added, each being commissioned by the Governor. After some time it was decided to expand the membership to include representatives of every county and city and as many smaller communities as possible. This was done by writing to the presidents of the universities and colleges in the state asking them to select from their former graduates "men and women who had already achieved some success in the fields of education, health, welfare, law, medicine, the ministry, industry, and business in general." The response was excellent and a membership of between one and two thousand persons was built up. "That process has been continued under practically all of the Governors since 1921, until today there is a membership of between 2,500 and 3,000, representing the best of both races in North Carolina. Throughout these years there have been only five chairmen: (1) a Greensboro banker, (2) a scientist and college president, (3) a college administrative dean, (4) the head of the Institute for Research in Social Science of the State University, (5) the Episcopal Bishop of the Diocese of North Carolina."

The major work of the Commission throughout the years has been a gradual individual educational process of conservations and conferences of its officers and members with leading industrialists, presidents of colleges and universities, and leaders in educational, religious, social and business activities of the state, "toning down" conflicts and misunderstandings, "toning up" the spirit of friendly cooperation.

The Commission has, however, carried out also certain definite undertakings. For instance, in 1937 the General Assembly authorized and the Governor appointed a committee to study the public schools and colleges for Negroes in North Carolina and to make recommendations to the Governor and the Legislature in 1939. This report was prepared by two senators and three members of the House of Representatives. "For several years the Student Workers Council composed of white and Negro students from North Carolina College for Negroes, Duke University, the University of North Carolina, as well as workers from the mills and factories of Durham and vicinity met regularly and discussed problems affecting the community. Under the auspices of this Council, a state-wide meeting of Students and Workers was held in Durham at which time national leaders from labor, government and other areas of life participated. The Council organized the Durham Housing Association and sponsored a program for Federal Housing Project (sic) in the city of Durham."[27] There is also a Durham Citizens' Committee on Negro Affairs which has a political committee as one section. This committee gets out the registrations and votes, scrutinizes the candidates and their records, and follows court cases involving racial issues. A subcommittee on civic and social affairs is working for the appointment of Negro Auxiliary Police, similar to the white auxiliaries under Civilian Defense, and of at least three Negroes as regular police officers.

South Carolina

South Carolina, though less effectively, is showing concern over the unequal citizenship of Negroes. Twenty-one leading white citizens of Columbia petitioned the state Democratic Convention in 1942 to appoint a committee to study the question and make plans to permit qualified Negroes to vote in the Democratic primaries, and the white papers of the state carried full reports of this action. Unhappily the Democratic Convention did not act at that time, and the South Carolina legislature has since moved to abolish primaries rather than to allow Negro citizens to participate in the selection of candidates. To their credit many white citizens of the state and of other southern states have repudiated this undemocratic action.[28]

Nevertheless Negro citizens of the state are facing their own problems and becoming articulate. In the winter of 1943 at the annual meeting of Negro college presidents, deans and registrars, one educator urged: "(1) that Negroes talk the language of citizenship; (2) that a true history of Negroes be placed in Negro and white schools; (3) that Negroes of South Carolina be totally organized and support some particular program; (4) that Negroes launch a progressive pro-

[27] A. Elder, letter, May 5, 1943.
[28] Stephen J. Wright, Field Report, October, 1943.

gram of social reconstruction; (5) that they promote a vigorous program of racial understanding."[29]

In the city of Charleston a period of unrest and disquieting rumors brought about the organization of a twelve-member committee drawn in equal numbers from prominent Negro and white citizens, with standing instructions "to investigate all reports of unrest, attempt to remove misunderstandings, and promote a better spirit of cooperation between the races." The committee operates with the full approval and cooperation of the mayor. Subcommittees have been appointed to deal with the proper authorities in each of these tension areas: (1) congestion and friction on buses; (2) discriminatory practices at the Charleston Navy Yard; (3) police brutality; (4) inflammatory articles in the local press; (5) attitudes of school-age children.[30]

Greenville, South Carolina, "was fortunate in having the Community Development Program for five years sponsored by the General Education Board." One of the objectives of the program was to improve the relations between the races, and for a time a Negro who held a master's degree in sociology from Iowa University was employed in this phase of the program. The repercussions of this program have continued and with the intelligent leadership of both races tensions have been lessened.

In Richland County the Committee on Interracial Cooperation has worked for: (1) action by the City Council to make available three sites suitable for Negro parks; (2) health and housing programs (discussed in other sections); (3) the encouragement of discussion groups among youth of the community to study interracial problems.

Rock Hill has a Council of Interracial Cooperation founded in 1943 through the efforts of representatives from the Negro and white ministerial associations. Twenty-eight civic leaders, professional and business men and women of both races, including the city manager and the city superintendent of education, are members of this council. At the time of the report the Council was working to relieve overcrowded conditions in two Negro schools, to provide bus transporta-

[29] *Christian Century*, December 15, 1943, p. 1,480.
[30] L. Howard Bennett, Field Report, May, 1944.

tion for Negro students, and to secure more space in the local paper for normal Negro community news.

Meanwhile the State Interracial Committee is working to foster similar groups in other counties. Those already functioning include committees in Columbia, Charleston, Greenville, Bamburg, Orangeburg, Greenwood, Florence, Sumter, and Rock Hill. The chairman reports that "our committee has taken up with the inter-state bus company the treatment of Negroes on buses." Other questions in which the committee has interested itself have been "the matter of representation on draft boards, in at least one case, the matter of clemency for a Negro where race feeling may have had a large part in his conviction, compensation of school teachers, the service of Negroes on grand and petit juries, and provision for allowing Negroes to take at least a small part in governmental matters."[1]

Tennessee

As in so many other cities, it took an atmosphere of tension, several acts of open violence, and fear of more general racial outbreaks to awaken in the Nashville community a desire to take action to improve race relations in the city and to get at some of the factors that were at the root of the disturbances. The precipitating factor was a near-riot arising out of the arrest of a Negro soldier by a white M. P. and the subsequent invasion of the area by white M. P.'s and the civilian police when some unknown person sent in an unnecessary riot call. Before the disorder was over a group of leading Negro and white citizens had called upon the chief of police. Recognizing the need to take some action beyond the immediate suppression of violence, this group later issued invitations to over two hundred Nashville citizens to hold a special citizens' meeting at a down-town Methodist Church. Over one hundred responded and came.

One of the problems that immediately came to light was the need for greater common knowledge of events. Utterly different accounts of the episode had appeared in the white and Negro papers, and many citizens were astonished at the record of the facts given to the joint group by eye witnesses and members of the original committee.

At this first meeting those present voted to endorse and follow up

[31] *Southern Frontier*, September, 1943.

a request for Negro M. P.'s; to appoint a nominating committee which should select thirty members equally divided between the two races as a permanent committee; and to instruct this committee as soon as organized to try to get Negro civilian policemen and policewomen appointed for Negro residential areas. Shortly afterwards, four Negro M. P.'s were stationed in the areas where Negro soldiers congregated; and in December when an episode, which might easily have taken on a racial slant, occurred at a bus station where an M. P. was called in to handle Negro troops, this white M. P. wisely called a Negro M. P. and the matter was settled in a normal way.

These first steps were taken in the spring of 1943. During the summer no new crisis arose; all activities subsided; and there seemed some danger that the Committee would die. In the fall, however, activity was renewed. Membership was increased to fifty so that men and women representing the churches, colleges, business, the professions, organized labor, the press, and civic and social action groups of both races could be included. By December of 1943 an Executive Committee had been formed. Subcommittees were at work on problems of transportation, press, institutions, police, and facilities for Negro troops in the city. Organized social workers of both races have also appealed for Negro policemen and policewomen and sentiment for this is spreading in the community.

Meanwhile, the Nashville branch of the N.A.A.C.P. has increased its membership to over eleven hundred, of whom about thirty are white. It is active in keeping the Negro community informed on civic and social issues, and in getting out the vote; it has subcommittees at work on such problems as getting more satisfactory conditions at the City Detention Home for Negroes and the State Reformatory for Negro boys and seeking improved services for crippled Negro children who cannot now get the services available to white children. Last year the N.A.A.C.P. won a suit for the equalization of salaries of Negro and white teachers, and in several court cases where danger of a racially prejudiced decision was involved it has provided counsel or court reporting.[32]

There are signs that Nashville is beginning to recognize that

[32] Margaret McCulloch, Field Report, January, 1944.

Negroes ought to participate in community planning which affects them. The local Housing Authority has one Negro member. When the Chamber of Commerce set up a Postwar Planning Commission with thirteen subcommittees, one subcommittee chairman included three Negroes in his group, which is studying problems of health and welfare. The other twelve, however, set up lily-white committees to plan for Nashville's postwar future.

Texas

When the city of Austin decided to form an over-all community planning committee, the question was raised whether to have two community councils, one white and one Negro, or a single joint council. The latter plan was wisely adopted, and the committee has been functioning for over a year. There are two Negro members among the twenty persons composing the council, about the ratio of Negroes in the population. The planning group has been given official status as part of the city-county OCD organization appointed by the city manager. Its meetings are held in the municipal building where a secretarial assistant is provided. It has become a clearing house and consultant for all planning groups in Austin. A great improvement in recreation facilities for Negroes has resulted and the city-wide youth survey now in process will doubtless result in other recommendations.[33]

In Tyler, Texas, another interesting venture grew out of the Tyler Council of Parent Education, founded in 1935. In 1940 this Council, a white organization, set out to develop a cooperative program that would interrelate and supplement all existing agencies. It would approach Tyler's problems on a total community basis. Tyler's population is about 20 per cent Negro, so, to make this real, the white Council called together a group of twenty Negroes and a parallel Negro Community Council grew out of the conference. A Negro library committee was formed, which eventually grew into an interracial committee. Meantime, the Negro Community Council had defined the eleven major problems which seemed to confront them. Towards the solution of these they had established by 1943: (1) a nutrition program, with a Negro project supervisor employed by the

[33] Robert L. Sutherland, letter, 1943.

Board of Education which was establishing neighborhood councils and clubs for home improvement in each of the Negro school districts; (2) a boys' shop which was under construction; (3) the beginning of new case work with juvenile delinquents; and (4) a library for Negroes that had been opened with 800 books and a trained Negro librarian in 1941, and now had 1,500 books and equipment.[34]

Virginia

Virginia has a State Commission on Interracial Cooperation and at least thirteen city and county committees. In December, 1943, the State Commission met and adopted a statement on methods with the following six points: "(1) study race relations; (2) disseminate the facts; (3) take steps to correct the wrongs; (4) formulate a constructive cooperative program for the entire community; (5) enlist the aid of all friends and community agencies; (6) cease attacking 'radicals and reactionaries' and conserve energy for own program."

According to a letter from the director, the commission plans to focus its work on five points of friction: (1) streetcar and bus transportation; (2) treatment of Negroes by law enforcement officers and the courts (3) training and employment of Negroes in the skilled and semi-skilled trades and industries; (4) provision for health and recreation services for both the civilian and military population; (5) adequate provision for education and, along with this, school bus transportation for Negro children.[35]

The members of the Commission who are working on this program include Negroes distinguished in the professions, especially in education, and such leading white Virginians as the President of Randolph Macon College and the editor of the Richmond *Times-Dispatch*.

Many of the local committees have limited their programs very largely to discussion, which serves the purpose, according to one chairman of "learning to know each other better and to acquire a broader viewpoint in thinking of these subjects."[36] However, in Arlington, across the Potomac from Washington, a twelve-man committee

[34] Lillian Peak, *Team Work on the Home Front.*
[35] Dr. Thomas C. Allen, letter, February, 1944.
[36] Dr. Frank M. Daniels, letter, May, 1944.

formed through cooperative effort of white and Negro ministerial unions, is working to "promote better housing for those dislocated by the federal government building program in the community" and to solve "problems connected with Virginia laws of segregation on public vehicles."[37]

SUMMARY

This has been a rather long and detailed review of the evidences in every southern state that Negro and white citizens are beginning to work together for the better and more democratic functioning of local communities, of states, and of the South as a whole. In some states we can note only incipient stirrings; in others men and women of both races have actually labored together to put through programs of action which have expressed democratic principles in concrete terms of more equal facilities, more equal justice, and wider opportunities for Negro citizens. In so doing, an encouraging number of these groups are beginning to recognize that the work they are doing is essential not only in justice to a minority group but for the progress and prosperity of the community and the region as a whole. As this recognition deepens we shall see an increasing number of these groups revising their objectives as the Southern Regional Council has already done, and beginning to push programs for the social, economic, and civic development of all elements in the population.

[37] Dr. Walter M. Lockett, letter, March, 1944.

CHAPTER II

THE PRACTICE OF CITIZENSHIP

CITIZENS AND THE BALLOT

"THE RIGHT of the citizens of the United States to vote shall not be denied or abridged by the United States or by any State on account of race, color, or previous condition of servitude."

So declares the Fifteenth Amendment to the Constitution. Yet every Southerner knows that Negro citizens in the southern states have for a long time past been rather generally deprived of their right to vote. We are all too familiar with the various means that are used toward this end: intimidation, overt or covert, is one; the white primary (now outlawed by the Supreme Court) is another; differential enforcement of qualifications for voting is a third—for example, literacy tests which are used to disqualify highly educated Negroes while not applied to whites at all; the so-called "poll tax" is another. While it is doubtful that the payment of one or two dollars a year is the actual direct deterrent from voting for many qualified voters, the poll tax has many vicious indirect effects. It is cumulative in certain states, so that a citizen who has not registered for some years must pay back taxes with interest in order to vote. Actually, the "tax" disfranchises poor-white Southerners even more extensively than it does Negroes; yet it is secondarily a means of racial discrimination also, as there is such a great proportion of Negroes within the lower economic class.

Against this background of widespread disfranchisement, some good practices stand out and seem to be slowly gaining ground. Before considering these in detail, it is well to remind ourselves that the right to be governed by representatives of one's own choosing is no mere academic freedom—important as that freedom is to the development of responsible citizenship. It is a right whose benefits can be seen in such concrete manifestations as sewers, street lights, and garbage disposal. In other chapters of this book we shall see again and again that in those states and communities where Negro citizens vote they also have better health facilities, better housing, and better schools. This is not just a coincidence. City councilmen and legislators who vote appropriations know what people elect them. And although clinics may be equipped and schools improved as a solace to uneasy consciences, it is not by chance that the best hospitals, the best schools, and the cleanest streets are found in those communities where Negro citizens vote in considerable numbers and where they are beginning to use their franchise with some intelligence and political wisdom.

In the rural districts, the small towns, the poverty-ridden Deep South, Negroes rarely vote. In the large cities, the upper South, and the more progressive states, they frequently do. For instance, in Nashville, Memphis, and Chattanooga, the largest cities in Tennessee, Negroes vote in considerable numbers. In Nashville, in 1943, a Negro ran for councilman and received a sufficiently large number of votes to place him in a run-off election. He lost the election, but by a rather small margin of votes. In Louisville, Kentucky, a white citizen reports: "The Negro is better off as to civil rights in Louisville than in most other places in the South. He exercises his franchise here in about the same proportion that the white population does." One Negro is in the legislature and one is on the Housing Commission. Louisville has Negro policemen and postmen and a Negro deputy city-county health officer; and there is no segregation in public transportation.[1]

In Virginia for more than a decade, the white citizens have generally ceased to oppose Negro voting, but the Negro vote in practice is generally small. Negroes in Virginia cities in some cases participate in state-wide primaries and in local elections. The Norfolk City Democratic Committee has one Negro member who attends all meetings and serves on the same basis as any other member. Democratic party leaders frequently consult Negro leaders concerning local ques-

[1] Mark Ethridge, letter, March 15, 1943.

tions which affect the city's interest, such as schools, teachers' salaries, hospitals, and recreation.[2]

In Baltimore, Maryland, Negroes vote; and in 1943 some of them organized a campaign to stimulate Negro citizens to register and vote. Approximately 5,000 registered in the first six months of this campaign.[3]

In North Carolina, Negro voting is general. Only in isolated regions is there any objection.[4] In Raleigh, where some 7,000 Negroes vote, Negroes are integrated into all parts of the city's civic and political life. The vote is large enough to constitute a balance of power when so used, and has consequently been courted by rival candidates. Largely as a result of this situation there are Negroes serving in a number of public positions: there is one Negro plain-clothesman, and more recently there have been added uniformed Negro police officers in Negro areas, a Negro justice of the peace, and several employees of the City Recreation Commission. Extensive recreation facilities are open to Negroes, the city auditorium is open to all at any time, and citizens of both races use the State House park. These good practices reflect not only the progressiveness of the state, but the activities of Negro civic and political organizations. In 1931 a Negro Voters' League was formed to revive the lagging interest in the Negro vote. As a result of a campaign which the League conducted, the number of Negroes voting rose from 200 to 1,500, most of whom registered as Democrats. Announcing that it would be impossible to challenge each registrant individually, white politicians had a great number of the names of these registrants stricken from the books. A group of interested Negroes acted to bring this matter before the Wake County Superior Court, which ordered the names reinstated. Following this, no further obstruction of Negro voting was attempted.

In 1941, two of the precincts were so arranged as to be wholly Negro "to eliminate white political manipulation"; fresh registrations were held to eliminate unqualified voters; and the judges of election and registrars in these precincts have since then been Negroes. There

[2] L. P. Jackson and P. B. Young, letters, March, 1943.
[3] J. Harvey Kearnes, Field Report, October, 1943.
[4] L. E. Austin, letter, April 12, 1943.

is also an active Young Citizens' Civic and Political Club in Raleigh working on the same problems, and there is evidence that both white and Negro citizens are taking their responsibilities as voters with increasing seriousness.[5]

In Durham, North Carolina, a somewhat similar situation exists. In the city and county, Negroes vote in both the primary and the general election without interference. In fact, in two of the precincts where both whites and Negroes vote, the precinct chairmen are Negroes. One of these precincts is at the county court house. The precinct chairmen serve as members of the County Democratic Executive Committee. They meet regularly with the other members and participate in whatever business is being transacted. Several Negroes from Durham County were elected as delegates and alternates to the Democratic State Convention held in Raleigh in 1942.[6] In Craven County, North Carolina, a Negro was unopposed in the 1944 election for one of the sixteen positions as magistrate. A candidate in the Democratic primary, Mr. McDonald was reported to be the first Negro to hold a political office in Craven County in over 50 years.[7]

Even more significant from the long term point of view are recent developments with reference to Negro participation in primary elections. One of the most effective instruments of depriving Negroes of actual political influence has been the white primary. Since most of the southern states have, for all practical purposes, only one political party, the primary election is the only one in which the citizen can exercise an effective choice. As long as Negroes could be excluded from the primaries, the right to vote was a mere form. In March, 1944, however, in the case of Smith vs. Allwright, the Supreme Court of the United States ruled that the constitutional protection of the right to vote regardless of race extends to primaries as well as general elections. Although this historic decision was greeted by vociferous protests from some southern white politicians, and although various devices to evade it were at once concocted and have yet to be legally tested, it appears that the result will be greatly to increase the

---

[5] Interview (undated and unsigned) with C. D. Halliburton; Forrest interview with George Mitchell; Newbold material by F. G. Carnage, attorney, April 16, 1943.

[6] Memo from A. Elder, May 5, 1943.

[7] *Monthly Summary of Events and Trends in Race Relations,* May, 1944, p. 5.

participation of Negro citizens in southern elections. Many southern white newspapers have declared that the decision should be accepted and acted upon; and there has been a striking increase in Negro political activity all over the South. In 1944, Negroes voted not only in the Texas primaries, on which the decision was based, but also, to a limited extent, in other southern primaries. Although Negro citizens holding registration cards were not permitted to vote in the Georgia primaries in July, 1944, there was a great increase in registration and political interest.[8] Citizens' Democratic clubs were organized in the major Georgia cities as well as in some of the smaller towns. High schools organized campaigns to register all students over eighteen. In Atlanta, a Negro announced his candidacy for the Republican nomination for Congressman, the first time since Reconstruction that a Negro had sought a position as Congressman from Georgia.[9] In Birmingham, Alabama, representatives of thirty-one Jefferson County Negro organizations made a concerted drive to secure as full a registration as possible of Negro voters. Canvassers were trained and educational materials prepared for distribution through churches and trade unions.[10] In South Carolina, Negro voters, excluded from the regular Democratic party councils, took the lead in organizing the Progressive Democrats of South Carolina, which sent a delegation to the Democratic National Convention in Chicago in July, 1944. Although the delegation was not seated, it did not fail to make an impression on the assembled Democratic leaders. In the 1944 general election, this group, which included white as well as Negro voters, entered a Negro candidate for United States Senator.[11]

The election of 1944 came too soon after the Texas Primary decision for its full effects to be reflected in actual Negro participation. It seems likely that the 1946 elections will show much more clearly the results of this decision, as well as the results of increased political consciousness on the part of labor. In the meantime, there are signs that both whites and Negroes in the South are awakening to the evils of the poll tax and other barriers to voting. Such leading white news-

[8] *Ibid.*, July 1944, p. 6.
[9] *Ibid.*, May 1944, p. 6.
[10] *Ibid.*, October 1944, p. 67.
[11] *Ibid.*

papers as the *Nashville Tennessean,* the *Virginian-Pilot* of Norfolk, Virginia, and the Louisville *Courier-Journal* are adding their voices to those of small but determined publications as the *Southern Frontier* and the *Southern Patriot,* representing respectively the Southern Regional Council and the Southern Conference for Human Welfare. A group of southern newspaper editors met in Atlanta in December, 1944, to consider the question of voting restrictions throughout the South; and the Governor of Georgia recently called for a factual study of the poll tax, conducted and financed by Southerners, to determine whether it actually is "injurious to our democratic institutions"![12]

CITIZENS AND THE COURTS

One of the phrases dear to American ears is "equal justice." Yet if the word justice means anything, it does not need the word equal to indicate that it makes no distinction between high and low, between rich and poor, or between a citizen with a white skin and a citizen with a skin of some other color. It is perhaps because this ideal of justice is the very cornerstone of our American creed that we are most reluctant to inquire too closely into the relation of reality to the ideal. Yet no one can read over the following list of instances, laboriously collected, in which justice appears to have triumphed over racial distinctions, without feeling that the search for such instances, to say nothing of the meagerness of its fruits, is in itself a sad commentary on some of our courts. However, it can be said that the number of these instances appears to be increasing all over the South, and that there are indications that in time they will no longer be news of the "Man Bites Dog" variety.

In some cases the trend toward impartial enforcement of the law has been due to federal intervention. The more active intervention of federal agents and officers has, for example, contributed to the marked reduction in lynchings. In Mobile, Alabama, where confessions were obtained from two Negroes under questionable circumstances, their execution was stayed by the United States Supreme Court until the case could be reviewed.[13] In Hattiesburg, Mississippi, federal investigation of the lynching of a Negro resulted in indictments

[12] Associated Negro Press report, December 20, 1944.
[13] *Daily Worker,* April 21, 1943.

against five white men, including a deputy sheriff charged with failure to use "reasonable means" to protect the prisoner.[14]

In many cases, however, these instances of impartial justice are wholly local and indigenous. A judge of the Circuit Court in Knoxville, Tennessee, awarded $400 in damages to four Negro war workers who had been put out of a bus to make room for white passengers.[15] In the spring of 1943 the prompt action of the sheriff and coroner in Manchester, Tennessee, saved a Negro from a threatened lynching by a white mob.[16] A Circuit Court judge in Mobile, Alabama, sentenced a twenty-year old white shipyard worker to two years in the penitentiary on a charge of assault to murder for striking a colored worker on the head with a hammer. This white worker was one of the mob which precipitated a race riot at the Pinto Island yard of the Alabama Dry Dock Shipbuilding Company in May, 1943.[17]

An instance of belated justice is reported from Atlanta. An all-white jury after nearly six hours of deliberation convicted a sheriff, a police officer and a special deputy—all white, on two counts. The first count charged them with acting to deprive Robert Hall, a Negro prisoner, of his life without due process of law. It carried a sentence of one year and a $1,000 fine. The second count was conspiracy. It carried a sentence of two years and no fine. Hall, twenty-nine years old, had been arrested on an allegedly faked warrant accusing him of the theft of an automobile tire. He was beaten to death while in the custody of the three police officers.[18]

From Memphis comes the report of a case in which local authorities intervened to protect a Negro from lawless practices. The Negro, who had been beaten on the farm where he worked, obtained a government release and went to Memphis, where he got a job. His formei white boss and a friend drove into town with two guns in the back seat, and tried to force the Negro into the car. Both of the white men were apprehended and fined.[19] On another occasion in the same city, two little Negro girls, twin sisters in their early teens, were set upon

[14] *Ibid.,* April 21, 1943.
[15] *Monthly Summary,* September 1943, p. 9.
[16] Margaret McCulloch, Field Report.
[17] *Interracial News Service,* September, 1943, p. 4.
[18] Grace T. Hamilton, Field Report, November 6, 1943, and press reports.
[19] M. E. Bicknell, Field Report, September, 1943.

and injured by a white man as they were walking along the street. They had been working after school for the family of this man, but had left their jobs. Apparently he was angered over something that had occurred before they left. Their mother brought suit and the white man was convicted and required to pay court costs and doctor's bills and damages.

An example of good handling of a dangerous incident, from police action on the spot through court disposition of the case, is reported from Pitt County, North Carolina. In the little community of Fountain, tension had been rising since early in the week when Negroes became resentful over a report that a white man slapped a Negro girl. On Saturday, June 17, 1944, a white man attacked a Negro whom he accused of "pushing" him as he was crossing the street. A free-for-all fight ensued in which participants used knives, rocks, sticks, bottles, and lumps of coal. A white man was cut on the face and a Negro was stabbed in the arm. The police (members of the North Carolina Highway Patrol and county officers) were called and arrived just as both Negroes and whites were beginning to appear on the scene with firearms. Eleven Negroes and ten whites were arrested and taken to court. There the bond on all the participants was fixed at the same figure—$500. At the trial in Pitt County Court, eight whites and four Negroes were sentenced for their part in the incident, while six Negroes and two whites were freed. The sentences ranged in severity from 30 days in jail to twelve months at hard labor. On the whole, the sentences meted out to whites were more severe than those given to Negroes.[20]

Although these instances are few and scattered, they could be multiplied many times if all good practices in this area were reported. They show a slowly growing determination in the courts to see that the law is enforced impartially and for the protection of all. An effective practical step toward such impartiality is the inclusion of Negroes on juries on the same basis as other citizens. Although this right and responsibility legally falls upon all citizens, in the case of Negroes it has until recently been generally denied by various means.

In October, 1943, Atlanta, Georgia, broke the taboo on the use of

[20] *Monthly Summary,* July, 1944, p. 11; and August-September, 1944, p. 11.

Negroes on grand juries. Birmingham, Alabama, took the same step almost simultaneously; for the first time since the Scottsboro decision two Negroes were empanelled on the fall grand jury.[21] In Virginia the practice of accepting Negroes for jury duty is becoming general. "Since the famous Cox case," wrote a field reporter, "when Attorney Charles Houston secured a mistrial for a Negro accused of murder on the ground that Negroes were excluded from jury service, Negroes have served on juries in the counties and cities of the state. This applies in the state courts as well as in the federal courts."[22]

When Judge Elmer Davies assumed office some years ago in Middle Tennessee Federal District Court, sitting in Nashville, he almost immediately directed that names of citizens be placed in the federal grand and petit jury boxes without discrimination. It is interesting to recall that Judge Davies was believed to have been an active member of the Ku Klux Klan and that his advent to the bench was looked upon with considerable dismay by many Negro citizens. In 1942, Jasper C. Horne, a Negro and the manager of a federal housing project in the city, was among the twenty-three federal jurors sworn in.[23]

A detailed report from Memphis, Tennessee, states that Negroes are called for service and serve on petit and grand juries in Shelby County. The number who serve is limited, however, in part because most of the persons called are relieved from service at their own request. The reporter did not know whether Negroes are called in proportion to their proportion in the population, but from casual observation thought this was probably the case. In Durham, North Carolina, Negroes are quite frequently called for jury service, and at least one has served on the grand jury of the county.[24]

Along with the sound practice of employing citizens on juries without racial discrimination is the developing pattern of affording the full rights and courtesies of the court to Negro lawyers. This practice does not yet prevail in rural regions and isolated small towns, partly because of the general backwardness of these areas, partly

[21] *Monthly Summary,* November, 1943, p. 2.
[22] Wiley A. Hall, October, 1943.
[23] *Nashville Tennessean,* 1942 (undated clipping).
[24] A. A. Latting, letter, October 1, 1943.

because the number of qualified Negro lawyers is still small and most of them practice in the larger cities.[25]

The situation described by a Negro lawyer practicing in Memphis will serve as a good example of customs in the larger southern cities. "There is absolutely no discrimination in the courts here against Negro lawyers. We have the same rights and opportunities as other lawyers, and we are treated with the same respect. There has been no discrimination against Negroes in qualifying for and taking the Bar examination." The reporter continues: "I have heard complaints about unfair practice in the grading of papers but have seen no proof of this. I am advised that Mr. Looby of Nashville (a Negro attorney) made the highest mark of applicants when he took the bar, and I made the third highest grade when I took the bar in 1935. This seems to negate the idea of unfairness." In Tennessee the white bar association does not admit Negroes, but Negroes have their own bar association. Some few Negroes are employed in probation and parole services, and some in correctional institutions for juveniles.

Nashville has several Negro lawyers practicing freely in the courts. Richmond, Virginia, has about a dozen. "It can be said generally today that a competent Negro lawyer can practice with dignity and substantial success in most of the large cities of the South. However, Negro law graduates still experience greater difficulty in being admitted to the bar in the southern states than elsewhere in the country."[26]

Before he faces the hurdle of bar examinations, however, the southern Negro who wishes to practice law has to solve the problem of securing a legal education. Some few, of course, can make their way to the law schools of northern universities. But entrance requirements, distance, and the relatively very high cost are all obstacles. Others may attend the Law School of Howard University in Washington, D. C., though again distance and costs are barriers to be reckoned with. To compensate for the inequality of offering a law school education to white citizens and none to Negro citizens, some southern states have begun offering scholarships to Negro citizens to study law outside the

---

[25] William H. Hastie, letter, October 14, 1943.
[26] *Ibid.*

state. The Supreme Court, however, has declared this practice un-constitutional as a substitute for genuine equality of educational opportunities.

As a consequence, two attempts to open law schools for Negroes have recently been made in southern states. At St. Louis, Missouri, following the Supreme Court decision in the case of Lloyd Gaines, the state organized a law department for Negro students in connection with Lincoln University. Unfortunately the entry of the United States into the war at almost the same time has drained off almost the whole supply of potential law students, so that the department has been obliged to close its doors temporarily (as has also, incidentally, the law school for whites of Vanderbilt University in Tennessee).[27]

The state of North Carolina has organized a law department at North Carolina College for Negroes in Durham. This school opened in 1940-41. Professors from the University of North Carolina, half an hour away by bus, have devoted part of their time to this school—possibly a more practical and promising beginning than in Missouri.[28] Tennessee has recently authorized the purchase of a law library by its state college for Negroes as a step towards the establishment of a law school.[29]

One southern university, that of Maryland, has faced its problem with refreshing realism, by admitting qualified Negroes to the existing law department of the state university. It is, of course, obvious that it is difficult, costly, and wasteful to establish duplicate state law schools, equal in all respects, one for whites and one for Negroes; and obvious also that if this is done, neither can rise to the quality that the state desires and that the citizens have a right to expect, especially in states where per capita income is relatively low. On the other hand, anything less than this is less than justice. The step taken by Maryland shows a frank recognition of the problem and a readiness to accept the most practical solution. Experience so far has brought no startling consequences. The few Negroes who have attended the law school have been well received and have made creditable records.

[27] *Ibid.*
[28] *Ibid.*
[29] E. W. Turner, letter, 1943.

CITIZENS ON PATROL

One of the most effective contributions to justice and to respect for law that the South has made in recent years is the employment of qualified Negro policemen in areas predominantly Negro. Many people do not realize how widespread this practice is. For this reason a list of cities where Negro policemen are successfully employed may be revealing.[30] Numbers are given where reported.

PLACE	TOTAL	IN UNIFORM	AUXILIARIES ONLY
Arkansas			
Little Rock	8	8	
District of Columbia			
Washington	113	99	
Florida			
Bartow			
Daytona Beach	4	4	
Fort Myers			
Jackson			
Lakeland			
Miami	12	12	
Sarasota			
Tampa			400
Georgia			
Atlanta (Requested by civic and church groups)			
Macon			65
Kentucky			
Lexington	3[31]	0	
Louisville	18	14[32]	
Owensboro	1	1	
Louisiana			
Baton Rouge			

[30] Compiled from *Southern Frontier*, Report of Greater Little Rock Urban League, and Field Reports.

[31] Includes one woman.

[32] Fifteen additional men to be appointed by order of December, 1943.

Maryland

    Baltimore 6

    Cambridge 1

    Easton 1

    Pocomoke City ....

Missouri

    St. Louis .... 24[33]   9

North Carolina

    Asheville (under consideration)

    Charlotte 4   4

    Elizabeth City (under
       consideration) ....

    High Point 2   2

    Raleigh 1

    Winston-Salem 1

Oklahoma

    Muskogee ....

    Oklahoma City 9   5

    Tulsa 8   7

Tennessee

    Knoxville 5   5

    Nashville (under consideration)

Texas

    Austin 3   3

    Beaumont 2   2

    Galveston 13   10

    Houston 4   3

    San Antonio 7   1

Virginia

    Newport News ....   100[34]

    Portsmouth   50

    Richmond (Requested by
       church, civic and social work
       groups) ....

[33] Includes two women.
[34] Also has two Negro women in Juvenile and Domestic Relations.

It is interesting and significant that while the materials of this study have been in process of collection repeated requests have come in for information on this point. The list has kept growing, partly by the coming in of reports of instances formerly unknown, and also by the appointment of Negro police in cities previously without them, and by the increase of such appointments in cities where a smaller number had previously been appointed on a more or less experimental basis. It is likely that this list does not include all the instances and is an understatement of the present numbers. Although Alabama, Louisiana, Mississippi, and South Carolina are missing from the list, it may be that even in these states the practice has begun in some instances not yet known to us. This practice, which is so patently reasonable, is being found so effective that it is spreading surely though slowly all across the South.

Since this is so, it is well to review the experience of some communities with these policemen.

Washington, D. C., has had the longest and most extensive experience in the use of Negro police. Negroes have served on Washington's Metropolitan Police Force since it was organized in 1861. The total police force of the city is 1,601, exclusive of 235 vacancies; of these 150 are regularly assigned to plainclothes duty. Of this force Negroes number 113, of whom 14 are detective sergeants and precinct detectives or engaged in other investigative duties in plainclothes. The remainder, including one lieutenant, are uniformed policemen. The present police chief reports them as "loyal, willing, trustworthy in all respects, and highly satisfactory."[35] The present number represents an increase of 71 since 1941.

The second oldest instance that has come to our knowledge is that of St. Louis, Missouri. Negro policemen have been employed there for more than forty years. Originally experimentally employed, they are now a permanent part of the force. There were by 1936, 24 Negro police; 9 uniformed men who patrol boats, 9 special officers, 1 sergeant, 1 lieutenant, 2 policewomen, and 2 prison guards.[36]

Tulsa, Oklahoma, has employed Negro police for more than fifteen years through the civil service system. Their services are restricted to

[35] Letter of chief of police, February 1944.
[36] Report by Atlanta correspondent, based on N.A.A.C.P. report of 1936.

Negro areas. Experience with them through the years is reported to have been "very fine. We have some very loyal and efficient Negro officers who take a great deal of pride in their work in apprehending Negro criminals and maintaining peace and order in their part of the city."[37]

"Daytona Beach, Florida, has employed Negro police for ten years. These police are restricted to Negro areas and have power of arrest over Negroes only. Under these conditions we have found the use of Negro policemen entirely satisfactory."[38]

Louisville, Kentucky, has employed Negro police for a number of years. Some are officers on patrol; some are detectives; two are on the vice squad. They are selected on the basis of merit and trained carefully before being placed on duty. Experience has shown their work very satisfactory, and there has been no opposition to them.[39] In December, 1943, the Office of Safety director announced plans under way to appoint an additional fifteen Negro policemen and two policewomen. Three officers from the present quota are to be raised to the rank of sergeant.

Texas employs Negro police extensively. Austin has Negro radio patrolmen. The San Antonio chief of police reports that his department has had "some very good Negro policemen, having ability, quality, and bravery. They have made a very enviable record. There has never been any racial antagonism in San Antonio, whether the Negroes be on the police force or off the police force. I am not considering attempting to run a police department without the efficient help of Negro members now employed on our force."[40]

Among the cities more recently adopting this practice reports are also good.

Lexington, Kentucky, has Negro radio patrolmen. The police are not in uniform but act as plain-clothes men. They serve in Negro districts. There is one policewoman, a college graduate and a woman of intelligence, who commands the respect of the Negroes of her district. The chief of police feels that crime has been curtailed in the Negro district during the last few years.[41]

[37] Report of Atlanta correspondent, based on letters examined.
[38] Field Report by student under Dr. Reid.
[39] Atlanta correspondent's report.   [40] *Ibid.*   [41] *Ibid.*

Charlotte, North Carolina, has four Negro police. An early report stated that they were not then under civil service as were other police officers, received only $110 monthly as compared with $165 received by the whites, and met with some antagonism among Negro citizens who objected to being arrested by Negro officers. Later reports from the chief of police and others state that the men serving at present are carefully selected on the basis of education, training, and temperament, though it does not make clear whether on a civil service basis or not, that equalization of salaries in the near future has been promised, and that the officers have been able to perform their duties in a thoroughly satisfactory manner. Their relations with the white police have been excellent and their cooperation has contributed both to the solution of many crimes and to the easing of tension between the races.[42]

The process of establishing the use of Negro police in any city seems to be fairly uniform as far as the reports received show. Some church or civic group becomes concerned over the differential rate and treatment of crime in the white and Negro sections of the city or over racial tensions. A study of the situation follows, revealing that the use of policemen of their own race promises to go far to dispel antagonism to law-enforcement in the Negro community, to build up in its place respect for law, and to ease tensions. Experience of other cities is studied and the successful use of Negro police discovered. Representations are made to the proper city authorities, and education of the city public is undertaken through church and civic organizations and the press. City officials agree to make a few experimental appointments. Where these are made on a sound basis with equal pay and equal requirements, uniformed status, and adequate facilities, the effects are almost invariably to reduce crime and ease tension. Further appointments are then requested and generally granted. It seems unnecessary to repeat this story in instance after instance. Initiative comes from an Urban League, now from an Interracial Commission, again from a church conference on social work, or from a branch of the N.A.A.C.P.

A second pattern is the use of auxiliary police under the Civilian

[42] Correspondence.

Defense Program. How durable and fruitful a practice this is, it will take time to learn. Tampa, Florida, has four hundred auxiliary police in four companies, uniformed and armed at public expense, who rendered the equivalent of 1,261 eight-hour days' service in 1943. They include also two men in traffic patrol duty and a medical unit.[43]

One other story of the use of auxiliary police and one of regular police will serve as illustrations. In Macon, Georgia, until a few years ago, certain Negro districts had been regarded as among the most difficult for law enforcement. In 1942 Macon appointed Negro voluntary police as auxiliaries to the regular force. By 1943 there were sixty-five of these. They work without pay, buy their own uniforms, pistols, and guns, and have tackled the most difficult districts in the city; yet they have set a remarkable record for efficiency. They are assigned to regular beats and receive some training in connection with civilian defense work. On April 27, two of the auxiliary police distinguished themselves in service by capturing a Negro convict who had escaped from the Florida State Prison at Raiford. This convict had a criminal record in two states and was under a twenty-year sentence in Florida. High commendation is given the whole auxiliary force by the chief of police and especial praise to J. W. Burnham and James Thomas who recognized, chased, and brought in this escaped convict. No one, of course, would commend as a permanently good practice that police be required to purchase their own uniforms and guns or to serve without pay. Yet the remarkably fine spirit and service rendered to their city by these Negro volunteer police is certainly a fine demonstration of how Negro police can work, and has earned Macon's Negro citizens the clear right to normal participation in the regular police force.[44]

Little Rock, Arkansas, has begun its experiment on a different basis. In 1941 the Secretary of the Urban League became concerned over a wave of homicides reported to be taking place among Negroes. He began investigating the causes and making his findings known as widely in the community as he could. At the same time, inquiries brought him reports of twenty-one southern cities successfully using Negro police in some manner, and he began to publicize this fact

[43] *Southern Frontier,* February, 1944.
[44] Associated Negro Press release; *Southern Frontier,* May, 1943, p. 1.

and to seek public support for a request for Negro police in Little Rock. In June, 1941, the Interdenominational Ministerial Alliance joined the Urban League in filing a memorandum with the Mayor and City Council on this subject. This memorandum pointed out that white officers are often unable to gather evidence relating to crimes committed by Negroes against Negroes, or can only do so with great difficulty. It recommended that Negro policemen be appointed to patrol areas where crime among Negroes was high, that punishment commensurate with the degree of the offense be given Negroes who commit crimes against Negroes,[45] and that the Mayor, Council, and private organizations and citizens cooperate in the interest of adjusting this serious problem.

The example of the twenty-one southern cities was cited, and a specific recommendation was made for the addition to the police force of four Negroes until an adequate number could qualify under civil service examination. In the same year requests were sent to the Commander of Camp Robinson and to Judge William H. Hastie, then civilian aide to the Secretary of War, asking investigation of the use of M. P.'s in Little Rock. White M. P.'s were being used in a section frequented by Negro soldiers. Neither request met with any response in 1941 or in the early months of 1942. During 1942, however, there were several conflicts growing out of these situations. Finally there followed the tragedy of the shooting to death of a Negro sergeant by a white city policeman. The policeman was exonerated; but the Negro citizenry was deeply disturbed and roused. Negro M. P.'s were then appointed to patrol the Negro business district, and the Urban League was requested to furnish the names of ten Negro men to be recommended for jobs as civilian policemen. Eight Negro special policemen were eventually appointed without examination, at regular rookie salaries.[46]

The latest instance reported follows the consistent pattern of satisfactory experience. In September, 1944, the city of Miami hired its first five colored police officers. By December, the chief of police

[45] It is common practice to give a lighter sentence for crimes against Negroes than for the same crime against whites by either whites or Negroes, thus giving the Negro citizens less protection of law and weakening respect for law in general in the Negro community.

[46] Annual Report, Urban League of Greater Little Rock, Arkansas, 1942.

and the City Safety Director were so pleased with the results that they hired seven more, more than doubling the original number.[47]

CITIZENS IN THE CUSTODY OF THE STATE

In every state, the state government assumes control over some of its citizens and takes them into custody for their own well-being and for the protection of society. Clearly justice demands that these wards of the state, temporary or permanent as the case may be, receive impartial treatment and care. Up to now, this has hardly been the general practice in the penal and welfare institutions of the southern states.

There is commonly one state prison in which both white and Negro convicts are imprisoned. All prisoners are under one administrative and supervisory control, and receive in theory at least identical food, clothing, and medical care. Frequently, however, accommodations for Negro prisoners are inferior to those for whites, and there is a differential in their work and in the treatment they receive. The entire staff, other than menial laborers, is generally white and frequently includes poorly paid, untrained and prejudiced white persons. This condition seems at present to be almost static. No change in the direction of more qualified personnel, or use of Negro personnel, was reported by any of the states replying to inquiry. One report of improvement alone was sent in.

This report is of a new policy in the Alabama State Prison. For some time it has been the practice to give white prisoners quite thorough tests on entry, including: (1) photography and finger printing; (2) physical examination and reference for treatment; (3) work placement, comprising case histories, I.Q., educational background, experience and aptitude tests. Work placements were made on the basis of the last group of tests; and the prison taught sheet-metal working, welding, machine-shop work and shoe repairing. Negro prisoners, however, received only the first two tests and were all assigned to the jute mill. But in December of 1943 it was announced that the state is now prepared to give Negro prisoners the same complete tests as whites, and to make work placements based on the

[47] Associated Negro Press release.

results, opening to them also the opportunity to learn trades that can be useful to them upon their release.

In regard to the care of juvenile delinquents, conditions are somewhat more variable; but there has been in the past a tendency to set up institutions either solely or primarily for whites. These had always an all-white staff. Negro juvenile delinquents were frequently not provided for at all, or were given an inferior section of the white institution under white personnel. Within the last few years, however, there has been a widespread awakening among Southerners, both Negro and white, to the need for correcting this situation.

A brief summary of the replies received from southern State Departments of Welfare and Institutions is indicative, though not exhaustive.

STATES WITH RECENT OR NEW PENAL AND WELFARE BUILDING PROGRAMS

Alabama: None.

Arkansas: None.

Delaware: "Yes"— for Negroes, unspecified.

Georgia: New school for delinquent Negro girls just opened.

Kentucky: All institutions bi-racial; improvements under way in Negro sections of all penal and welfare institutions; a new fireproof hospital for the insane planned; new men's reformatory and new women's prison for both races recently completed.

Louisiana: All institutions are now bi-racial but the legislature has appropriated funds for a home to be built for delinquent Negro children.

Mississippi: Legislature has authorized the building of a Negro juvenile reformatory.

North Carolina: Legislature has authorized a state training school for Negro girls.

Oklahoma: None.

South Carolina: None.

Tennessee: Improvements just completed costing several thousand dollars at a colored girls' industrial home; has one new brick building, replacing derelict frame shacks, underway at the state reformatory for boys at Pikeville, and a second authorized.

Texas: Funds appropriated for a home for Negro delinquent girls, but its construction has been delayed by the war.

Several other states are studying phases of this general problem. In Maryland better handling of Negro delinquent boys and provision for Negro feeble-minded are being studied and projected. In North Carolina a special legislative committee has been appointed to study the needs of the Negro feeble-minded and to make recommendations. In South Carolina welfare workers have laid before the State Department of Welfare recommendations in regard to the needs of the Negro population. In Nashville, Tennessee, white and Negro citizens are urging the further development of a child-placement program recently launched for all children but not yet functioning for Negro children, and are seeking related improvements in the state, city, and private child-care institutions for Negroes. The question is also being raised of provision by the state for Negro feeble-minded children.

Here then is a field where the public conscience is awake and where there is every reason to believe that within the space of a few years, if public-spirited citizens will concern themselves with the problems, improved institutional care can be achieved for all citizens, including improved and largely equalized care for Negro citizens.

There is another encouraging aspect of this improvement in state institutions for Negroes. This is the rapidly increasing use of trained Negro personnel in such institutions. A summary of reports from southern states bears this out. It should be borne in mind, however, that all-Negro personnel in institutions for Negroes only is a good practice only within the framework of segregation. It is axiomatic that under other conditions civil service examinations open to all, with appointments based not on race or color but on ability and qualifications, would produce the highest quality of public servants, and would serve the best interests not only of the wards of the state but of the commonwealth as a whole.

SOUTHERN PENAL AND WELFARE INSTITUTIONS EMPLOYING NEGRO PERSONNEL

(as reported, 1943)

Arkansas: Negro Boys' Industrial School, all except the director. School for Negro Blind. School for Negro Deaf would use Negro personnel if they could find trained Negro teachers.

Delaware: Girls' Industrial School, all-Negro personnel and bi-racial Board of Directors.

Georgia: School for Delinquent Negro Boys, all-Negro personnel. School for Delinquent Negro Girls (just opened) all-Negro Personnel.

Kentucky: Negro sections of State Institutions for the Insane, Feeble-minded and Delinquent.

Louisiana: All institutions are bi-racial; no use of Negro personnel reported. New institution planned for Negro delinquents to have Negro personnel. Department of Public Welfare employs some Negro social workers as field workers, case workers, case supervisors, and child welfare workers.

Maryland: All but two institutions are bi-racial; no reports of Negro personnel in these. School for Colored Girls has an all-Negro staff. School for Colored Boys has a bi-racial staff, soon to be all-Negro.

Missouri: All institutions bi-racial; all staffs white except State School for Epileptic and Feeble-minded, where one building is for Negroes and has an all-Negro staff.

North Carolina: Some institutions for Negroes have white staffs. Morrison Training School for Negro Boys and the two state orphanages for Negroes have Negro staffs throughout. Negroes are employed under the State Board of Charities and Public Welfare as case workers, probation officers, child welfare workers, case-work aides in sufficient numbers to be fairly representative, chiefly in the large urban centers. The State Board makes extensive studies of Negro Welfare in which Negroes participate.

Oklahoma: Training Schools for Negro boys and girls, all Negro staffs; white directors recently replaced by Negroes.

Tennessee: Vocational school for colored girls, all-Negro personnel.

Virginia: Most staffs white. The two reform schools for Negro juvenile delinquents have all-Negro staffs.

Texas: Most staffs white. School for Negro Blind employs all-Negro staff. No Negroes now serve in State Department of Welfare but employment of some has recently been authorized.

Here again is a record of progress so pronounced as to constitute a definite trend. Indeed the practice of employing trained Negro personnel in welfare and correctional institutions which have Negroes in their charge has become so general that the states where it is not to be found in at least some of the institutions are now the exceptions.

Back of these encouraging trends in the field of welfare and correction—prisons being as yet unaffected—lie several factors. One is a general advance in social work in the South. As this work is rapidly being raised to a professional level, a new degree of intelligence, education and social vision is brought into it, broadening the recognition of community responsibility, pointing out gaps in the institutional and welfare programs, and offering expert counsel for their correction. A second factor is the increasing body of trained Negro personnel available and prepared in recent years to enter these services on a high professional level. A third very important factor is active and cooperative citizenship, the growth of which has already been traced.

Let no one suppose, however, that a "trend" in social affairs means that improvements come about automatically. Far from it. What appears as a trend when observed in the mass is shown on closer examination to be made up of innumerable instances of individual and group achievement, brought about by the persistent, unremitting, not-to-be-discouraged efforts of courageous and patient men and women of both races. The story of three such efforts, one on a state-wide scale, one in a local department of welfare, and one still in process in a Council of Social Agencies, will illustrate what it takes to make a "trend."

"NOTES ON THE HISTORY AND BACKGROUND OF THE GEORGIA TRAINING SCHOOL FOR NEGRO GIRLS"[48]

"The Georgia Federation of Colored Women decided to try in some way to help the delinquent colored girls of Georgia (date of first interest unknown). There was no institution where these girls could be sent. If probation proved unsuccessful, they were sent to prison. This procedure was deplored by judges and probation officers, but nothing was done to correct the situation. Then Mrs. W. A. Hunt of Fort Valley, who had cherished the hope for years that a state institution would be provided, stimulated the Federation of Colored Women to go to work on the problem. They were encouraged in this by the example of colored women in others states—Alabama, Virginia, Texas, Mississippi, and South Carolina—who had helped in the estab-

[48] By an Atlanta University student under Doctor Reid's supervision.

lishment of State Training Schools; and although they were well aware of the many difficulties involved, they were determined to try.

"The Federation first raised the money to buy 130 acres of land for the proposed school, in Bibb County near Macon. They raised $3,000 in cash and made the down payment. Then, with the aid of a WPA grant, they built a brick building of modest proportions that would house about 75 girls. After all debts were paid, they presented this building to the state. This was not the end of their struggle; it was only the beginning. An appropriation was needed to run the institution. The women had hoped when they gave the state the building, which had cost $27,000, that the legislature would appropriate the money for upkeep and running expenses. But in 1937, the year the building was turned over to the state, the legislature failed to pass any such appropriation. One reason for this was probably lack of organization and confusion in procedure. The women found themselves very much handicapped by their lack of experience in political strategy. They therefore appealed for help to the Commission on Interracial Cooperation, and its Director, Mrs. Ames, on the basis of her legislative experience, undertook to arrange for the necessary preliminary steps.

"In 1939, when the Legislature met again, the bill was re-introduced. But plans for sponsoring it had not yet been perfected, and for the second time it failed to pass.

"In spite of two setbacks, work and plans went forward with increased vigor. The white women of the state now joined in the effort. Civic and religious institutions helped. Key white women, club leaders in 15 Georgia cities, lent their efforts to get the cooperation of their legislators. Newspaper editors heartily sponsored the cause. Ralph T. Jones, in his column in the *Atlanta Constitution* on January 25, 1940, published a strong appeal for the passage of the appropriation.

"In 1940 the Governor of the state was to be elected. The fact that it was an election year raised great hopes for the passage of the bill; indeed, Governor Talmadge, campaigning for re-election, promised his support.

"Mrs. Ames went to Macon and had pictures made of the school;

she talked with important political figures and made other contacts. The 1939 Grand Jury in Dekalb County had recommended the appropriation, on the ground that there was no place to send Negro girls, and had selected a committee to interview the Governor. This proved to be the opening wedge in securing the support of a number of judges, including Judge Graham, Oconee judicial court, McRae; Judge R. Eve, superior court, Tifton; Judge C. H. Porter, Rome judicial court; and Judge Telford of the Hall County Juvenile Court in Gainesville. Judge Holliday, of the Bibb County Juvenile Court, was of immeasurable assistance.

"In the meantime, Governor Talmadge was re-elected. In preparation for the 1941 session of the legislature, white women in every city interviewed their representatives, and hopes for the final passage of the appropriation were high. Ralph Jones, writing again in the *Atlanta Constitution* on New Year's Day, 1941, said: 'It won't be long now. Soon the Georgia legislators will be gathering at the State Capitol for their regular session . . . (One of the important issues is the appropriation for the Georgia State Training School.)

" 'There is a lot involved, much more than appears on the surface, in this request. It could easily mean tremendous things for Georgia in the future, if the legislature looked with sympathy and understanding in this instance, instead of surrendering intelligence to outworn prejudice.'

"To their credit, the legislators did 'look with sympathy': the appropriation was passed. But on March 27, 1941, 'just within the deadline for executive action, Governor Eugene Talmadge vetoed the appropriation to open the training school for delinquent Negro girls.' (*The Georgia Observer,* April, 1941—Georgia's Governor Fails Georgia Women.)

"Meanwhile, the building put up by the Federation of Colored Women stood empty. In 1941, the Bibb County Commissioner decided to use it temporarily as an orphanage for white children. Mrs. Hunt again sought help from the Commission on Interracial Cooperation. It seems that the Juvenile Society and Executive Secretary of Bibb County had secured permission from the court to use the building for a white orphanage. Mrs. Hunt and Mrs. Ames conferred with

Judge Holliday of the Bibb County Juvenile Court, an agreement was reached under which the injunction was withdrawn, plans for the white orphanage were abandoned and the institution remained closed.

"Plans for a new appropriation were made. Ellis Arnall, candidate for the governorship, was interviewed. Mr. Arnall declared his approval of the appropriation and promised that the training school would be opened if the legislature passed the bill. Old plans and hopes were revived, and again the political machinery was set in motion.

"In 1939 the appropriation for the training school was to have been from any unexpended funds in the state treasury. In 1941 there was a straight appropriation bill. Now candidate Arnall said that if the legislature passed the bill, he would get the appropriation from the Educational Fund.

"In 1942, after Governor Arnall was elected, a letter was sent to him about the appropriation. In June, 'ten months after his inauguration, under authority granted him by the assembly,' Governor Arnall opened the school.

"Still the work was not finished. The next question confronting the board was the selection of personnel to direct the training of the girls. It was decided that by all means the supervisor should be a Negro. The Commission on Interracial Cooperation arranged for a conference with Miss Stevenson, from Virginia, who had training in such work as well as experience as matron of the school for delinquent girls in Virginia. However, Miss Stevenson refused to consider the original salary offer of $1800. After consultation with Governor Arnall, the board wired Miss Stevenson an offer of $2100. This she accepted, and has since served as an able and competent supervisor.

"The next question was the furnishing of the building. No appropriation had been made for its equipment. Again the colored and white women all over the state set to work with fresh determination. The necessary furnishings were decided upon at bi-racial committee meetings, and all groups joined in the project. Showers were given; church women of both races contributed. The outcome of this joint undertaking was not only the furnishing of the building, which was successfully accomplished, but a genuine increase in interracial understanding and good will, brought about by cooperation on a common project, and respect for the qualities demonstrated by women of both races."

A similar effort on a smaller scale is described in the following report from Greenville, South Carolina:

"Recognizing the dire need for an additional social worker to work with Negro children, and the fact that proof would have to be furnished before one could be secured under the Lanham Act, a committee composed of the executive secretary of the Family Welfare Society, the Negro case worker, the chairman of the Negro advisory board, the director of the Phillis Wheatley Center, and the county director of the Department of Public Welfare, assembled the following memoranda:

"1. Statement of local Negro child welfare needs, by F. S., Negro case worker.

"2. Testimonial of need and promise of cooperation from the Negro Advisory Board—signed by the members.

"3. A statement from the Interracial Committee chairman commending the request and promising cooperation.

"4. A statement from the Juvenile Court Judge emphasizing the need and pledging cooperation.

"5. A statement from the superintendent of the city schools stating the need as revealed by his Negro visiting teacher and pledging her assistance.

"6. A statement from the Phillis Wheatley Board emphasizing the need and offering office space free of rent for such a worker.

"7. Statistics from the medical social worker at the General Hospital showing increase in number of unmarried Negro mothers.

"After these reports were assembled, they were forwarded to the county director of the Department of Public Welfare with a letter requesting that she take the matter up with the Chief of the Child Welfare Division of the State Department of Public Welfare. This she did personally with the added emphasis of a letter from her board.

"This step was followed up by a personal letter and then a visit to the Chief of the Child Welfare Division from the Chairman of the

Committee. The executive secretary, the Juvenile Court Judge, and one of his probation workers accompanied the chairman on this visit to the State Capitol. The technique was effective. In late January, 1944, a Negro child welfare worker was assigned to Greenville and her coming was welcomed by all of the cooperating agencies. She began active duty on February 8th as the first Negro worker appointed in South Carolina under the Lanham Act."[49]

Often these developments have their origin in the efforts of private local agencies to meet the needs of the citizens whom they are trying to serve. This kind of beginning is glimpsed in the following field report from Memphis, Tennessee:

"The Negro Welfare Committee of the Council of Social Agencies has made a report to the Council of their six months' study of social work for Negroes. It was possible in this report to bring to the attention of the white members of the Board of Directors of the Council (there are no Negro members of this Board) some graphic evidence of the need for expansion of services. The report was received with great respect and there is promise that it may bear some results.

"The Committee is also being asked to work with the Venereal Disease Division of the U. S. Public Health Service on a study of this problem among Negroes. This is due to the reputation that the Committee has gained through the preceding study. This is the first time that Negroes have been given a participating role in such investigations of their own needs.

"Another result of the previous study is the appointment by the Division of Vocational Rehabilitation of a Negro physician to care for needy crippled Negroes, and the cases are being taken care of financially from federal funds."

November report: "The Negro Welfare Commission has been increased by the addition of two colored persons and one white. It now consists of 5 Negroes and 4 whites. Two of the latter hold executive positions on the Council."[50]

In Nashville, Tennessee, the Council of Community Agencies is organized on a community basis without racial discrimination. Negro

[49] *Monthly News Letter*, Family Welfare Society, Greater Greenville, South Carolina, March, 1943.
[50] M. E. Bicknell, Field Report.

agencies are represented on the same basis at white; Negroes serve on the Research and Planning Committee and Executive Committee of the Council; meetings are held in the white Y.M.C.A. and are unsegregated.[51]

Other southern cities are following this pattern in increasing numbers. We shall mention only one more—the Social Planning Council of St. Louis, Missouri. Six of the agencies which are members of the council serve Negroes only. Of these, two are operated by Catholic Sisters, two by bi-racial boards of directors and two by Negro boards of directors. Each agency has two representatives on the Board of Delegates which is the corporate body of the Social Planning Council. There are no Negro members of the board of directors nor on the paid staff. Each division of the Council, however, has a divisional executive committee; some of these committees have Negro members, some have not, in a constantly changing pattern. Where there is an outstanding Negro professional person or layman in a particular field, he or she is likely to be on the executive committee in that division. There are also forty or fifty working committees. When these working committees deal with problems involving a racial angle, they are always bi-racial; at other times, they frequently have Negro members. Negro social workers are extensively used and are on the increase. Week in, week out, these workers plan together to meet community needs and solve community problems.[52]

It is by such steps, often slow and painful to the workers concerned, that forward moves are made—here, there and everywhere—until to the casual observer the growth seems spontaneous and effortless, a "social trend."

CITIZENS ON PUBLIC CARRIERS

There was a time in frontier days when a man could build his own stretch of country road and his own bridge across a stream and it was his privilege to charge what he pleased for travel over it. Gradually roads and bridges have become the handiwork and property of the government, city, county, and state; and it is the public duty of all citizens to support them, the public right of all citizens to use them.

[51] Walter L. Stone, letter, 1943.
[52] Myron Gwinner, assistant director, Social Planning Council, letter, April, 1944.

So, too, there was a time, not so long ago, when private individuals dreamed and adventured for the making of railroads. These, too, though the work of many hands and heads together, were at first essentially private undertakings. But as they became increasingly essential means of transportation for all Americans, governmental aid and governmental regulation began to be extended to them in the public interest. They stand in relation to the citizen midway between the ancient private and the modern public road, institutions with a private aspect in finance, profits, management, and charges for services; institutions with a public aspect as carriers of United States mail, of government officials and armed forces and their supplies, of essential freight and passenger traffic, interference with which would disrupt the public life. Even closer to the public are the buses operating over tax-supported roads and so benefitting from the public pocket. So it becomes decreasingly a matter of private privilege, increasingly a matter of public justice, that there should be equity in the services rendered by these "common carriers" to all citizens. Increasingly in interstate travel, this is becoming the case. Decisions of the United States Supreme Court have declared it unconstitutional for trains and buses operating in interstate transportation to discriminate in the quality of service offered. Segregation has not been ruled out; but accommodation offered must be equal and equally available to citizens regardless of race. In intrastate travel no such federal rule holds, although "separate but equal" is the traditional illusion entertained with respect to all segregated accommodations.

To convert a ruling into a practice, however, is quite another matter.[53] As yet very little progress has been made, but a few tentative steps in this direction have been taken.

Prior to 1943 the Gulf, Mobile, and Ohio Railroad system had, despite numerous protests, barred Negroes, including men in the armed forces, from its dining cars. The road operates between Mobile, St. Louis, and New Orleans. Two southern officials of the N.A.A.C.P. then made a trip over its lines, and sent a report of their findings to the legal staff of the N.A.A.C.P. in New York; this in turn filed an

[53] Carl A. Hausaker of Chicago, Illinois, has recently published a small fifteen-cent pamphlet for the Bansberry Foundation entitled *Interstate Jim Crow Laws Abolished.* This is a manual of procedures for Negroes in obtaining the protection of the law.

informal complaint with the Interstate Commerce Commission in Washington. The Commission took up the matter with the railroad and requested a reply. Today Negroes are served in diners of this road on the same meal calls as other passengers.[54]

Two other roads operating in the South have recently made similar moves towards compliance with the law. On the Southern Pacific since the war started, the traffic between Houston and Dallas has grown heavy. The train making this run now divides one of its deluxe coaches between whites and Negroes by a movable curtain which is moved forward or back as the need demands. In some instances the conductors give up their seats in order to see that all passengers are accommodated. The Rock Island road which makes this same run has also recently provided equal accommodations for Negroes.[55]

In one instance the backward step of a new Jim Crow law was averted, and in two instances abandonment of the whole mechanism of compulsory segregation laws in transportation has been advocated with considerable support. In Jacksonville, Florida, overcrowding, combined with segregation customs, was creating tensions on the buses; so the city council passed an ordinance segregating the races on public carriers and sent it to the Mayor to sign. The Mayor, believing there was a better way to handle the problem, called a conference. To this conference came by invitation representatives of the City Council, the police department, the Motor Transit Company, the Ministerial Association and every considerable Negro organization in the city. In a series of sessions an agreement was reached to handle the whole matter by education, custom, and common consent rather than by law. Whites would be asked to seat themselves from the front towards the rear, Negroes from the rear to the front. The arrangement was accepted by both sides and to the satisfaction of the whole community, the ordinance was returned unsigned.[56]

Still more recently a similar situation in Virginia became acute, but Virginia already had laws requiring segregation on intrastate buses. These were causing, as in many other states, great inconvenience

[54] Similar action earlier in 1941 had led to equal pullman accommodations on this same road. Field Report.

[55] J. Le Flore, Field Report, November 7, 1943.

[56] *Southern Frontier*, March, 1945.

to both white and Negro passengers who may not seat themselves as they enter or as seats fall vacant but must be forever pushing past and scrambling over each other, hopping up and down to move forward or back or keeping each other standing when there are vacancies. Facing the issue squarely, Virginius Dabney, editor of the Richmond *Times Dispatch,* came out in favor of repeal of the obnoxious laws. To the surprise of those who believe that southern habits of thought cannot change, letters of agreement from white as well as Negro citizens came pouring in.[57]

In Maryland both whites and Negroes have moved to have the Jim Crow transportation laws repealed. In fact, a bill to this end was introduced in the legislature in April, 1944. At a public hearing on the bill a delegation of some thirty-odd persons of both races urged passage of the repeal. The passenger and freight agent of the Baltimore and Annapolis Railroad who was present stated that his company was anxious for repeal of the law because wartime travel had made its enforcement impossible. These are a few small instances of justice rolling forward on wheels.

CITIZENS IN A NATION AT WAR

The Armed Forces

It is impossible to think of relationships in the world today, and ignore the war. Yet the war and its repercussions are only on the fringe of this story. Primarily we are trying to portray the normal, peaceable, progressive and cooperative developments within the South. The war effort, organized largely on a national rather than a local or regional basis, is an interruption of these normal processes, and an exception to them. Gigantic programs of army, navy, marines and air forces, of WACs and WAVES and SPARs, of taxation, of rationing, of industrial production, of rent control, of war bond drives, scrap-metal collections and air raid precautions, are initiated, planned and enforced by centralized agencies of the government in the nation's capital. What happens under them is therefore not typical and often not indigenous for any state or region. For this reason we are touching only very lightly on these programs and wartime practices. They

[57] *Monthly Summary,* December, 1943, p. 2; January, 1944, p. 17.

cannot, however, be altogether ignored; southern citizens of both races participate in them both under compulsion and voluntarily; southern citizens have a voice with the rest of the nation in shaping the broad outlines of the war program; and within the general framework set up by the national government there is room for a good deal of local variation. Also it must be said that even an interruption and an exception, if it is as violent and pervasive as a global war, is bound to have its effect. Things may return to normal when the war is over, but "normal" will never be quite what it was before. This is as true of the South as it is of the rest of the country; and it is therefore important to inquire what practices growing out of the war program contribute to increased Negro participation in the main stream of American life.

Let us look first at the Armed Forces. The Selective Training and Service Act of 1940 states: (Section 4a) "In the selection and training of men under this Act, and in the interpretation and execution of the provisions of this Act, there shall be no discrimination against any person on account of race or color." It is a matter of common knowledge, of course, that segregation and discrimination do exist in every branch of the armed forces, and that in some branches this discrimination is extreme. Yet the balance will certainly show that the training and experience of Negroes in the armed forces during this war have given a tremendous impetus to their achievement of equal citizenship in fact as well as in law. To quote the report of the Julius Rosenwald Fund for 1942-1944: "A million Negroes—practically all the young men of the group between eighteen and thirty—have been given an education far beyond any school or college. They have been well housed and well fed. Their health has been safeguarded and their strength built up. They have been trained and disciplined—for the most part in wholesome fashion. They have seen other parts of the country and of the world. Along with slights, most soldiers have sensed wide horizons and have had some warming experiences of respect and administration as they moved over America, through the Pacific, and in Europe. Coming back from such experience, the whole young male population of the race will never again fit into the serfdom of southern feudalism or into second-class status in northern industrial cities . . . "

Negroes have served in every branch of the services. The Marines, which at the beginning of the war did not accept Negroes, later en-enlisted them. The Navy broke its long-standing tradition against the use of Negroes as anything but mess boys and had thousands of colored sailors and a few colored officers. At the last report the Coast Guard had 698 Negro officers and 4,000 Negro men working and fighting side by side with their white fellows, without segregation and without friction. Negroes learned to fly in the army air corps and engaged in a number of foreign missions: and in the army they may rise through the various ranks of officers, the highest rank now held by a Negro being that of brigadier general. Negro officer candidates in the army are sent to training schools where they study, eat, and live with other officers without segregation or discrimination. One of these schools at Fort Monroe, Virginia, and one at Fort Benning, Georgia, and relationships were excellent in both.[58]

Negro soldiers served in every theatre of war. General MacArthur praised their zeal and gallantry in Australia and the Solomon Islands, and General Eisenhower cited the same qualities in their service in North Africa and in France. Negro women, too, served in uniform. The WAC almost since its inception recruited Negro women and trained them along with whites at Fort Des Moines, Iowa. The WAVES for a long period did not accept Negroes, but before the end of the war began to do so.

When every day brings forth some new instance of discriminatory practices, by which equal sacrifice is repaid with unequal treatment and honorable service rewarded with humiliation, it is difficult to realize that progress is being made. Yet slowly and haltingly those responsible for the armed services seem to be moving toward thinking as Americans, rather than as racists, and toward the recognition that men who are called to arms to defend democracy need to know that democracy exists for them. On July 8, 1944, a War Department order was made public which explicitly forbade discrimination and, in some instances, segregation, on army posts, in post exchanges, officers' clubs, theaters, and in government-owned and -operated buses throughout

[58] From reports in the *Journal of Negro Education, Crisis, Interracial News Service, Opportunity,* and the general press.

the country. Although the order was greeted with angry protests in some quarters, and although there is reason to believe that in some places it is not enforced, reports indicate that in many southern camps it is being accepted and carried out. The October, 1944, *Monthly Summary* states: "The order was publicly announced and emphasized at the Columbia (South Carolina) Air Base. At Congeree (South Carolina) Air Base it was included on all bulletins. At Fort Jackson (South Carolina), Negro WACs have experienced no difficulties in attending movies and in making use of the PX's." However, Negro men reported that there were attempts to discourage their use of common facilities.

In the United States Merchant Marine, not a part of the armed forces but essential to them, Negroes are playing an important and honorable part. At least eight of the Liberty ships built since the war began have been named for Negroes, leaders in the struggle for liberty. These are the *Booker T. Washington,* the *George Washington Carver,* the *Paul Laurence Dunbar,* the *Frederick Douglass,* the *John Merrick,* the *Robert L. Vann,* the *James Weldon Johnson, and the John Hope.*[59]

Two of these ships have been commissioned under Negro captains and, like most other ships of the Merchant Marine, operate with crews made up of many races, creeds, and nationalities. In part this is due to the strong anti-discrimination policy of the National Maritime Union, C. I. O., which has a large membership in the Merchant Marine.

The *Booker T. Washington,* the first Liberty ship to be commissioned under a Negro captain, Hugh Mulzac, was launched in September, 1942; before July of 1943 she had travelled over 15,000 miles, from Los Angeles through the Panama Canal, around the Caribbean Islands to New York, across the Atlantic to England and back. Her crew of forty-two men included Filipinos, Danes, Russians, Hondurans, Panamanians, Irish, Jews, Spaniards, and Americans, among whom were two Texans and twenty Negroes. The crew was conscious of its unique character and, with its captain, sought to render distinctive service. Every week there was a meeting aboard,

[59] *Southern Frontier,* January, 1944; *N.A.A.C.P. Bulletin,* January, 1944; **OWI** Maritime Commission, Release N-391.

the skipper taking part like any other crew member, and any crew member being eligible for chairman. The men early agreed that since the world would inevitably be noticing them, there should be no drunkenness and no fighting among members of the crew. Throughout their voyages they stood solidly together. In North Africa, when someone objected to the entry of Negro crew members into a tavern and started a fight, the white crew members who were with them joined in overpowering the aggressors, and served notice that this crew was "all for one and one for all."[60]

In 1943 the first warship ever to be named for a Negro was named for a naval hero of this war, Leonard Roy Harmon. Harmon was a mess attendant, first class, from Cuero, Texas, who lost his life in a naval engagement off Guadalcanal. Secretary Knox approved the naming of the ship and awarded Harmon the Navy Cross posthumously.[61]

Wherever these experiences of common effort, common hardships, and common sacrifice take place, men inevitably progress in mutual respect and understanding. Unfortunately, practices in the armed services which have resulted in racially segregated units and assignment of duties on a racial basis have limited the number of such experiences. In the forward areas, however, distinctions tend to break down, and on all the fighting fronts white soldiers and Negro soldiers are learning to work and fight together. Such a distinguished Southerner as the Governor of North Carolina has stated publicly that letters he has received from southern white soldiers indicate that they will return from the war with a new realization of the demands of justice and fair play toward their Negro fellow-citizens.[62]

Soldiers and Civilians

As Negroes serve in increasing numbers, many of them have distinguished themselves for bravery and countless more have made an honorable record and earned promotions. Increasingly the southern white press is giving them recognition. Where a few years ago Negroes were seldom referred to except in comic strips or reports of

[60] *Negro Digest*, July, 1945, pp. 37-40.
[61] *Southern Frontier*, June, 1945.
[62] *People's Platform* Radio Broadcast, December 16, 1944.

crime, today notices appear of Negroes serving in the armed forces, featured along with those of whites, using the proper titles and sometimes adding photographs. Almost always these accounts are of home-town boys.

By 1943 the Commission on Interracial Cooperation had compiled the following instances of such recognition:

"1. Southern white newspapers known to be printing news and photographs of local Negroes in the armed forces: Shelby, North Carolina, *Star;* Lumberton, North Carolina, *Robersonian;* Oxford, North Carolina, *Ledger;* Waycross, Georgia, *Journal-Herald;* Augusta, Georgia, *Herald;* Raleigh, North Carolina, *News and Observer;* Mount Airy, North Carolina, *Times;* St. Petersburg, Florida, *Times;* and Waco, Texas, *News-Tribune.* (To these should be added at least the Greensboro, North Carolina, *Daily News;* the Durham, North Carolina, *Morning Herald;* and the Orange, Virginia, *Review.*)

"2. Southern white newspapers carrying such news without photographs: Columbia, South Carolina, *Record;* Mullins, South Carolina, *Enterprise;* Kaufman, Alabama, *Herald;* Mobile, Alabama, *Register;* Georgetown, Texas, *Sun.*"

Occasionally other papers which do not regularly include local Negroes in their reports break silence to do so. Both the *Tennessean* and the *Banner* of Nashville, Tennessee, carried the picture of Lieutenant William J. Faulkner, Jr., of Nashville and announcement of his receiving his commission in the Air Force, noting that his father was Dean of the Chapel at Fisk University. The *Tennessean* caption referred to him as a Negro; the *Banner* caption did not even make reference to his race. With few exceptions in these paragraphs, parents are referred to with the normal courtesy titles of "Mr." and "Mrs."

While these examples are pathetically few, they demonstrate the independence of local communities and local editors where good will does prevail.

An unusual instance of recognition of achievement was the designation of December 12, 1944, by Mayor Kaufman of St. Louis, as a day of official tribute by the city of St. Louis to Captain Wendell O. Pruitt, St. Louis Negro pilot who won the Distinguished Flying Cross and the Air Medal with Four Oak Leaf Clusters. The St. Louis

Post Dispatch hailed the action of Mayor Kaufman as an example of good Americanism and the democratic way of "judging a citizen by his individual worth."

Negro participation in the war was now and then recognized on the radio. For example, in October, 1942, the Mutual Broadcasting System put on a program featuring the exploits of Negroes in the armed forces and the Merchant Marine. The program had the cooperation of the Army and Navy Departments, and was sent out from Baltimore with pick-ups in Chicago, New York, Fort Dix, and Washington.[63]

All over the country, it has been the duty and pleasure of Americans to extend hospitality to members of the armed forces stationed nearby, usually far from their own homes and desperately needing a friendly welcome and some entertainment or occupation for their few leisure hours. But Negro soldiers off duty have not on the whole had happy experiences. Instead of whole-hearted endeavors to cooperate in welcoming troops of both races, a few scattering instances of rather belated efforts to alleviate tensions are all that can be reported.

One of the best of these reports came from Augusta, Georgia. As early as the fall of 1942 "the commanding officer at Camp Gordon made arrangements with the city police authorities to open head-quarters for a Negro military police patrol. Negro soldiers are under the protection of Negro military police in the colored section of the city, together with any white soldiers who may be found there, although this area has been put out of bounds for white soldiers. This step on the part of Police Headquarters has unquestionably reduced friction and made it possible for any trouble arising between soldiers and civilians to be stopped in its beginning or certainly before getting beyond control. Many of the white citizens of Augusta are getting used to seeing Negro military police."[64] Local citizens of both races joined in the establishment of a USO Center in the Negro district which has conducted excellent programs for the Negro troops. Joint staff-conferences are held each week at the white and Negro centers alternately. Incidentally, a by-product seems to be an increasing readiness on the part of the more intelligent and educated white people of the city to consider the possibility of Negro civilian police.

[63] OWI Release, October 5, 1942.
[64] E. C. Peters, letter, October 2, 1943.

We have already seen how Little Rock, Arkansas, met the tragedy which occurred there, using the interval during which troops were removed from the area to plan for Negro military police, special transportation and postal facilities, reading and recreation rooms, theaters, and a hotel for Negro soldiers' families.

At Lake Chickamauga, Tennessee, there was stationed a unit of the Coast Guard in command of a white officer from Memphis. In this unit were two Negro members. The officer made contact with the Negro citizens of Chattanooga asking that the two Negro members be cordially received when off duty in the city, and stated that his sworn duty required him to see to it that these Negro members received the same treatment as other guards. They slept, ate, and took part in the other activities of the station without difference.[65]

The program of the USO provides theoretically for all troops; but it also provides for accepting local practices in the communities in which it functions, unsegregated in the North, segregated in the South. It does, however, follow a policy of weekly staff councils in which Negroes and whites responsible for the local program confer together on the planning. This gives an opportunity for at least presenting the needs of Negro soldiers and seeing that some of these are met. Now and then this has effects beyond the immediate setting up of wartime recreational facilities under the USO. The director of Field Operations reported in March, 1943, on one such instance. "An interest on the part of Negro citizens for additional USO services, in a community in the deep South in which Negroes made up approximately half of the population, warranted a visit from the USO field representative, who held conferences with Negro and white representatives, separately and jointly. The conferences resulted in a joint meeting of the Negro and white Ministerial Alliances, at which these groups, together with the local N.A.A.C.P. went on record as favoring cooperation to the end that maladies existing among the community's colored citizens might be relieved and ultimately cured, and agreed to address themselves cooperatively to bringing about the establishment of a USO center with dormitory as well as recreational facilities for the use of Negro soldiers. Other objectives set for this body were

[65] T. D. Upshaw, Jr., letter, March 24, 1943.

securing of additional government housing projects; securing federal funds for the erection of additional school buildings for children of colored defense workers; adding their weight to the elimination of discrimination against colored workers in war industries in their community; improving race relations; providing more adequate defense training projects for colored people of their area, etc."[66]

Progress made in these general community projects was not known to the writer. He reported, however, that some months ago the authorization for establishing the USO had been approved. A building had been located, renovations begun, and workers assigned.

From Charleston, South Carolina, comes the report of an interesting and unusual episode of cooperation between soldiers and civilians across race lines. The Burke Industrial School at Charleston is a school for Negro boys, with an enrollment of thirteen hundred and eighty. Early in the war, white soldiers from the North were encamped near Charleston at Storey Field. Some of them became interested in the Burke School, stimulated the school officials to ask the cooperation of the unit in putting over a special program of health, physical development, and military training for the boys of the school. The boys were patriotic, had already taken part earnestly in the city's salvage drive and in Red Cross and Civilian Defense activities. They were then organized into a victory corps and troops and boys worked together harmoniously for some months. Then the northern white troops were ordered elsewhere and a contingent of southern white troops moved in. The boys were concerned, anticipating an unpleasant time, but the relationship was continued as before and they found no difference in the attitude of the soldiers.[67]

One of the focal points of soldier-civilian contact is the draft board in each community. The following excerpt from a letter of Lieutenant Col. C. C. Johnson, March, 1943, gives the general picture of race relations in the draft boards.

"In the Selective Service system's attempt to live up to the spirit as well as the letter of the democratic provisions of the law, nearly 2,000 Negro men and women are serving at National Headquarters, State Headquarters, and with local boards throughout the country as

[66] Ray Johns, letter, March, 1943.
[67] W. H. Grayson, Report, April 17, 1943.

members of local boards, members of appeal boards, members and associate members of registrants advisory boards, examining physicians and dentists, members of medical advisory boards, and clerks and stenographers. Although Negro members of local boards are found principally in northern, western, and border states, such southern states as Virginia, North Carolina, and Kentucky have Negro local board members. All southern states have Negro members or associate members of registrants advisory boards and Negro examining physicians and dentists. So well has it succeeded that every poll, official and unofficial, confidential as well as public, has stated that the racial policy of the Selective Service is worthy of commendation. Two regulations which aid democratic policy are:

"1. Any case seeming to involve discrimination may be reviewed by National Headquarters, no matter where the case originates.

"2. Although the governors of states have sole right to nominate members of the Selective Service System within their states, any member may be removed from office by the Director with or without reference to the Governor of the state.

"From the experiences of the bi-racial boards have come respect for the ability of colored men and a sense of community responsibility on the part of the colored man that only comes from sharing and exercising important community functions.

"Although a considerable number of the registrants are white, some local boards are made up entirely of Negro personnel, others have a majority of Negro members, still others have a minority of Negro members. There are several chairmen of mixed boards. On one board in Louisville, Kentucky, with one Negro and two white members, the Negro member has been chairman since the beginning of the Selective Service System."[68]

THE CIVILIAN WAR EFFORT

Back of the armed effort stands the economic effort. Negro participation in war industry and labor organizations will be discussed in the section on Economics; but here it should be noted that Negroes have been more ready to serve than whites have been to accept them in the whole production program. In the financing of the war, too,

[68] Lt. Col. C. C. Johnson, letter, March, 1943.

they have participated wholeheartedly in war bond drives and have raised large sums of money for the war. Even a partial report on Negro life insurance companies by October of 1943 showed that at least $1,300,000 of the money of Negro policyholders went into putting the bond drives over the top. In one drive the Atlanta Life Insurance Company purchased $650,000 worth of war bonds through its agents in nine states. Its total investment in war bonds was then $1,528,500. This same company had more than 100 employees in the armed forces. North Carolina Mutual Life Insurance Company, a Negro company, had at the same date a total investment of $2,120,300 in war bonds and its president, C. C. Spaulding, was serving as a member of the local draft board. In one drive, Memphis Negroes underwrote the sale of $2,000,000 in war bonds to themselves, "to buy a Flying Fortress to add to their bomber 'The Spirit of Beale Street' already purchased with a million dollars' worth of bonds bought in the second bond drive."[69]

The handling of rationing was so gigantic a problem that it was conducted largely on a basis of expediency—"sometimes expediency dictated that Negroes and whites register at separate schools, at other times, in separate places in the same school, at still others, that they form a common line."[70]

Some of the casual but friendly contacts that grow out of these necessities of war are suggested by the following glimpses of activities of various committees. In Chattanooga, Tennessee, registration for selective service, gasoline, and food rationing were handled in both the Negro and white schools. Citizens were told to register at their nearest school regardless of race.[71] In a rural Tennessee county a Negro volunteer registrar for Ration Book Two found herself the only Negro volunteer among a group of whites at the county office where they received their materials and instructions. She was received in a friendly and unstrained manner and they all went quietly to work together. In one village the Negro worker and a white worker went together in the former's car, in another they went separately. At the last town both white and Negro registrants were to

[69] *Southern Frontier,* October, 1943, pp. 1-4.
[70] Arthur Raper, letter, March 27, 1943.
[71] T. D. Upshaw, Jr., letter.

register at the local high school, and the colored worker was asked to help the colored registrants; but a large crowd had already gathered and as the people poured in both whites and Negroes lined up at each desk as they came without thought of race, and the whole registration went off in an orderly and pleasant way.[72]

In Norfolk and Hampton Roads, Virginia, Negroes have been well integrated in the Civilian Defense and rationing program. There are functioning Negro auxiliary firemen, policemen, and zone wardens. The director of Civilian Defense in Norfolk is also city manager and he has an advisory committee of ten, two of whom are Negroes. Norfolk has two rationing boards. The personnel of one is all white, of the other all Negro. Both boards serve both races. Portsmouth at the time of reporting was considering also setting up a Negro rationing board.[73]

In Tuscaloosa, Alabama, Negroes participate in civilian defense as auxiliary policemen, wardens, and the like, and on occasions, whites and Negroes have paraded together. The Hamilton County-Chattanooga Defense Council in Tennesseee has twelve Negro members, one of whom serves on the executive committee. Meetings are held in the Chamber of Commerce. Negroes served as air raid wardens, auxiliary police and firemen, and as such were not confined to Negro sections but were assigned wherever their services were needed.[74] In Charleston, South Carolina, the local War Services organization was composed of both white and Negro citizens and worked in conjunction with Selective Service Officials sponsoring a program for draftees rejected because of educational limitations. These classes when first begun were financed and supervised by the WPA Educational and Recreational Division. Since the discontinuation of WPA, the State Education Department has taken over the financing of this program. In 1945, six teachers were employed and classes were held two hours a night, four times a week, Mondays through Thursdays, at the Burke Industrial School.[75] In Williamson County, Tennessee, and in Jackson, Mississippi, mass meetings were attended by citizens of both races to discuss

[72] Letter in W. E. Turner report.
[73] P. B. Young, letter, March 29, 1943.
[74] H. H. Harlan, letter, March 11, 1943.
[75] W. H. Grayson, Report, April 17, 1943.

ways of helping in the war effort. In these programs both white and Negro speakers addressed the audiences; and in the Tennessee meeting Negroes sat freely where they chose, while Negro speakers occupied the front seats along with white speakers.[76]

The Red Cross

Negro participation in the activities of the American Red Cross has taken long strides ahead since the days of the first World War. This is true for the United States as a whole and for the South in particular.

In March, 1944, there were a total of 117 American Red Cross Negro workers overseas: Eleven field directors and assistant field directors and 106 workers in clubs. These latter comprised 20 club directors, 17 assistant program directors, 13 personal service workers, and 21 staff assistants. Recruiting of 97 more overseas workers was in process.

For the first time in its history the American Red Cross appointed a Negro to its national staff, Mr. Jesse O. Thomas, assistant to the Administration of General Services. Since his appointment, Negroes have been employed for the first time in the following chapters: Savannah, Georgia; Birmingham, Alabama; Dallas, Texas; New Orleans, Louisiana; and the District of Columbia. The inclusion of a Negro in the overseas personnel as qualified public accountant is the first occasion in the history of the American Red Cross that a Negro has held this position. On the governing board of the American Red Cross there is also a Negro for the first time, President F. D. Patterson of Tuskegee, and at Tuskeegee there is an all-Negro chapter of the Red Cross.[77]

While most chapters in the South are white and the setting up of additional chapters locally is subject to their approval, they do include Negroes in many of the service activities and Negro response and sharing in these has been greater than ever before. For instance, Negroes are engaged in First Aid and Water Safety Training, Nutrition and Home Nursing Courses, as Nurses' aides in at least fourteen

[76] Report of Mrs. Eva Myers Lee, July 23, 1943; *Clarion Ledger,* Jackson, Mississippi, May 28, 1943.
[77] Jesse O. Thomas, letter, March 11, 1944.

Negro hospitals in Alabama, Florida, Georgia, Mississippi, North Carolina, South Carolina, and Tennessee, and as Junior Red Cross members in Negro schools. The Junior Red Cross unit in a Birmingham, Alabama, school was responsible for 1,000 pairs of convalescent slippers for use in Army and Navy hospitals; the Junior Red Cross program in a New Orleans high school included trips to hospitals to sing for the patients, making of covers for the Junior News in braille, and making ping-pong tables which were being sent to the army overseas. State A. and M. College in Alabama was one of the first Negro colleges to organize a Red Cross college unit, and one of the first eight of all colleges in the southeastern area; North Carolina College for Negroes and Tennessee State A. and I. College sponsor courses in first aid, water safety, and accident prevention; and at these the National Organization of the Red Cross conducts each summer the National Aquatic Schools for Negroes in the South.

In fund-raising, smaller communities generally conduct a single campaign and one cannot calculate the giving by races; but many large communities have separate Negro divisions and these have shown larger returns than ever before. Especially good campaigns were carried on by the Negro units in Atlanta, Georgia; Charleston and Columbia, South Carolina; Birmingham, Alabama; and Nashville, Tennessee.[78]

Between January, 1942, and January, 1944, nearly 1,100 Negroes qualified as first aid instructors. They taught a total of 1,659 first aid classes. Some of these instructors were extremely active; for instance, seventeen have taught 12 or more classes. One of these in the Prince William County, Virginia, chapter, taught 23 classes, and one in the District of Columbia taught 25 classes.

Fifty-one Negroes qualified as water safety instructors and taught a total of 70 swimming, life saving, and water safety classes since January 1, 1942. They have been particularly active in Washington, D. C., Richmond, Virginia, Indianapolis, Indiana, and Charleston, West Virginia. To the two aquatic schools already listed, a third was added at West Virginia State College in 1943.

[78] Mr. Nat C. Wilson, letter, March 29, 1944.

In the eastern area there are 46 authorized Negro instructors in Red Cross Home Nursing, of whom 31 are active; Virginia leads with 18 active instructors.

More could be added to this list but enough has been recorded to show how Negroes have been sharing in the work of the American Red Cross all over the South.

CHAPTER III

EMPLOYMENT

MAKING A LIVING

FROM ONE END of the South to the other, whites and Negroes live and work in an economy based on the land. The South is still overwhelmingly agricultural and, compared to the rest of the nation, decidedly poor. Problems of making an adequate living from the soil, problems of promoting industrial development, problems of earning enough on which to live, and of stretching a meagre budget are basic for all of the South's citizens.

Within this economy, however, the Negro bears a double burden. An overwhelming proportion of Negroes are still engaged in two pursuits, agriculture and domestic service; only slowly and with great difficulty are they winning a place in industry. Southern economic progress in the past has been heavily handicapped by the state of mind that saw in this whole situation not one problem facing all the people, but a problem, on the one hand, of white progress, and, on the other, of keeping the racial situation stabilized, sometimes referred to as keeping the Negro "in his place." Probably the most significant development of the last decade has been the rise of the new southern viewpoint which thinks in terms of the southern region as a whole, and which sees that its problems can never be solved save as they are tackled as common problems of all the people who live in the South.

This new viewpoint is expressing itself in varied forms and with increasing effectiveness. Such scholars as Howard Odum and others of his school of thought have contributed to it by their studies of American regions; the federal government, by the development of the Tennessee Valley as a regional entity, has given a hint of what might be accomplished; private citizens, through the Southern Conference on Human Welfare and now through the Southern Regional Council, are thinking in terms of cooperative planning and action to improve social, educational, and economic opportunities for all Southerners; and labor, as represented primarily by the C. I. O. and to a somewhat more limited extent by the A. F. of L., has moved to organize southern workingmen together irrespective of race, on the principle that any organization of workers which excludes a part of the labor force is doomed to defeat.

Such recognition is in itself an intellectual revolution; and that it should already be expressing itself in actual organizations, institutions, and social experiments gives evidence of its vitality. It cannot be expected to sweep all before it suddenly. The timid, the dwellers in backward areas, the race-bound spirits of both races are sure to resist the change.

It is necessary to bear this in mind as we survey the economic field, for as yet signs of progress in this area are few, with the striking exception of some labor organizations in the industrial field. We are at the beginning, not on the full tide, of progress in economic cooperation.

EVERYBODY'S HOME

If agriculture is excepted, the vast majority of Negroes are engaged in domestic and personal service. Yet in this field there is scarcely even a straw blowing to indicate any progress. The whole level of comfort and economy in the homes of the white South and the whole level of wages and working conditions and consequent home conditions among Negroes hinge upon the intelligence and efficiency with which this matter is handled. Yet it is virtually taboo even to discuss it, and there is no evidence of any serious effort anywhere in the South to consider it from an intelligent, objective point of view. Indeed, any suggestion that this be done is commonly looked upon with suspicion and alarm by members of both races. White women react with panic to wild talk about Eleanor Clubs of Negroes organized to leave them servantless and to the idea that servants may be about to form a union; Negroes react with fear that any stirring of the issue may lose them their jobs and with resentment at the suggestion that they may need training to fit them for work they have always performed untrained. If the two sides are ever brought together to discuss the matter, the

discussion nearly always degenerates into an airing of personal griev-
ances against maid or mistress. One of the biggest contributions that
could be made to the whole level of southern living, white and Negro
alike, would be a serious, impersonal, large-scale approach to this
problem, and the working out of practical improvements that would
lead away from merciless hours, starvation wages, old clothes, "hand-
outs," and "food-toting," on the one hand, and inefficient, irresponsible
service, on the other, to a high level of home economy and satisfactory
working relationships.

Nationally, the American Association of University Women, the
Y.M.C.A., and the National Committee on Household Employment
have pioneered upon this problem. A set of standards has been drawn
up and approved by a widely representative group of workers. The
Southern Regional Council, carrying on the interest of the Commission
on Interracial Cooperation, has brought the problem to the attention
of its members through a recent issue of the *Southern Frontier*.[1] As
far as action and practice go, however, only two small indications of
progress have been reported from southern states.

In June, 1942, a group of Baltimore household employees organized
a union. In September they were chartered by the C. I. O., "the first
local industrial charter in this field." Membership has gradually increased. Through the union some four hundred placements had been
made by March, 1943, with no cost to either employer or worker.
Hours were cut from around 70 to 48 for full-time workers, and wages
increased. Sunday work was ruled out except in rare emergencies.
Meantime, the union worked on its training and selection program,
and on a system of priorities by which employers who are themselves
employed, especially in defense industries, receive special attention.
At the end of about nine months, the experiment seemed to be giving
satisfaction to both sides. Should it continue to succeed it may well
point the way to similar developments in other cities.[2]

One other straw shows employers taking the initiative. At a con-

[1] "What Can Be Done About Domestic Employment," *The Southern Frontier*,
August, 1944.

[2] Jean C. Brown, "Household Employers Join the CIO," reprint from *Journal of
Home Economics*, Vol. XXXV (March, 1943). J. H. Kearnes, Field Report, October,
1943.

ference of Methodist women of the eastern jurisdiction, held in January, 1942, in Nashville, Tennessee, the following statement was drawn up and issued: "Realizing that we are employers of labor, we recommend: that we work to improve the hours, wages, and working conditions in domestic service, and that definite studies be made by local societies, using as guides, *What Are Real Wages?* and *What Price Domestic Service?*" (two pamphlets prepared by the Commission on Interracial Cooperation). Should this resolution prove to represent a genuine purpose and be carried into effect, it too might go far towards the transformation of outlook that must precede any extensive change of practice in this field.

FIELD AND FARM

The second major occupation of Negroes in the South is agriculture. Here, too, the evidences of changes are few and small, but there is at least more stirring than in the case of domestic service. And when we remember that, historically, farming areas have been conservative and slow to change, that the South as a whole is still agriculturally and educationally backward, and that Negroes began their life as free laborers only about eighty years ago, the present seems less discouraging. Through federal and state agricultural programs, through projects stimulated by private foundations and church groups, and on the initiative of the farmers themselves, forces are at work which, if given a fair chance, may change the southern agricultural patterns which have bound whites and Negroes, tenants and owners alike, in a network of poverty and frustration.

FEDERAL FARM PROGRAMS

Within the Department of Agriculture there are a number of programs designed to help farmers, white and Negro, meet their problems more adequately. One of the oldest of these is the Agricultural Extension Service which works through farm and home demonstration agents throughout the country to improve the quality of farming and farm economy.

To a large extent, traditional patterns still prevail in the Extension Service. The needs of whites are generally considered first; white agents outnumber Negroes out of all relation to their proportion of the population, and Negro agents are everywhere under white supervisors. But there are signs of change. As far back as 1893 some individuals in the Department of Agriculture showed interest in tackling the problem of helping Negro farmers through the employment of competent, qualified Negroes as demonstration agents. In 1906 the first Negroes, nine of them, were appointed to field service in the South. By 1943 this number had increased to 281. (This was still in contrast, however, to the total of 1,298 white agents with 505 white assistants.) In general, the Negro demonstration agents have given valuable service, helping croppers and tenants, mitigating the more vicious forms of exploitation, raising the level of living, and encouraging cooperative action.

Recently, there have been efforts to enlarge the number of Negro agents in every southern state, and to increase their efficiency. Before the war began, special training schools for Negro agents were conducted at Tuskegee Institute, Alabama, and Prairie View, Texas. After the war began, some training programs were offered for local neighborhood leaders, with emphasis on food production.[3]

It must be noted that while this extension program is sponsored by the federal government, its support is federal, state, and local; the agents are generally southern men and women, and their program is wholly dependent upon local cooperation. In Arkansas, for example, the Agricultural Extension Service cooperates with counties in employing eighteen Negro home demonstration agents working in 19 counties, and sixteen Negro county agents working in 16 counties. It also employs two traveling school agents, a man and a woman, equipped with a panel-body truck and demonstration materials, who work largely in fourteen counties where the percentage of Negro families is relatively small. The Service also employs a Negro as a district agent and a Negro woman as district home demonstration agent to supervise the work of the county and home demonstration agents and the traveling school agents. The programs of both the white and Negro county and home demonstration agents are coordinated by a staff of white extension specialists; and the two colored

[3] President F. D. Patterson, letter, Tuskegee, September 22, 1943.

district agents attend the monthly state staff conference along with the white agents.[4]

Arkansas is by no means unique among the southern states in this program. Louisiana increased her force of colored agents by about one-third in just two years. A recent report listed 26 Negro agents, 17 men and 9 women. All but three of the parishes with a large Negro population were served by Negro agents, and in one of these three an agent was to be added shortly. The demonstration agents in Monroe and Shreveport, with the cooperation of the ministers, recently did an outstanding job in the state in the recruitment of emergency farm labor.[5]

Other agencies of the Department of Agriculture have also made advances in the employment of clerical and professional Negro personnel, in service to Negro farmers, and in increased participation of Negroes in federal programs. The Bureau of Animal Husbandry has recently employed a number of Negroes. An interesting individual achievement is the appointment of Carra Dell Owens, of Houston, Texas, as a technician in the Bureau of Animal Husbandry, the first Negro woman to receive such an appointment. She works in the pathological division of the Bureau, preparing culture media for bacteriological purposes.[6]

More significant in relation to the southern scene may be the fact that a number of southern regional officials are breaking away from antiquated local customs and housing their Negro employees in the same building with the rest of the staff. Such practices have been noted, for instance, in Atlanta, Little Rock, and Raleigh.[7]

While it still requires a breaking down of customary ways of thinking for some of the older bureaus to consider farmers as farmers, and not as Negro farmers and white farmers, the newer Farm Security Administration has made a definite effort to consider equally the needs of all low-income farmers, to have Negroes participate in proportion to their numbers, and to stimulate a community rather than a racial basis of farmer organization. This philosophy entitles the FSA to a separate section.

[4] Kenneth B. Roy, letter, November, 1943.
[5] H. C. Sanders, director of Agricultural Extension, letter.
[6] Atlanta, Georgia, *Constitution,* April 4, 1943.
[7] Thomas N. Roberts, June 2, 1943, and Erwin H. Shinn, October 19, 1943, letters.

THE FARM SECURITY ADMINISTRATION

Some of the most hopeful instances of new agricultural vigor in the South have developed in connection with purchasing and marketing associations stimulated through the program of the Farm Security Administration. True, this is a federal rather than an indigenous program, but the men and women, white and Negro, who are participating in it are Southerners, many of them with little education or knowledge of the outside world. Yet they are demonstrating their ability to shake off fixed ways of thinking and doing, both racial and agricultural, and to share and even assume leadership in projects which offer a way out of the vicious circle of debt and soil depletion. To many low-income southern farmers of both races in these poll tax states, these associations bring the first experience of practical democracy in which each man has an effective vote and voice in matters of importance to himself and to his community.

The general plan of these organizations is as follows: ten or fifteen families are formed into a local neighborhood action group which meets regularly to discuss common problems; the membership of the local group is usually of one race. Each local group elects representatives to a county board, which includes both white and Negro members as they may be elected by the various local groups in the county. This board is responsible for the purchase of necessary supplies and equipment, for marketing products from the farms of members, and for any new ventures such as leasing a warehouse, a processing plant, or needed transportation equipment. In this board the farmers meet not as Negroes and whites but as men with common problems coming together as representatives of their local communities to work out a cooperative solution.

This pattern is the ideal rather than the rule. The surprising thing is that it has been successfully carried out in a number of rural southern communities. In areas of big plantations and low-level share cropping, it is almost impossible of attainment; where small farms run by both Negroes and whites prevail, the development of democratic procedure is greatest. Yet we shall take as an example a county in which, although only a small percentage of the farmers are Negroes, the one Negro on the board is one of its most active and influential members.

SEVIER COUNTY, ARKANSAS

In this southwestern Arkansas county, in 1940, there were 1,648 farmers, of whom only 173 were Negroes. The average size of farms is about 96 acres, although most of the Negro farms fall below this average. Neighborhood action groups were started in the county in 1942 and a county purchasing and marketing association was established. There are white neighborhood action groups and several Negro neighborhood action groups. There is one Negro member on the board of directors, elected through the vote of the Negro neighborhood action groups. He takes a leading part in the activities of the association.

Last year the member families purchased all of their seed and much of their fertilizer through the association. In the Silver Ridge community, where most of the Negro farmers live, one neighborhood group has purchased an assemblage of hay-making equipment, including tractor, hay-baler, a mower, and a rake. White groups have followed the leadership of this group in buying similar equipment in their communities. Working with the county officials of the FSA and Soil Conservation Service, the Association has worked out a county-wide soil conservation and improvement program. Large-scale terracing equipment has been hired and the whole county surveyed for terracing purposes. A plan for planting soil-conserving and soil building crops has been adopted and is being carried out on most of the farms, both Negro and white. Recently, enthusiastic discussion was going on in the various neighborhood groups regarding the purchase and operation of a dairy plant which would provide a market for surplus milk and cream. Negro and white neighborhood meetings are attended regularly, and the FSA assistant supervisor reports that frequently white leaders from other neighborhood action groups attend the meetings of the Negro group. "Free and friendly relations have been developed which have been a decided contribution to racial understanding and cooperation in the community."[8]

[8] From "Race Relations at the Grass Roots," *Monthly Summary of Events and Trends in Race Relations,* January, 1944.

In the state of Arkansas, Negroes serve on the boards of eight of these County Purchasing and Marketing Associations. A Negro also holds the position of cotton receiver for the State Central Association which handles large scale purchases and sales for the county associations. In this capacity he not only classifies and records cotton receipts from member associations, but is responsible for drumming up additional business among the local associations and increasing the receipts of cotton.[9]

During the war, when the emphasis everywhere was on increased food production, Negro farmers who had a fair chance to do so did more than their share in stepping up their production of livestock and food and feed crops important to the prosecution of the war. For example, a comparison between the record of Negro FSA borrowers in Alabama, Arkansas, Georgia, Louisiana, Mississippi, and South Carolina, and that of farmers in the nation as a whole shows the following facts: All farmers in the nation as a whole shows the following facts: All farmers in the nation increased milk production 3 per cent (1942 over 1941); these Negro FSA borrowers increased their milk production 33 per cent. All farmers increased pork production 13 per cent; these Negro farmers increased their pork production 33 per cent. All farmers increased production of chickens 50 per cent—and so forth. The evidence shows that where Negro farmers operate fairly adequate units, where they have converted former cotton acres to food production, and where they have had adequate financial aid and guidance, they can not only improve their own family status immeasurably but make a significant contribution to the nation's food supply and the sinews of war. It should be noted that other Negro farmers who are not FSA borrowers are also making significant increases in food production where they are able to obtain necessary financing and the help of their county agents and the vocational agricultural teachers in their communities.[10]

The story of one farm woman fittingly illustrates this section. Mrs. Violet Wade, a Negro living in Person County in North Carolina, is a widow who bought her home through the Tenant Purchase

[9] Giles Hubert, Lecture, July, 1944.
[10] Giles A. Hubert, "The Negro on the Agricultural Front," *Journal of Negro Education*, Summer, 1943.

Program of the Farm Security Administration and has been co-operating with its "Live at Home" program. In 1941 she canned 1,500 quarts of food, including 375 quarts of tomatoes and 100 quarts of pork and veal. In addition, her family butchered five hogs that dressed out 1,950 pounds, milked three cows and raised two heifers for additional dairy cows, kept a flock of pure-bred laying hens throughout the year, and produced an adequate supply of wheat, garden vegetables, and cane for home use. Before she took part in this program, raising tobacco had been Mrs. Wade's only source of income.[11]

STATE AGRICULTURAL PROGRAMS

In addition to its cooperative relationship with the federal program, every southern state has, of course, a State Department of Agriculture, State Agricultural Experiment Stations, and state agricultural colleges for whites and for Negroes. As a rule, however, state departments of agriculture have all-white personnel and state agricultural colleges for Negroes are not up to the level of those for whites, although there is a trend in that direction in line with the general movement toward equal educational opportunities.

In North Carolina the Department of Agriculture makes it a policy to "serve all the people of the state without discrimination as to race or creed." It has sponsored employment of Negro agricultural agents in all counties with substantial Negro population. It holds annual Field Days at all State Agricultural Experiment Stations, to which both Negro and white farmers are invited—on the same day when facilities permit, on the day following the white farmers' visit when facilities are not adequate for both at once. Negroes are employed at the State Office in Raleigh and at all of the experiment stations. Employment and pay are on the basis of qualification—Germans, English, French, Syrians, and Jews, as well as Negroes, have been employed. All are selected, paid, and promoted on the same basis.[12]

The agricultural program of South Carolina as it touches Negroes is described by the State Commissioner of Agriculture as follows:

"South Carolina maintains a Normal, Industrial, and Agricultural

[11] Newbold materials.
[12] W. Kerr Scott, letter, November 8, 1943.

College for Negroes located at Orangeburg, in which are offered liberal courses in vocational education, in agriculture, home economics, mechanic arts, teacher training, business, and other applied arts and sciences. The college also directs the work of the Negro farm and home demonstration agents and the Negro agricultural, home economics, and trade teachers in the public schools."

In 1942 the college enrolled 1,000 regular students and 1,268 summer students. The plant and other facilities are being improved each year.

"The State Department of Agriculture is administrative in South Carolina and the County agricultural agents are employed jointly by the state through its Land Grant College in cooperation with the United States Department of Agriculture. Working in this capacity are nineteen Negro men agricultural agents in as many counties and one Negro man supervisor. In addition there are thirteen Negro women and one Negro supervisor employed in as many counties where there are the largest Negro populations.

"In addition to these, approximately two hundred and fifty Negro teachers of home economics and agriculture are employed in the Negro schools of the state, their number being about equally divided between men and women."

The coming together of white and Negro farmers at fairs and similar occasions is a symbol of the approach toward a common meeting ground on the basis of common interests. In Williamson County, Tennessee, on the Farmers' Mobilization Day, white and Negro farmers met together and took seats as they happened to come. Farmers of both races talked on the program, and men, women, and children, both white and Negro, sang and recited. In Hamilton County, white and Negro farmers met together to fix quotas on crops, and to pool deliveries of farm supplies and lime. In the same county there is an annual ten-day tri-state fair serving Georgia, Alabama, and Tennessee. All buildings in the fair are open to both races, and although there is a separate exhibition building for Negroes, more white than colored people visit it. In Madison County there is no separate colored hall—both races display their prize exhibits in the same building during the harvest festival.[13]

[13] W. E. Turner materials, October 26, 1943.

STIRRINGS IN THE COTTON FIELDS

Not all the initiative for changes in southern agriculture have come from governmental agencies. The widespread displacement of southern farm workers that took place in the thirties gave rise to various attempts at unionization. Inevitably, all such unions are interracial, since the intense competition and pressing labor surplus, particularly of Negro labor, would make it impossible for either group to gain anything by excluding the other. The best known and the strongest of these unions is the Southern Tenant Farmers' Union, with headquarters in Memphis.

No one with any acquaintance with sharecropping in the tri-state area of Mississippi, Arkansas, and Tennessee can question the need for action to raise the level of living of these destitute and exploited people, white and Negro. Thousands upon thousands of them go through their lives under a system crushing to body and soul, which permits the barest existence at an almost subhuman level, devoid of all that makes life worth living or that could stimulate manliness, self-reliance, initiative, or determination to succeed. Indeed, the problem seems so hopeless that most people give it up. All the more interest is attached to the courageous venture of the Southern Tenant Farmers' Union.

This union is about twelve years old. It was founded in 1934 by a group of Negro and white sharecroppers living in eastern Arkansas. Its first efforts were directed toward protecting the rights of sharecroppers and tenants under the AAA cotton control program. Both as an organization of croppers in defense against generations-old exploitation by planters, and as a union composed of both races, the S.T.F.U. at once attracted the wrath of the white planters. In such areas as this the planters are the judges, sheriffs, and all other officers of the law; they own the land, they own the stores, and they virtually own the people. A challenge to their power could not be expected to be peacefully received. It was not. Violence broke over the heads of organizers and unions. Meetings were broken up by armed men. Members were beaten, shot at, thrown into jail. Still they persisted and the organization spread throughout the tri-state area and beyond. Today the Southern Tenant Farmers' Union is established in the large plantation areas of Alabama, Arkansas, Mississippi, Oklahoma, Louisiana, and Texas. Over twenty thousand farm families, tenants, sharecroppers, and farm laborers hold membership in 142 local organizations. Approximately 75 per cent of the membership is now composed of farm laborers; about 50 per cent of the members are Negroes. The leaders are native Southerners of both races. The Union serves its members in protecting their legal rights and helps them with transportation and resettlement in cases of extensive migration, with aid in cases of eviction, and with education in the democratic process of organizing to forward their common interests. At the same time, by publicizing their plight, the union has helped indirectly to correct or at least to check some of the worst abuses of the plantation system. Compared with the total number of the victims of this system, twenty thousand members are only a handful; yet the fact that, among an utterly depressed and generally apathetic people, twenty thousand white and Negro farm workers have joined together for the improvement of their lot is an omen of no small significance for the future of southern agriculture.[14]

Support for the work of the Southern Tenant Farmers' Union has come indirectly from leading Southerners, both white and Negro, through the National Sharecroppers Fund. The Fund grew out of six years' experience with National Sharecroppers Week which was instituted in 1937 to obtain financial support for the S.T.F.U. The Fund still gives a helping hand to the S.T.F.U. but it has broadened its approach to include "the support of other non-profit making democratically controlled organizations in and of the South, having as their main purpose the amelioration of economic, social, and educational conditions among the sharecroppers, tenant farmers and agricultural workers of the South."[15] Recently, the Fund has sponsored a proposal to extend federal aid to veterans of the armed services with farming experience to enable them to secure ownership of "family-size farms." It is emphasized that in the administration of such benefits it is essential that there be no discrimination between Negro and white. The proponents of this "Magna Charta for Southern Agriculture" feel that

[14] H. L. Mitchell, letter, April 7, 1943.

[15] Miss Eileen Fry, Executive Secretary, National Sharecroppers Fund, letter, June, 1944.

it offers an historic opportunity to attack the "sharecropper system" at its roots.[16] Although the Fund is a national organization with representatives from all parts of the country on its national board, it is significant that this Magna Charta has been signed by distinguished southern white editors, educators, and lawyers.

Here and there in the South there have been spontaneous experiments in cooperative farming. Such have been the Delta Cooperative farm, in Mississippi, south of Memphis, and the little Koinonia Farm program in Americus, Georgia. The former was a fairly large-scale program for the resettlement of evicted white and Negro sharecroppers on a jointly-held cooperative farm. The latter is a small venture of four families, two white and two Negro, and two white high school boys on a farm conducted on the basis of Christian brotherhood and sharing. Small straws, their significance lies less in the degree of practical success achieved than in the challenge of their bold experimenting to the thinking of whites and Negroes about the South's most pressing problem — the future of her low-income farm workers of both races.

Reference has already been made to cooperative purchasing and marketing associations. Not all of these are started under government sponsorship. A small credit union, begun twelve years ago at Bricks, North Carolina, with $86 total resources, has grown into a chain of twenty-three such credit unions with deposits amounting to $186,000. This union, which has enabled its members to buy farm machinery, repair their dwellings, and improve their farming methods, was started by a small group of Negro farmers with the guidance of a field representative of the American Missionary Association (Congregational). Throughout eastern North Carolina many other such unions have been formed by farmers' groups in a movement which, though still small, shows steady growth and progress. The same community at Bricks also started a cooperative store which has prospered and stimulated the organization of other stores which did a combined business of $200,000 in 1943.[17] These cooperative ventures have as yet hardly

[16] *An Appeal to America,* open letter of the National Sharecroppers Fund, November, 1944.

[17] Interview with Miss Ruth Morton; Reports of the American Missionary Association.

made a dent in the vast field of southern agriculture, yet their accomplishments on a small scale seem to point at least one possible way out of the tangle of exploitation, individual helplessness, and inadequate financial resources. From the point of view of race relations also, these credit unions and consumers' cooperatives give promise of better understanding through working together for the common welfare; for although the local associations on a neighborhood basis tend to be of one race, county and state-wide associations automatically become interracial, while the cooperative philosophy with its emphasis on democracy and the worth of each individual is in itself a denial of racist theories.

Mention of the American Missionary Association brings up another important chain of influences in the rural South. These are the farm schools, demonstration centers, and rural community projects of private educational institutions and philanthropic and religious founddations. Some of the schools and centers sponsored by the American Missionary Association will be found described briefly under Religion. The work of two privately supported educational centers, Tuskegee Institute and Penn Normal Industrial and Agricultural School are discussed in the section on Education. Many more could be mentioned, but perhaps it is enough to say here that these institutions have served as experimental and demonstration centers for methods of agricultural education and development of rural community life, and that the ideas which they have promoted have been potent influences working towards newer and better ways of living all over the South.

IN THE FACTORY

The increasing industrialization of American life is a commonplace. More and more men and women earn their living by machine operations which require skill, training, and experience, and increasingly they are organizing themselves into unions to advance their interests and protect their rights. Is the Negro moving out into the main stream of this industrial life?

Early industry was largely northern, its skilled ranks filled by native whites, its unskilled ranks by newcomers from Europe. Prior to the last World War the stream of industry swept by, while the Negro, predominantly rural and southern, was left on the banks.

Toward the end of World War I the demands of northern industry drew many Negroes from the plantations to the factories, but the vast majority were unaffected. Still today the North is more industrialized than the South; the bulk of war industries have developed there; and where southern Negroes have broken into industry on a large scale, it has been by migration to the east coast, the west coast, or to northern cities. Even there they are still meeting many difficulties: they are underemployed as compared with their proportion of the potential labor force, they are largely restricted to unskilled and semi-skilled jobs, and they meet opposition to upgrading from both employers and fellow workers. Nevertheless, by July 1, 1943, the War Manpower Commission was able to report that of 14,683,000 employees in 16,000 establishments, Negroes had risen in six months from 5.8 per cent to 6.7 (their per cent of the potential force being about 9.8). One of the biggest jumps recorded was in the aircraft industry where general employment increased 35.4 per cent and Negro employment 96.1. In shipbuilding the increase in Negro employment in six months was 62.8 per cent, and in tank factories 100 per cent. (Of course these huge percentage increases themselves reflect the almost complete exclusion of Negroes from these industries at the beginning of the defense program.) In the mining of bituminous coal, Negroes exceed their per cent of the labor force, constituting 23.1 per cent of mine workers; and in blast furnaces, steel works, and rolling mills they are 12.2 per cent.[18] As far as this is from complete absorption into the main stream, it does show that Negroes have come some distance in terms of mass employment in industry.

Negro women also are being employed in increasing numbers as production workers in aircraft factories, ordnance plants, shipyards, and garment factories. Sixty-four important war plants in eighteen states reported in October 1942 that they were employing Negro women as electricians, welders, sheet metal workers, assemblers, machine tool operators, lathe hands, drill press operators, power machine operators, aircraft production operators, explosive operators, rubber workers, and in a number of other skilled and semi-skilled lines. Three of the eighteen states from which reports were secured were

[18] *Pittsburgh Courier*, July 1, 1943.

border or southern states: Kentucky, Maryland, Missouri. While the numbers are not given, the facts that most of the occupations listed call for skill and training and that Negro women are here entering the industrial field in significant numbers are developments of major importance.[19]

One more statistical observation illustrates what is happening all over the nation. Between May and September, 1943, employment of Negroes in five shipbuilding yards alone increased by 5,864. One of the yards, in a border southern state, increased its Negro force from 50 to 1,600.[20]

Although most of these industries are outside the South or barely within its borders, southern workers, white and Negro, are flowing into them by the thousands, acquiring wages, new skills, and habits of working together on the job. Such sweeping changes in our national life do not leave the South altogether unaltered.

In other ways the South is participating in this nation-wide development. Where ancient relics of racialism have blocked the way to full utilization of manpower, the nation has had its agencies and commissions at work on the problem — the War Labor Board, the War Man-power Commission, the Fair Employment Practice Committee, and the United States Employment Service, to mention only those most directly concerned. On all of these, Southerners, some of them Negro Southerners, have served or are serving with marked distinction, working for a national, rather than a racial industrial life.

Southern white industrialists, it must be admitted, have been slow to launch themselves on this main stream. There are only exceptional instances of steps being taken either to upgrade workers on the basis of merit and seniority or to hire workers on the basis of industrial need and worker skill. Racial prohibitions still resist the demands of sound economy, patriotism, and democracy in this area.[21] Yet over against this picture we must marshal what evidence we can secure of Negro participation in the main currents of southern industrial life.

OLD LINE JOBS

The history of Negro skilled labor goes back deep into slavery days

[19] *PM*, October 28, 1942, citing OWI-4056 Y-5092.
[20] OWI Release, N-156, X-3825.
[21] *Monthly Summary*, January, 1944.

as is attested by fine iron-work and masonry in many of the older southern cities. But the immediate effect of emancipation was to crowd Negroes out of skilled occupations rather than to widen their opportunities. Even so, "In the South the Negro worker is a familiar figure of long standing in iron and steel production, tobacco processing, shipbuilding, saw-mills and lumbering, coal mining, and turpentine production. His ability to perform skilled work has long been accepted in this section."[22] The extent and growth of this labor force is a factor not to be overlooked in our quest for more recent progress.

It is not easy to get dependable, exact information on Negro employment in southern industrial establishments, and most of the firms from which reports were secured asked not to be identified. In the examples of southern establishments given below, therefore, only the type of industry will be reported with the individual firms indicated by a letter. The examples are drawn from Alabama, Arkansas, Georgia, Louisiana, Tennessee, and Virginia.

SHIPBUILDING

A. "This company has employed both white and Negro employees for over fifty years. The experience has been very satisfactory, and no so-called 'race problem' has been evidenced. The rules and regulations apply to all employees as do rates of pay or piece work prices, without regard to race or color. An independent union has a substantial majority of employees as members and has sole collective bargaining agreement with the company. Both white and Negro employees are members, serve on committees, and are officers of the union. The present roll is approximately 28,000 of which 7,200 are Negroes."

B. "This company took over the management of this shipyard on February 1, 1943, at which time there were employed in the yard a total of about 400 clerical workers and a small number of semi-skilled workers. At that time, we suggested to the union and other agencies interested in employment practices that we follow the rule of no discrimination as to race and give the colored race an opportunity in the skilled crafts.

"Due to geographical location, we have always felt that inter-

[22] Robert P. Weaver, "With the Negro's Help," reprint from *Atlantic Monthly,* June, 1942.

mingling is not conducive to the best interest, and we therefore set aside our third shift for Negro workers in the skilled classifications. We presently have in the neighborhood of 1,000 skilled Negro mechanics principally in the welding and ship fitting classification, whose opportunities for advancement and whose rates of pay are on a par with those of the white race. The same conditions and opportunities are given to the Negroes that are extended to the white workers. The unions have set up an auxiliary local for the colored workers, with their own business agents and officers, and they have been cooperating with us in every way. Since we started the employment of Negro skilled workers we have extended them to the second shift as well as to the third shift in the Welding Department, usually segregating them on a specific job. We have had satisfactory results."

MINES AND METAL WORKING

C. This mine employs 1,500 men. Seventy-five per cent of these are Negroes. Negroes work in all jobs except as supervisors and get the same wages as whites. In the union, a Negro serves as vice-president, one as financial secretary, and another as recording secretary. Also Negroes serve on the bargaining committee.

A second mine in this area employs 1,300 men, of whom fifty per cent are Negroes, and a third, 400 men, of whom fifty per cent are Negroes. In this last Negroes serve as head miners, track foremen, and timber foremen over Negro groups.

D. This sheet mill plant employs about 1,100 workers, of whom seventy-five per cent are colored. Wages start at a basic minimum of 46 cents for all workers.

E. This coal and iron company employs about 15,000 men, of whom about 6,000 are Negroes. Negroes and whites start at the same basic wage. Probably about half of the Negroes are in skilled or semi-skilled work; they rise as high as subforemen, and make as high as $14 or $15 a day. In some cases the work is departmentalized by race; in some cases Negroes and whites work side by side.

F. This bridge company employs about 420 workers, fifty per cent of them Negro. About a third of the Negroes are in skilled jobs. This plant is 100 per cent organized.

G. This metal working company employs about 1,050 workers, of whom about 200 are Negroes. The starting wage for both is 45 cents. Two out of twenty workers in one highly skilled occupation are Negroes; two out of five in another; hardly any Negroes are left in the 45-cent class. Negroes are advanced as rapidly as they can handle the work. The personnel manager is proud of his skilled Negro workers and says that neither he nor the white employees would trade them for whites.

H. This hardware company employs 250 men, fifty per cent of them Negroes. Both start at a wage of 48 cents; they are segregated on the job by race; and only twelve Negroes are in semi-skilled jobs.

I. This iron-work company employs 400 whites and 400 Negroes. They start at the same basic wage of 40 cents. Negroes rise into some highly skilled work and get as high as 60 cents per hour; but whites in similarly skilled jobs get 91 cents per hour. Whites and Negroes work side by side without friction. Experienced Negroes sometimes teach young white boys just out of high school to do skilled work, then the white boys are moved up above them though the Negroes may have been there for years.

LUMBER, WOOD-WORKING AND FURNITURE

J. In this plant there are about 600 Negroes and 500 whites. All start at the same basic wage of 50 cents. Both are upgraded a little way according to ability, many Negroes rising to the 65 cent bracket, but no Negro gets above the semi-skilled bracket. The informant attributes this to lack of the necessary training. White and Negro employees work side by side on the same jobs with little or no friction.

K. In this furniture company there are 300 employees, 164 Negro. They are not organized. Negroes start at 40 cents, whites at 42.5 cents. The highest for Negro women is 43 cents, for Negro men 47 cents; most white men get approximately 50 cents. Negro and white men work side by side without trouble.

Two variants on this pattern are one furniture company which has employed a Negro shipping clerk for many years and another wood-working company employing twenty-five workers, of whom five are Negro. Finding that the field reporter speaking to him was working for Negroes the personnel manager of the latter plant refused further information, saying he "wasn't gonna help them none" and adding that "no niggers are gonna work with white men in this plant."

MISCELLANEOUS

L. Two large firms located in the same city employ thousands of white and Negro laborers in the same plants. Neither will release information, but one is reported to departmentalize its work in such a manner that racial segregation is almost complete. Yet it starts them all at the same basic wage. The other imports whites from mountain and farm areas, despite the existence of large reserves of local Negro labor, has experienced Negroes train these green whites, and then makes foremen of the newly-trained white hands, putting them sometimes over the very Negroes who trained them.

M. This plant carrying on extensive chemical processing employs about 900. Of these, 400 are white, 500 Negroes. Whites start at a wage 14 cents higher than that of Negroes. Many Negroes have worked at the same wage for fifteen years; very few have ever been ungraded. In one department, however, whites and Negroes do the same work, get the same pay, and work side by side without trouble.

N. Another plant also using extensive chemical processes, employs 1,200 people. Of these about 40 per cent are Negroes. Many Negroes do skilled work in the plant but are not classified as skilled.

Two or three things seem evident from this motley array of examples. In the first place, it is a common southern practice to employ Negroes in industry, and to employ them in the same factories as whites. A second statement we can clearly make is that Negroes cannot move freely on the industrial scene, nor have they reached the top in any of the examples reported. A third point is that there is no uniformity in the practices. We find some plants paying the same basic wage, others a differential. Some do not upgrade Negroes at all, some very rarely, some freely in the lower brackets, some freely in the semi-skilled, some occasionally into skilled ranks, and a few freely into skilled jobs. Some carry differential rates of pay on up the line; some evade this by using Negroes in skilled roles but not so classifying them; some few pay equally for equal work throughout.

A few factories employ Negroes and whites in complete segregation; more, in partial segregation, a few, without segregation. This kaleidoscopic variety is inconsistent and irrational, yet not without its promise. For one thing it means that one rigid caste pattern is not uniform throughout the South; there are as many varieties of practice as there are firms; and changes are taking place which, small as they may seem, move in the direction of justice and integration. Blocked here, meandering there, bogged down somewhere else, yet ever creeping on, the currents of Negro industrial experience are flowing into the main stream of southern industrial life.

SPECIAL MENTION — THE SHIPBUILDING INDUSTRY

The building of the *Booker T. Washington,* mentioned previously as the first Liberty ship, highlighted the significance of the Maritime Commission's construction program, on which members of all races are employed at equal pay for equal work. Chinese, Filipinos, Mexicans, Negroes, and Caucasians helped to build the *Booker T. Washington.* More than five hundred skilled, semi-skilled, and unskilled Negroes were employed in the work, including electricians, stud gun weld operators, shipwrights, painters, welders, burners, chippers, and buffers.[23] It is impressive to realize, parenthetically, that this ship was commissioned under a Negro captain and that his crew included Brazilians, Filipinos, Scandinavians, Spaniards, West Indians, Peruvians, and (in the majority) Americans. Among the latter were "white men, born and bred in the South, who took orders from Negro officers, ate and slept alongside Negro shipmates, went ashore in foreign ports with Negroes — and on occasion knocked down those who wanted to make something of it."[24]

The President's Fair Employment Practice Committee recommended as "worthy of praise" in the employment of Negroes the North Carolina Shipbuilding Corporation in Wilmington, North Carolina, the Newport News Shipbuilding Company in Newport News, Virginia, the Higgins Shipbuilding Company, New Orleans, Louisiana, and the J. E. Jones Company, Brunswick, Georgia. The North

[23] OWI Release, N-158, X-38999; W. K. Graham, letter, November 22, 1943.

[24] John Beecher, "S. S. Booker T. Washington," *The New Republic,* October 2, 1944.

Carolina and Newport News shipyards, employing thousands of Negroes, received special commendation for efficiency of production in building Liberty ships.[25]

The Higgins Shipbuilding Company has received too much publicity to need to have its identity concealed. Employing many thousands of workers—estimates running as high as 40,000—its president has announced from the outset his policy of employing Negroes without discrimination. The company employs thousands of workers of both races, operates separate training programs for them at its own expense, and works on a basis of equality of opportunity and equal wages for the same skill. Just one instance of its policy was the hiring of fifty-one skilled Negro welders in July, 1943.[26]

SIGNS OF LIFE

There are other signs that the South is not standing still in its employment policies — few and small, but worth noting.

In April, 1943, the United States Employment Service reported that "employment of Negroes in other than common labor operations is increasing among southern storage and warehousing firms . . . Negroes are being employed as truck drivers and helpers in several Tennessee establishments, while a New Orleans company lists 450 Negroes among its 550 employees. Seventy-five of the Negro employees were engaged as truck drivers."[27] One of these smaller firms employs forty whites and fifty Negroes, with a starting rate for both of 40 cents. Most of their work is filling orders; Negroes and whites work side by side, and get along together without friction. A few men of each race get 50 cents an hour.[28] A second firm employs 75 workers, about 50 of them Negroes, and has two Negro foremen.[29]

From here and there come instances of new positions, or of upgrading on a merit basis:

An engraving company in East Texas which turns out work for 600 printers and for newspapers in forty-eight states employs two

[25] OWI Release, N-405, X-14515.
[26] R. Weaver, "With the Negro's Help," *op. cit.;* A. J. Higgins, letter, November 15, 1943; C. S. Johnson, *Monthly Summary,* October, 1943, p. 2.
[27] OWI Release, N-377, X-13181.
[28] Cecil Thomas, Field Report.
[29] *Ibid.*

Negro engravers on the same basis as the white engravers in the company's employ. The employer stated: "We have no favorites and we practice no favoritism in our business. . . . The matter of race does not enter our consideration." This company has customers of both races as well as employees.[30]

A cotton-seed oil company employing Negroes is starting to upgrade them.[31]

The Louisville and Nashville Railroad has recently hired eleven Negro firemen, the first to be hired in seventeen years on its Mobile and New Orleans division.[32]

Negro telegraph messengers are being employed for the first time in several southern cities. In Baltimore, Maryland, the Urban League and other civic organizations worked for six months and succeeded in 1941 in getting the Postal Telegraph Company's local branch to employ six Negro boys.[33] In 1942 the Postal Telegraph Company in Nashville, Tennessee, was employing thirteen Negro messenger boys and finding them satisfactory.[34] In 1943 the Western Union Telegraph Company in Durham began employing "one or two" Negro messenger boys.[35]

In 1943 several laundries in Memphis, Tennessee, began using Negro women as "checkers" and Negro men as supervisors.[36]

In Newport News, Virginia, in October, 1941, the first Negro sales girls ever to be so employed were employed in a chain store, through the joint efforts of the Newport News Youth Council and the faculty of Huntington High School.[37]

In St. Louis, Missouri, in the 1942 Christmas rush, ten Negro girls were employed sorting mail, the first ever to be employed in a clerical position in that post office.[38]

In Memphis, Tennessee, in 1943, Travellers' Aid Association added

[30] Associated Negro Press release, November, 1944.
[31] Cecil Thomas, Field Report.
[32] C. S. Johnson, *Monthly Summary*, January, 1944, p. 4.
[33] *Baltimore Afro-American*, October 11, 1941.
[34] *Pittsburgh Courier*, October 24, 1942.
[35] L. E. Austin, letter, April 12, 1943.
[36] Benjamin F. Bell, Jr., Field Report.
[37] *Norfolk Journal and Guide*, October 11, 1941; in *Interracial News Service*, December, 1941, p. 3.
[38] *Pittsburgh Courier*, January 2, 1943.

three Negro workers to its staff, the first time that this has been done.[39]

In Atlanta, Georgia, and in Dallas, Texas, aviation plants have recently begun to employ Negroes.[40]

The Tennessee Valley Authority has for some time employed Negroes in seventy-five different classifications, given them training on the job and upgrading them, thereby helping to relieve critical manpower shortages in dam construction, power operation, and the production of war chemicals. Beginning in 1944, it is upgrading Negroes to clerks' and stenographers' positions on the basis of tests.[41]

These are just a handful of scattered instances but they serve at least to show that the South can venture on new steps when it will — and that it sometimes will.

WAR WORK

War work in its details is a military secret. So we can report here only a few items already public knowledge; a few released by proper authorities, a few with identities wiped out. The gap is less important because war work represents the least essentially southern and least essentially permanent gain. Much of the employment of Negroes in war industries in the South has been a reluctant yielding to much-resented pressures. Almost all of it is essentially temporary, and the workers must find new employment now that the war is over.

In one ordnance plant located in the South, Negroes were at first not employed. The local Urban League held a long series of conferences and communications with plant and government officials, union officers, local Negro workers, and others, and was eventually called upon to select and refer the first group of twenty-five women. This order was filled in four days. By January of 1943, one hundred Negro women were working on the assembly line and giving satisfaction.[42]

An army specialized depot, opened during the war in a southern city, employed 1,400 workers, of whom 350 were Negroes. These were in unskilled and semi-skilled work and though segregated received the same pay and same upgrading as whites in the same work.[43]

[39] M. E. Bicknell, Field Report.
[40] Clifton Jones, notes; National Urban League Report, 1942.
[41] OWI Release, N-390, X-103708; *Nashville Tennessean*, February 16, 1944.
[42] References suppressed. In abstract file.   [43] *Ibid.*

Sixty-two Negro women were employed in a bomber plant in the South in skilled capacities.

In another airplane factory in the South, a Negro riveter won a letter of commendation from the Labor-Management Committee for an idea to speed up production.[44]

In another southern state an explosive company that employed no Negro labor in January, 1942, employed Negroes as 17 per cent of its force in 1943.[45]

Another ordnance company employing large numbers of Negroes employed a Negro in its personnel department.[46]

At a bauxite plant, both white and Negro workers are employed. All start at the same wage. One department is all Negro and Negroes are upgraded within it.[47]

TRAINING FOR THE JOB

To do a skilled job well a man needs specific training, and generally his educational background also helps. Negroes, with less industrial experience and in general less educational background than whites, have been in special need of vocational training to enter the newly-opened positions in industry, but they have found it hard to get. School boards have been reluctant to set up expensive vocational training programs for Negroes when industrial owners and managers would not employ them when trained. Owners and managers have found lack of training a good excuse for excluding Negroes. So Negro workers were caught in a vicious circle.

The first real break in this circle was the vocational training program of the N. Y. A., growing out of the nation's experience in the depression. The W. P. A. helped with an older age group. Then came federal defense training. As a result of these programs, the number of Negro mechanics has been trebled. There had been trained by April, 1943, 8,000 Negro machinists, millwrights, and toolmakers, 5,000 plumbers and steamfitters, 6,000 blacksmiths, foremen and hammer men, and 25,000 iron and steel workers. In 1941, 56,000 Negro students completed trade and industrial courses and between

[44] *Ibid.*
[45] *Ibid.*
[46] *Ibid.*
[47] *Ibid.*

55,000 and 60,000 Negro students enrolled in defense training courses.[48] Among those trained were Negro girls and women in a great range of skills ranging from sewing and clerical activities to aircraft sheet metal work and automotive mechanics. While most of the placements of these girls have been in the North, some have been in the District of Columbia.[49] In 1945 more than twice as many Negroes as in the previous years were enrolled in pre-employment training courses of the Vocational Training for War Workers program, and three times as many Negroes were enrolled in the courses of the Office of Education supplementary training.[50]

We do not know accurately how far the South is participating in this program. Only a few reports of special instances here and there have come in.

Tuskegee Institute, of course, established a civilian air-training center, and later a military one. Around these training centers controversies have raged fiercely because of their encouragement of segregation in a new field where Jim Crow had not yet planted his feet firmly. But they have supplied training for both civilian and military air service in increasing numbers, opening to these young men new ranks of skilled labor.

In Atlanta, cooperating with the Council on Defense Training, the Urban League registered five thousand applicants for war-training; and after nine months of strenuous effort these organizations, the United States Office of Education, the State Department of Vocational Education, their friends, and the FEPC secured the establishment of the Washington High Aircraft School, the first such school for Negroes in the South. The initial equipment cost $10,000. The training, given by the United States Office of Education in cooperation with state and local departments of vocational education, began in October, 1942. In spite of handicaps, classes have been kept filled. The report adds: "It is hoped that Negroes thus trained will be employed in semi-skilled jobs by the Bell Aircraft Company in Marietta, Georgia."[51]

[48] W. S. Meacham, "Democracy and the Negro." Founders' Day address at Hampton Institute, January, 1943.
[49] *California Eagle* (no date on note).
[50] C. S. Johnson, *Monthly Summary*, August, 1943, p. 11.
[51] Urban League of Atlanta; *Timeless;* Cy Record, letter, April 8, 1943.

In Charlotte, North Carolina, the local National Association for the Advancement of Colored People reports helping to secure training for Negro youth as machinists equal to that offered whites.[52]

From Birmingham, Alabama, comes a report that Negroes are planning a school, possibly at the local high school for Negroes, to train Negroes to be foremen, welders, mechanics, and other skilled operatives.[53]

In the meantime, Negroes are trying to train themselves to hold the jobs they have. As the latest comers to industry, colored workers are on the whole least skilled, least organized, least experienced, least accustomed to the necessary job disciplines of regularity, punctuality, orderly conduct, neatness, accuracy, etc., in their work. For these reasons, as well as because of prejudice, they face the likelihood of being the first laid off in many instances, after the war is over. Recognizing this, a group of Negro leaders has sponsored a National Hold-Your-Job Committee. This Committee, spear-headed by the National Council of Negro Women, with headquarters in Washington, has been conducting a nation-wide campaign among Negro women through pamphlet and questionnaire material, in co-operation with Negro women's organizations, branches of the N.A.A.C.P. and Urban League, teachers' associations and the like all over the United States, helping to educate Negro workers to fit themselves to hold their jobs.[54]

LABOR

Working together in tobacco plants, coal mines, steel mills and in many other industries, Southerners have begun to recognize their common interests and aspirations as workers, underlying the superficial differences of race. The amazing growth of organized labor within the past decade and the participation in it of southern Negroes embodies this realization in practice. A southern white editor recently estimated that since 1935 nearly a million white Southerners have joined trade unions with a hundred thousand Negroes.[55] At the September, 1944, convention of the C. I. O. the claim was made that

[52] N.A.A.C.P. *Bulletin* (no date on notes).
[53] Cecil Thomas, Field Report.
[54] Jeannetta W. Brown, letter, October 15, 1943, and reports of the committee.
[55] *Atlanta Constitution*, June 23, 1943.

the dues-paying membership totaled 5,850,000, of whom 700,000 were Negroes. The A. F. of L. in 1943 claimed over 300,000 Negro members in twelve southern states.[56] A more conservative estimate, by the Douglass-Washington Institute in Chicago, set Negro membership in all trade unions in the fall of 1943 at a little over 400,000.[57]

Whatever the exact figures, which are as difficult to obtain locally as nationally, the fact remains that the biggest single forward surge of Negroes into the main stream of American life in the past ten years has been their movement into the ranks of organized labor. This participation has meant for hundreds of thousands of Negroes not only a basic minimum wage, some approximation to equal opportunity in the lower ranks of labor, and a new level of economic security, but also their first participation on a democratic basis in any large organization of men and women of both races. For a few Negroes, union membership has meant a chance for upgrading to new levels of work and a chance to develop and exercise qualities of leadership in an interracial group. The opportunity afforded by labor organizations of both whites and Negroes to work together for common ends without condescension on the one hand or a sense of being patronized on the other, makes this movement perhaps the best channel so far developed for interracial cooperation on a natural and dignified human basis. For in this area the Negro knows that his welcome is based on a need for his bargaining power and a respect for his skill, rather than on that rather burdensome motive, a sense of duty.

The biggest and most vital movement has been that of the Congress of Industrial Organizations, and closely similar in a more limited field that of the United Mine Workers. Some unions within the American Federation of Labor have been as forthright as the C. I. O. in carrying out non-discriminatory policies, but on the whole the A. F. of L. unions have increased their Negro membership reluctantly and often only when forced to do so by the competition of other unions or the circumstances of the labor market.

THE CONGRESS OF INDUSTRIAL ORGANIZATIONS

The constitution of the C. I. O. sets forth as one of its chief pur-

[56] Policy Committee Report.
[27] *The Negro Handbook*, 1944, p. 202.

poses to " . . . bring about the effective organization of the working men and women of America regardless of race, color, creed, or nationality. . . ." Nor is this a mere phrase. Although there are instances of unfair treatment by individual C. I. O. union members ". . . no national C. I. O. union excludes Negro workers from membership nor segregates its colored members into Jim Crow local unions. Moreover, the national officers of the C. I. O. unions have, by and large, a consistent record of practicing what they preach in regard to the treatment of Negroes."[58] At its September, 1944, convention in Chicago, the national C. I. O. convention reaffirmed its stand against race or color bias, urged legislation for a permanent Fair Employment Practice Committee, and called for a clause in all future labor contracts forbidding discriminatory policies by employers. Extending its policy to a recognition of responsibility in the larger fields of political life and social welfare, the C. I. O. has supported efforts to abolish poll taxes and to register union members as voters in the South without regard to race, and has begun to scrutinize the practices of those community chests to which C. I. O. members make large contributions from the standpoint of the equalization of their services to all citizens irrespective of race.[59]

It is only fair to say that as a new movement, the C. I. O, in adopting a policy of non-discrimination, did not have to contend with traditions and practices of long established local organizations; and that while craft unions may profit, at least in the short run, from exclusionist policies, unions organized on the industrial basis, which is the cornerstone of C. I. O. policy, must take in all elements of the working force.

Regarding the growth of the C. I. O. in the South, one of its southern officials writes:

"There is no southern state in which the Congress of Industrial Organization does not have an established union of some of its affiliates. However, there are a number of southern states where only one or two groups are active, such as Mississippi where we have only textile and lumber. We have the greatest membership in the

---

[58] Herbert R. Northrup, *Organized Labor and the Negro*, pp. 14-15.
[59] *CIO News, passim;* W. H. Crawford, letter, April 30, 1943; *Opportunity; Service Men's Manual,* C. I. O., pp. 64-66.

United Steel Workers, the Textile Workers, the Agricultural and Canning Workers, Lumber Workers, Smelting and Mining. In the very beginning there were no white employers who were cordial or cooperative in their readiness for collective bargaining with C. I. O. unions. In fact we would have been just as welcome had we walked in with leprosy or smallpox. However, this has decidedly changed in the last three years. Today we have very pleasant relations with a large number of corporations and business men who have learned that organized labor increases production, improves quality, and is beneficial to them in many other ways. In every city we have firms employing both white and Negro workers whose employees are members of the C. I. O. In many of these, Negroes are holding jobs that they never thought of holding in the past. As an illustration, in the...........plant of the............corporation, there are six full Negro crews with the exception of engineers, something I do not think you will find in any other part of the United States."[60]

One of the areas where the C. I. O. has contributed most is in the Birmingham, Alabama, district. Here many thousands of workers are engaged in coal, iron and steel work and related industries. In 1933 the workers were almost wholly unorganized. At that time miners were paid in "clacker" (company money). They had to live in company houses and trade at the company store, paying whatever the company chose to charge. In the early organizing days, one of the organizers went about making stump speeches with a chain of clacker money around his neck. The success of the drive changed the whole picture. Now most of the company stores are gone and those that remain have to compete with ordinary stores. Union contracts stipulate that all wages be paid in United States currency. Tens of thousands of the men have been organized and placed under the protection of collective bargaining, with white and Negro workers together in the same unions, under contracts which call for equal pay for equal work and equal protection for all workers regardless of color.[61]

[60] C. R. Beddow, letter, September 13, 1943. Plant identity suppressed by editor in accordance with the usual preference of firms.

[61] Cecil Thomas, Field Report. Informants: William Mitch's assistant, Carr Haigler, and others.

The story of a Negro steel worker illustrates what all this means to the individual:

"A colored worker had for a number of years, even before the union was formed, held a job as jobbing mill shearman at the........ company. The job paid about $10 a day, and the worker was an ardent union man. A white worker, a non-union man, persuaded the superintendent of that department to give him the job, stating that he was better qualified for it physically and mentally. The colored worker appealed to the mill committee, all southern born white men, claiming that his seniority rights under the contract had been violated. The committee upheld his contention and demanded that he be put back on the job. The white man hurriedly joined the union and appeared at the next union meeting to ask the local to override the decision of the mill committee. There were two-thirds more whites than colored present when the white worker took the floor to tell why he should have the job. The committee countered that they were carrying out the terms of the contract and that the colored worker was entitled to the job on the basis of seniority. The local, by an overwhelming majority, voted to sustain the committee and uphold the seniority right of the colored worker."[62]

The validity of this story is borne out by a statement by Herbert R. Northrup in his recent book, *Organized Labor and the Negro:*

"One of the outstanding gains which unionism has brought to steel workers is grievance machinery for appeal from the decisions of foremen or other persons in supervising positions. Traditionally the underdog, concentrated in unskilled jobs where his place can be easily filled, and confronted by nominal superiors of another race, Negro steel workers have found that the union has provided them with the first real means of protection against unfair and arbitrary treatment. Moreover, representation upon grievance committees has taught the Negro worker how to stand up for his rights and how to express himself.[63]

"One more statement as to how the United Steel workers carries out its non-discriminatory policies in southern localities is inter-

[62] W. H. Crawford, director, United Steelworkers, District 35, C. I. O., letter, April, 1943.
[63] Herbert R. Northrup, *op. cit.,* p. 181.

esting: 'Locals were encouraged to elect a white president and a Negro vice-president. This allowed Negro recognition on the executive councils of locals, but avoided unnecessary friction in union management relations since the local president handles much of the negotiating.' "[64]

The C. I. O. also reports recent progress in interracial cooperation in Georgia. It has organized numerous plants in which both Negroes and whites are employed. There is no segregation or discrimination of any kind against colored workers in holding office or participating on the grievance committees. It is reported that prejudices of white workers against Negroes are being overcome and that Negroes, although they do not yet have complete confidence in the unions, are beginning to trust them more as the C. I. O. works with some industrial training programs for Negroes.[65]

Memphis has a large number of Negroes employed in its widely varied industries and almost all of them were unorganized prior to the coming of the C. I. O. to that city. The existing locals were, for the most part, craft organizations and the members were white. Negro workers received very low wages and even after the passage of Federal Wage and Hour legislation many of them were reported to have received less than the minimum stipulated by the legislation. Workers who protested were threatened and in some instances left the city in fear of violence and other reprisals. When the C. I. O. unions extended an open invitation to Negro workers, they joined in large numbers, and for a period the Negro membership exceeded that of the white. These unions have continued to grow. Some of them enroll their white and Negro membership in the same local and have common meetings. Some of the unions now are predominantly white, because the employment in the plants concerned is predominantly white. A few are exclusively Negro, and still others are about equally divided in membership between white and Negro workers, according to employment practices. In the mixed locals it is a common practice to elect a white president and a Negro vice-president. There are some Negro union officers in practically all locals in which there is any con-

[64] *Ibid.*, p. 180.
[65] C. H. Gillman, letter, May 12, 1943.

siderable Negro membership. The result of this policy is summarized by our informant as follows:

"(1) Negro workers have secured better wages and more security on the job. (2) Negroes' civil rights are better assured and they are guaranteed protection in observance of federal laws protecting wage earners. (3) The relationship between white and colored workers has definitely improved and there is a far greater feeling of solidarity as workers."[66]

In the same area, the United Cannery and Agricultural Workers (UCAPAWA), a C. I. O. affiliate, is organizing agricultural, canning and packing workers in mixed unions.[67] This same union has recently made progress in organizing tobacco workers in the South:

"Prior to August, 1943, the UCAPAWA's contracts in the tobacco industry covered locals composed almost solely of one race—those in Richmond, Virginia, having an all-colored membership, and one in Middletown, Ohio, having an almost all-white membership. Since then, it has won bargaining rights for the 12,000 white and Negro workers employed by the R. J. Reynolds Company in Winston-Salem, North Carolina, as well as for the all-colored labor force employed by two independent stemmeries in that city."[68]

In shipbuilding, where for the most part Negroes are newcomers, the Industrial Union of Marine and Shipbuilding Workers of America, the C. I. O. affiliate, has not only succeeded in organizing numbers of Negro workers along with whites but in certain border ports it has helped materially to open up new jobs for them. Two examples are cited:

"In March, 1943, approximately 10 per cent of the 6,000 workers employed at the Dravo Shipyard, Wilmington, Delaware, were colored. For the most part, Dravo's Negro employees were denied upgrading beyond semi-skilled levels. In May, 1943, the Negroes took their complaints to the IUMSWA, which had held bargaining rights in the yard for more than a year. After a conference in which Negro,

[66] Identity of source suppressed.
[67] A. J. Marcus, letter, April 3, 1943.
[68] Herbert R. Northrup, *op. cit.*, p. 117. (Note: That such a development faces many difficulties is evidenced by the recent arrest and detention of a Negro organizer in Winston-Salem on obviously trumped-up charges of assaulting a white woman worker, member of a company union, in a crowded courtroom.)

union and company officials participated, the Dravo company began upgrading Negroes and employing Negro women production workers, including welders. Since then the IUMSWA local has taken the lead in an attempt to eliminate segregated toilets, eating places and other vestiges of Jim Crow."[69]

"The industrial secretary of the Baltimore Urban League reported that Local No. 43 of the IUMSWA was 'the most important factor' in obtaining employment for Negroes in the Fairfield yard (the Bethlehem-Fairfield Shipyard). Moreover, the grievance committee of Local No. 42 have assisted newly employed Negroes to secure training for, and upgrading to, skilled positions. Despite the opposition of some union members, which once resulted in violence, and which necessitated the calling of Coast Guard reserves to prevent a threatened riot, both local and national IUMSWA leaders have remained firm. As a result, Negroes continued to be trained and upgraded."[70]

Of individual C. I. O. unions, the National Maritime Union takes particular pride in its record in race relations, as its vice-president testified at a hearing before the Fair Employment Practice Committee:

"The National Maritime Union is particularly proud that it has succeeded in wiping out discrimination of race in the South where it is so often said: 'It cannot be done.' It is not strange that many American vessels sail out of Baltimore, Norfolk, Wilmington, North Carolina, Charleston, South Carolina, Jacksonville, Florida, Houston, Texas, Texas City, Texas, Corpus Christi, Texas, with Negro and white seamen—men from the South—joining the ships together, working together, living together, fighting together, all in the interest of America.

"Discrimination does not exist on the American flag merchant vessels for which N. M. U. is the collective bargaining agent. Negro and white seamen work side by side, eat together in the same mess room, and are quartered in the same fo'c'sl, and die together on the high seas in defense of America. Many stories could be told of the heroism of our Negro brothers on merchant ships who gave their lives for the cause on which this war is predicated."[71]

[69] *Ibid.*, p. 224.
[70] *Ibid.*, p. 225.
[71] Institute of Labor Studies, *Labor Views on Current Issues*, October, 1943, p. 4.

This union is reported to have a membership of some 50,000 men, of whom about ten per cent are Negroes.[72]

The influence of the C. I. O. in one southern city deserves mention. In New Orleans, Louisiana, in 1936 there were some unions— A. F. of L. and independent — but none organizing whites and Negroes together. Towards the end of 1936 the C. I. O. entered the region; but it was 1938 before it secured a real foothold. In the five years that followed, locals were organized of the National Maritime Union, the United Cannery, Agricultural, Packing and Allied Workers, the International Longshoremen and Warehousemen, the Textile Workers of America and the Amalgamated Clothing Workers. The Celotex workers have also been organized, originally in District 50 of the United Mine Workers and now as independent. All of these are mixed unions. The N. M. U. has about 70 per cent white members, 30 per cent Negro. The Celotex workers are about 60 per cent white, 40 per cent Negro. In many instances members of these unions work together unsegregated on the job, and in the Industrial Union Council of New Orleans, which takes in all local C. I. O. unions, 15 per cent of the members are Negroes. Two Negroes were recently elected by the Council members to its executive board. The C. I. O. has held two big mass meetings in New Orleans, one a parade and open air meeting in which members participated with no segregation, the other at the Municipal Auditorium. This last was also unsegregated and attended by some 1,500 persons. The police protested but did not break up the meeting, perhaps because the mayor had given his consent to the use of the hall with full knowledge of the nature of the gathering.[73]

These achievements in organizing mixed unions in the South have required high courage and persistence. They have been won in the face of opposition from employers, from local police, and from older unions set up on a racial basis, while at the same time they have had to overcome the initial fears, habits, and prejudices of the white and Negro workers themselves. They have involved struggles with all these elements, strikes, picketing, union rivalries, police objection, and

[72] *Pittsburgh Courier*, September 5, 1942 (but the *Negro Handbook*, 1944, says there are only about 2,000 Negroes in the N.M.C.).

[73] Horace Mann Bond, Field Report, Spring, 1943.

internal union problems. Yet from this bed of nettles has flowered a new understanding and cooperation between white and colored workers.

THE UNITED MINE WORKERS

Throughout the history of the United Mine Workers of America, the organization has accorded full membership to Negroes. Its constitution includes a clause providing that benefits accrue equally to all members. All workers are paid the same basic wage for the same job, sometimes working side by side regardless of race, sometimes in crews or teams of one race. Negroes have been advanced as high as machinists, electricians, and other skilled jobs. It is claimed there are Negro foremen in non-southern states. In Alabama the ruling out of Negro foremen is due neither to company policy nor to the attitude of the white workers but to a state examination which is required for the position and the state examiners will not permit Negroes to take the examination. Checkweighmen, with one exception, are white, most grievance committees are white, and most but not all local presidents are white. Beginning from scratch in 1933, Alabama membership in the U. M. W. has grown to over 20,000, a vast majority of miners in the state, nearly half of them Negroes. At first local officials in various cities tried to break up mixed meetings. Today, though segregated seating is required, mixed meetings are generally allowed; in fact, the mayor of Birmingham recently attended and addressed such a meeting.[74]

An appraisal of the miners' formula of equalitarian unionism by a student in this field adds a few details:

"When the 1933 organizing campaign was initiated in the South, the U. M. W. did not deviate from its equalitarian policies. The success of the campaign was indeed a tribute to the forthright manner in which its representatives faced the race issue and preached the necessity of interracial cooperation.

"More important than the success of the organizing campaign. however, has been the ability of the UMW district leaders in the South to devise a workable system whereby the two races could cooperate effectively and yet not antagonize the public by encroaching too sharply upon the customs of the communities. In West Virginia,

[74] Cecil Thomas, Field Report. Two miner officials informants.

where rigid separation is not the rule, and where race patterns are relatively fluid, the problem was not so serious, but in Alabama a good deal of both tact and courage was required.

"For example, when the time came for the election of local officers, the Alabama district leaders advocated the selection of whites as presidents and Negroes as vice-presidents, and this procedure was followed in locals even where the Negroes were in a majority. . . . It was felt that the employers should be accustomed to the novelty of joint grievance committees before being subject to the still more novel experience of having to deal with Negroes as equals. At the same time, the election of Negro vice-presidents and of other Negro officers provided the colored miners with representation in the policy-making decisions of the locals.

"The results of this policy of gradualism are already discernible. According to a number of informants of both races, 'Negro members of grievance committees who a few years ago would have risked physical violence had they raised their voices in joint union-management meetings, now argue their cases quite as freely as their fellow white members'. Local meetings are no longer featured by such 'formal' relationships between the races as, according to Dr. G. S. Mitchell, was the case in 1934-35. White members no longer hesitate to call a Negro unionist 'brother', or to shake hands with Negro delegates without displaying embarrassment. And now, Negro delegates contribute rather freely to discussions."[75]

THE AMERICAN FEDERATION OF LABOR

The A. F. of L. is, of course, less centralized than the C. I. O., and it takes the position that it cannot enforce policies on member unions or their locals; similarly, it opposes the enforcement of non-discriminatory policies on its unions by a government agency such as the FEPC, on the grounds that "Government controls, interfering with the self-government of labor organizations, must not be permitted."[76] Consequently, one must take as an expression of a wish, rather than a statement of effective policy or practice, such pronouncements as "The American Federation of Labor has been in the past,

[75] Herbert R. Northrup, *op. cit.*, p. 166.
[76] Associated Negro Press report of November, 1944, Convention of the A. F. of L.

and is today, unalterably opposed to any forms of discrimination because of race, creed, color or sex. However, certain of the member unions of the A. F. of L. have a fine record of democratic practice, and the fact that a white union delegate at the national A. F. of L. convention meeting in New Orleans introduced a resolution designed to make discrimination by unions on the grounds of race a criminal offense indicates that a strong leaven of democracy is working within the organization.[77]

In January, 1943, the A. F. of L. sponsored a Southern War Labor Conference in Atlanta, Georgia. It was estimated that at least 250 of the 1,000 delegates were Negroes, representing carpenters, longshoremen, common construction laborers, plasterers, bricklayers, painters and a few other A. F. of L. unions. The convention as a whole revealed a sharp awareness of the need to offer Negro workers a greater degree of economic equality. The following statement was adopted unanimously:

"This conference declares that it is in hearty accord with the fundamental principles of the A. F. of L., that the labor movement should serve the workers without regard of race, creed, or color, and further declares that there should be a condition of absolute equal rights on jobs and job opportunities without any discrimination whatsoever between the workers on account of race, creed or color."[78]

While such general statements as these have no binding force, and while no explicit stand was taken against segregated unions, the enunciation of policy at least gives the official sanction of the Federation to those individual unions which do wish to make progress.

A few A. F. of L. unions organize Negroes and whites together in mixed locals, in southern as well as northern plants. In the border cities of St. Louis, Kansas City, and Baltimore, Negroes employed in the clothing industry are admitted to locals of the International Ladies' Garment Workers Union along with white workers. However, they are generally restricted as to the kind of jobs they may hold and often segregated in the shop. In Kansas City, Negro pressers and floor help have been used in the garment industry for many years, and in some

---

[77] Associated Negro Press report of November, 1944, Convention of the A. F. of L.
[78] *The Negro Handbook*, 1944, p. 207.

locals picnics and parties have long been conducted without segregation. Recently, a few Negro women have been employed as operators. However, in at least one case the white workers objected so strenuously to this new pattern that the Negro operators were moved. In Baltimore also, Negroes have long been used as pressers, but only recently as operators and finishers. At least one walkout occurred when Negroes were introduced, although they were segregated. But in this case the employer sent for the union officials, and they succeeded in getting the workers back to their jobs without removing the Negroes. In Atlanta, the ILGWU has followed local custom in organizing separate locals for Negroes and whites. After some reluctance, white delegates are meeting colored delegates on the joint executive board.[79]

The Bricklayers, Masons, and Plasterers' International Union, A. F. of L., is a rare instance of a craft union in the building trades which has constitutional provisions, pretty generally enforced, against discrimination by reason of race or color. The national union has on a number of occasions fined locals for discriminating against Negroes, or forced them to honor the traveling cards of colored members. Even in southern cities, with the exception of Charleston, Atlanta, and Richmond, mixed locals of the Bricklayers are the rule. "In ten cities, all in the South, mixed locals were found in which Negroes were in a majority. In all of these, the business agent was colored, an assurance that Negroes receive a proportionate share of work. The strongest is the Louisiana Local No. 1, New Orleans, which was founded in the 1890's. Approximately 60 per cent of its 300 members are colored. It was the first local in Louisiana to adopt apprenticeship standards. In September, 1941, it had twenty-three apprentices, including seventeen Negroes, indentured for four-year terms." A gloomier side of this picture is that the proportion of Negro bricklayers is currently declining, largely because of the greater emphasis upon formal training and the difficulty experienced by Negroes in securing vocational training or in being accepted as apprentices.[80] One other A. F. of L. craft union in the building trades, the Plasterers, makes mixed locals,

[79] Herbert R. Northrup, *op. cit.*, p. 126.
[80] *Ibid.*, 38 ff.

regardless of race, its general policy, and fines its locals for discrimination on account of color. In 1940, 54.5 per cent of the plasterers and cement finishers in the South were Negroes.[81]

Of the unskilled building laborers in the South, 45 per cent were Negroes in 1940. Since 1936, the International Hod-Carriers', Building and Common Laborers' Union, A. F. of L. has made great strides in organizing these unskilled building laborers. In 1941, it claimed 250,000 members, including 70,000 Negroes and has since continued to prosper. The union has always organized workers without regard to race. A Negro is a member of the national executive board, and 250 Negroes were among the delegates to the 1941 convention.[82]

Despite these instances of good practice, reports from a few southern cities give a picture of the situation in the A. F. of L. union in these areas which seems to suggest a reluctant yielding to necessity, rather than a genuine acceptance of common interests.

In Birmingham, the freight workers' local of the Teamsters' union is a mixed union about 50 per cent Negro, with Negro officers and committeemen, and a uniform basic wage. The hod-carriers have a big union, about three-quarters of whose members are Negroes, while about half the officers are Negroes. Whites and Negroes work together on the job. The carpenters have two locals, one Negro and one white; Negroes do not come on a "white man's job." The Negro carpenters' local has a white business agent. In spite of everything, Negro membership in A. F. of L. unions in Alabama has grown enormously in recent years. Sixteen years ago there was just one Negro A. F. of L. member in Birmingham. In 1944, in the state of Alabama as a whole, there were 35,000 Negro members of a total membership of about 124,000. Three of the fourteen state vice-presidents were Negroes, and two organizers worked out of the regional office. Negro delegates attend the state conventions, although they are segregated.[83]

A few other instances of individual forward steps in race relations within A. F. of L. unions illustrate the various ways in which such progress is made.

In 1943 a non-discrimination clause and a pay increase provision

[81] *Ibid.*, p. 42.
[82] *Ibid.*, pp. 46-47.
[83] Cecil Thomas, Field Report, March, 1944. Informant, M. O. Hare.

ranging from 5 to 30 cents an hour were contained in a contract signed by the Southern Car Manufacturing Company and a Birmingham local of the International Association of Bridge, Structural, and Ornamental Iron Workers, A. F. of L., covering all production and maintenance employees in the plant. The non-discrimination clause provides that "the shop shall be classified without regard to race, color, or creed."[84]

Following the failure of the C. I. O. Steelworkers' Union to better the occupational position of Negro workers in two plants in the Birmingham area, the workers in these plants switched their allegiance to an A. F. of L. rival, which promised to press for reclassification of jobs done by helpers, a general upgrading without regard to race, and the opening of the plants' apprentice training systems to Negroes. After the A. F. of L. union had won two NLRB elections with the Negroes' help, it fulfilled the promise.[85]

In Memphis, three of the largest laundries have recently signed temporary contracts with the A. F. of L. Laundry Workers' Union, composed of both whites and Negroes.[86] This union generally adheres to a policy of mixed unions and non-discrimination. "Separate colored and white locals were established in Miami, Florida, but their charters were recently revoked, and a new charter for a mixed local granted instead. In most of the local organizations, Negroes are well-integrated, holding various offices and being well represented as shop stewards."[87]

The North Carolina State Federation of Labor, following the lead of Alabama, elected its first Negro vice-president in 1942. He was a tobacco worker of the Liggett and Myers Tobacco Company in Durham, long active in the union in organizing, in office work, and as a local shop committee chairman.[88]

War employment has increased the opportunities for southern Negroes in the building trades, but in most crafts they have had to fight hard for the opportunity to organize even in separate Negro

[84] Associated Negro Press release, December, 1943.
[85] Herbert R. Northrup, *op. cit.,* p. 186.
[86] *Monthly Summary,* January, 1944, p. 4.
[87] Herbert R. Northrup, *op. cit.,* p. 133.
[88] Dean A. El, letter, May 5, 1943.

locals, and then for a fair share of the work. Two stories illustrate this uphill progress.[89]

"In June of last year [1943], Negro carpenters in Chattanooga and Nashville, whose union has jurisdiction in the Hopkinsville, Kentucky, area, complained that they were being kept from employment on a cantonment construction job in the Hopkinsville area by the local [white] carpenters' union. [The matter was given to a mediator to investigate and adjust.] It was first determined how many Negro carpenters were available for work on this particular job. Then the representatives of the Negro and white carpenters' union were called into conference and an agreement was reached whereby the 120 Negro carpenters who were available in the area would be the next additional carpenters to be employed. The result was that within a period of a week, all available Negro carpenters were employed."

A similar story came from Georgia in 1943:

"Approximately thirty Negro carpenters are now employed by the MacEvoy Shipbuilding Company of Savannah, Georgia, which is engaged in the construction of concrete barges under contract with the Maritime Commission. Prior to July of 1942, Negroes were employed only in unskilled jobs with a few exceptions. Responsibility for this condition lay with the Metal Trades Council of the American Federation of Labor and its affiliated locals in Savannah, which barred Negroes from skilled jobs at the MacEvoy Company. The company followed no policies which would restrict the employment of Negro carpenters, being under a closed shop agreement with the Metal Trades Council of the American Federation of Labor.

"Efforts were made over a period of several months to secure a modification of the restrictive policies of the Savannah Metal Trades Council, but without success. The white carpenters' union and the Metal Trades Council representatives were summoned to appear before the FEPC, when it held hearings in Birmingham. As a result, the Metal Trades Council was ordered to permit the local union of Negro carpenters to become parties to the contract between the Metal Trades Council and the MacEvoy Company. The Metal Trades Council refused to accept the directive of the Committee, although agreeing

[89] Cy Record, letter, April 6, 1943.

to do so at the time of the Committee hearing . It became necessary eventually to issue another directive to the Metal Trades Council and compliance was finally secured with the result that Negro carpenters are now being employed by the MacEvoy Company."[90]

In Kansas City, Missouri, in New Orleans, Louisiana, and in Baltimore, Maryland, initial opposition of white locals to organization of Negroes in the building trades was gradually broken down and Negroes were organized largely through the activities of the Urban Leagues of these cities, backed in some instances by the new federal war agencies. These negotiations and struggles took from months to several years according to the local conditions.[91]

A heartening indication that the A. F. of L. is growing stronger and more American in its outlook was the recent action of its president, William Green, in the case of A. Philip Randolph's Memphis speech. Randolph, nationally known president of the Brotherhood of Sleeping-Car Porters, was scheduled to speak at a labor meeting in Memphis in the fall of 1940. Memphis' political machine leaders called the Memphis Trades and Labor Council president into conference, and the meeting was called off. Randolph, not to be put off, went to Memphis and met with such other groups as would receive him, also registering a protest with William Green. Green replied that he considered that "cancellation of Randolph's appearance represented violation of constitutional rights of free speech and assembly." The Tennessee State Federation of Labor stepped up and planned a mass meeting for April, 1944, to be held in Memphis with Randolph as principal speaker. Green publicly announced in March his approval of the meeting, and despite the protests of politicians and the refusal of the local Trades Council to have anything to do with the meeting, it was successfully held and Randolph delivered his speech unmolested.[92]

[90] *Ibid.*

[91] The A. F. of L. general constitution makes it mandatory to receive permission of the existing local before being considered for a charter. This enables prejudiced old-line white locals to block Negro organizations.

[92] *Nashville Tennessean* (AP), March 7, 1944.

SUMMARY

The changes that are being brought about in southern ways of thinking and acting through the development of organized labor, and especially of industrial unionism, are profound and remarkable. It is common to think that prejudice is strongest among humbler people and those with limited education and that persons who enjoy economic security and have had educational opportunities to learn the facts about individual and racial differences are more open-minded and willing to discard outworn fears and beliefs. We expect, too, to see persons with strong religious beliefs in human brotherhood and the principles of Christianity take the lead in recognizing the equal worth and equal rights of all individuals. But it is not in the churches, nor among the economically secure, nor even among the intellectuals that these principles are most clearly recognized and acted upon. It is by wage earners and laborers who in the common struggle for the security and decent conditions of work which all men want have learned that at the work bench, on the assembly line, in the union meetings, and in negotiations with employers the color of a man's skin is not as important as his character, his ability, and his intelligence.

BUSINESS AND FINANCE—A PROMISE FOR TOMORROW

For a well-balanced economy all groups must share not only in the work of farm and factory, but also in the work of store, office, and bank; not only in labor but also in management and finance. As yet it can hardly be said that Negroes have entered the main stream of American business life anywhere in the nation, North or South. Still there is some promise for tomorrow.

There are, of course, small Negro business establishments all over the South, especially barber shops and beauty parlors catering to Negroes. There are small grocery stores, cafes and restaurants, cleaners and pressers, generally reflecting in their facilities the depressed status of their customers. Here and there are firms of Negro contractors and builders doing a good business, small printing establishments and the like.

It is in the fields of insurance and banking, however, that the greatest progress has been made. Negro insurance firms began with the launching of the North Carolina Mutual Insurance Company in Durham in 1895. "With no capital, and their only resources faith, initiative, ability, and three stiff white collars, John Merrick, a barber, A. M. Moore, a physician, and Charles C. Spaulding, a ten-dollar-a-month dishwasher in a small hotel, founded the North Carolina Mutual Company."[93] Mr. Washington Duke, of Durham, became interested in the three young men, one of whom was his barber, and gave them his friendly counsel throughout the early years of their struggle to establish themselves. Today the association conducts an extensive insurance business, operates a bank and a building and loan association, and employs 112 persons in the home office in Durham alone. This home office building also houses a clinic, a research library, and agent training classes. Following the lead of this company, other large and successful Negro insurance companies have been built up.

It is true that these companies as yet, and the somewhat smaller Negro banks, operate almost wholly within the Negro group. Strictly speaking, therefore, these achievements cannot be classed as evidences that Negroes are entering more fully into American life, or of progress in race relations. Yet they are preparing a basis for future progress. White businesses do not yet give Negroes the opportunity to gain even the rudiments of business experience in their firms; and whites controlling capital have a natural reluctance to lend it in any considerable amount to inexperienced Negroes. Negroes individually are seldom wealthy enough to provide adequate capital for launching even small businesses. So the existence of these successful Negro business ventures serve as a function of the highest importance. Here hundreds of young Negroes get experience as stenographers, clerks, tellers, bookkeepers, cashiers, salesmen and on up to district managers of insurance companies and presidents of banks. Here also Negro-owned and Negro-controlled capital is being accumulated which can be made available for Negro business ventures as these trained young Negro business men and women begin to venture on enterprises of their own. From these sources also come persons able and ready to fill new posts opening in unsegregated areas of the nation's economy, as yet chiefly in federal agencies.

[93] "They Call Him Cooperation," *Saturday Evening Post,* March 27, 1943.

This function gives to Negro insurance companies, and to a lesser degree to Negro banks, a peculiar tone and significance lacking in their white counterparts. Their leaders often feel a special sense of responsibility and endeavor to use their enterprise to educate Negroes in thrift, home-buying, and in self-reliance and ambition in business as a service to the race. Similar functions are served by the National Negro Business League, with headquarters at Tuskegee Institute. The League was organized in 1900 by Booker T. Washington to serve as a medium of expression and cooperation for Negroes engaged in business and for others interested in furthering Negro economic progress. Although the activities of the League are mainly devoted to assisting individual Negro enterprises to follow recognized standards of business efficiency, and to increasing consumer support, it also serves a useful function to the larger community, local and national. The League maintains active relations with the United States Chamber of Commerce and the United States Department of Commerce. During the war, in cooperation with the Adviser on Negro Affairs of the United States Department of Commerce, the League has conducted several war-time business clinics, which have interpreted to Negro business men the various war-time regulations and the part which all businesses can play in the national war effort.[94]

The achievements already made by Negro business in the South, under the most difficult conditions, make it appear inevitable that southern Negroes will in time venture into new fields of enterprise and will be successful. The question remains to be answered whether this program will take the form of setting up a segregated Negro business and commercial life parallel with the white, or whether in time the South will open the doors of its economy to all men irrespective of race. Tradition has put many obstacles in the way; but neither American businessmen nor American consumers have ever shown much liking for being restricted as to where they may sell or where they may buy.

[94] Albion W. Holsey, executive secretary of National Negro Business League, letter May, 1944.

CHAPTER IV

EDUCATION

"SEPARATE BUT EQUAL"—THE PUBLIC SCHOOLS

THROUGHOUT THE SOUTHERN STATES a long and arduous venture has been under way since 1865. Poverty-stricken and backward at the beginning of the era and never able to close the gap since, the South has nevertheless had to tackle the problem of educating its children. Because of its racial views, two sets of schools have been required, one for whites and one for Negroes. In the constitution of almost every southern state it is decreed that these two sets of public schools shall be "separate but equal." They have been separate, but they have not been equal. In view of the relative political, economic, and social strength of the two groups, this is not surprising. But the American conscience, sluggish as it often is, is seldom permanently satisfied to determine public policy on the basis of power alone. Spurred from without by Federal Court decisions and from within by their own sense of the gap between democratic theory and practice, southern legislators and administrators in almost every state in the South have taken some action toward making "separate but equal" mean what it says.

To understand today's developments, one must know what lies behind them. The public school system of the South began, in general, only after the Civil War.[1]

"By 1870, practically all southern states had adopted basic laws providing for public schools. . . . At first, the Negroes got a fair share of the new public funds. Colored schools sprang up rapidly; their terms were of the same length as those for white; colored teachers were on the regular scale."

At first, also, separate schools, although the prevailing pattern, were not required by law. In many states it was not until around 1900

[1] Edwin R. Embree, *Brown Americans* (New York, Viking Press, 1943), p. 92.

that segregation in schools and other public facilities was made a legal requirement.

The strain of taxes for the dual educational system soon became so great that the impoverished South began to economize where it felt there would be least effective protest. One easy economy seemed to be the education of Negroes. In the first place, they had been effectively deprived of political power. In the second place, white Southerners were inclined to feel magnanimous in providing any sort of education for their former slaves; and the freedmen, rejoicing over any schools at all, were not disposed to be critical. Negro schools had to begin at the bottom with the three "r's" taught by white teachers to unclassified pupils of all ages in a church building, an abandoned plantation house, or unused barracks. Missionaries from the North began to train promising Negroes to become teachers for these schools. Often in early days, these teachers had no more than a grade of schooling beyond their pupils. So great was the struggle to make any beginning at all, so remarkable the progress made in a few short years, that few whites or Negroes paused to scrutinize the word "equal" in "separate but equal." The states successively undertook primary, elementary, high school, then college education for Negroes, while the missionary schools provided even higher levels of education, each time shedding the more elementary work as the states took it over. It has been a great story of achievement. As a supplement to the large contributions of northern churches and foundations, and appropriations from southern taxes paid by both whites and Negroes, it is estimated that since 1865 Negroes have contributed $50,000,000 for their own education and are still raising $3,500,000 annually for the support of their own schools.[2]

Today, however, the framework of the two parallel systems is nearly complete. Both whites and Negroes have begun to take the words "separate but equal" more seriously, and to insist that all the children of the state shall in fact enjoy equal educational opportunities. At first, this demand was voiced by individuals here and there; then organized groups began to exert their influence. The Commission on Interracial Cooperation, representing both Negroes and liberal white

[2] Fred L. Brownlee: unpublished report. Based on Work, pp. 210-211, *Negro Year Book*, 1930-31.

Southerners, made a study of the discrepancies between white and Negro schools, and carried these facts to the public through pamphlets, articles, and classrooms. Concern over the more obvious inequities became increasingly general until some states and local boards began to act on their own initiative. But in the South as a whole, action lagged. It took a jolt brought about by the challenging tactics of a pressure group to precipitate the growing sentiment into widespread action.

This jolt was given by the case of Lloyd Gaines versus the State of Missouri, sponsored and contested by the National Association for the Advancement of Colored People, and tried out in a border state as a test case. In December, 1938, Lloyd Gaines, a Negro college graduate in Missouri, desired to study law. Missouri provided a law school for its white citizens but none for Negroes. Gaines' application for admission to the only state-supported school of law was rejected on the grounds of his race and of the existing segregation laws. Gaines then entered suit which was eventually carried to the Supreme Court of the United States and the Supreme Court ruled that it was unconstitutional for the state of Missouri to deprive a citizen of his rights on the grounds of race. The Court held further that a scholarship to an out-of-state university was not sufficient to comply with the Constitution: the state must either admit Gaines to the existing law school or establish another law school for Negroes equal in every way to that provided for whites; public education might be kept separate on the basis of race, but it must be equal in fact and not in name alone.

Following this ruling, the southern states began to take action. Missouri established a law school for Negroes at Lincoln University; North Carolina founded a law school at North Carolina College for Negroes in Durham; Maryland, taking a more practical view, admitted the few qualified Negroes to the School of Law of its state university; Tennessee and Texas are taking steps to meet the problem, as we shall see in more detail later; the lower house of the Kentucky legislature in 1944 passed a bill (later defeated in the upper house) to admit qualified Negro students to the graduate and professional departments of the public universities and colleges of the state.[3]

Along with the process of equalizing graduate opportunities has

[3] *Nashville Tennessean,* February 27-28, 1944.

come the movement for the equalization of teachers' salaries. In many places there has also been some provision for equalization of other aspects of schooling such as buildings, equipment, and length of school term.

The United States Office of Education reported recently that from 1930-40 the average annual salary of the Negro public school teacher in the seventeen states with compulsory segregation laws increased from $432 to $601; in 1939-40 the corresponding figure for white teachers was $1,046. In 1931-32 average salaries for white teachers in these states were 103 per cent greater than those for Negroes; by 1939 this difference had been reduced to 74 per cent—still a wide gap. But four years later, by 1943, the gap was narrowing. Salary discrimination had been practically wiped out in Maryland and Oklahoma. Kentucky and North Carolina had adopted statewide equalization programs to wipe out these differentials within the next few years; and Negro teachers had won equalization of salary suits in six southern states, Virginia, Florida (in four cities), Louisiana, Kentucky, Tennessee, and Texas. Before the year was out, Tennessee and Texas had also adopted state-wide equalization programs and were at work on them.

Other discrepancies to which attention is being given are those in school terms and in pupil-load. For thirteen of these states and the District of Columbia the average school term in 1939-40 was 156.3 days for Negro schools and 170.8 days for white schools; the number of pupils per teacher was 37.7 for Negroes and 29.2 for whites; the per pupil expenditures on teachers' salaries was $13.35 for Negroes, $35.86 for whites; while the per capita value of school property and equipment per Negro child was far lower than for white children, "the ratio sometimes being as high as 7 to 1."

Equalization is not, of course, the only problem. Along with better training facilities, the number of trained Negro men and women ready to assume the responsibilities of helping to direct and administer educational institutions has steadily increased. Negro teachers entered the picture very early. But the white South was slow to recognize the importance of having Negroes share in shaping the policies of institutions which serve their children and to which they contribute in taxes and in many other ways.

In the state by state summaries which follow, we shall see progress being made along all these lines: increasing provision for graduate education, equalization of salaries, equalization of facilities and length of term, Negro participation in policy-making. The shape and tempo of the advance varies from state to state and from locality to locality. Some states have a highly centralized educational system; in others the control is almost wholly local and there can hardly be said to be a state policy in educational matters. The first states reviewed below are those in which the local school board provides the real control.

ARKANSAS[4]

"State aid is sent out by the state board of education under the common school law on a percentage basis with no racial discrimination. The financing of our schools, however, is determined almost wholly by the 2,500 local school districts of the state. We have an equalizing fund which is also sent out by the state without regard to color. Some of our Negro schools will receive as much as 75 to 80 per cent of their annual percentage from these state funds.

"Acts passed by the state legislature in 1943 and 1941 set up the Arkansas Teachers' Salary Aid Law which is doing much to relieve any deficiency in teachers' salaries through the state. It is difficult to say exactly how this works out but our records show the greatest percentage in increase in Negro teachers' salaries during the past school year in the history of the state and for the first time the percentage was greater for the Negro teachers than for the white.

"Our movement for consolidation which began about fifteen years ago has increased greatly the number of Negro school board members in the state. We now have approximately 500 Negro board members serving in more than 125 school districts.

"We have established branch libraries in our county library program for special use of the Negro population. One of these at Conway, Arkansas is functioning very effectively. We need to expand this type of service to our Negro population.

---

[4] Ed McCuistion, letter, November 13, 1943.

"There are many other instances of increased interest and cooperation to develop better opportunities for our Negro population:

"1. We have greatly increased the size and equipment of our state
A. M. and N. College for Negroes at Pine Bluff. We have received
approximately 25 per cent increase in appropriation for support of the
school and are already developing a state-wide service program.

"2. Through the organization and effective management of the
Urban League of Greater Little Rock we have gone furthest toward
equalization in this area.

"3. We have recently organized an interracial commission for
Greater Little Rock and hope to extend this interracial commission to
cover the entire state to serve as an over-all council agency in developing increased support for mutual understanding and general welfare."

VIRGINIA[5]

In Virginia, likewise, local control predominates and there are one
hundred counties, each of which is a law unto itself in educational
matters. In 1943 twenty-six of these counties either had equalized
salaries or were well on the way to doing so, while nineteen additional
counties had adopted equalization plans.

LOUISIANA[6]

"Louisiana has not adopted any state policy for the equalization of
salaries, school terms, buildings, transportation, equipment, current per
capita expenditures between the Negroes and whites.

"We are continuing from year to year the improvement of education for Negroes and whites in all the respects mentioned above.
While no particular statistics are available, I am sure that the differential is being gradually decreased.

"At the present time, the Negro public schools of the state, in most
parishes, participate in the state library fund on an equal basis with
the white schools; for example, a parish school superintendent allots
to his Negro school libraries the same per capita amount as he allots
to his white schools. Several parishes have branch centers of the Louisiana Library Commission established and operated on a cooperative
basis by the parish and the state. Gradually more of this service is

[5] *Southern Frontier,* December, 1943, pp. 3-4.
[6] J. E. Williams, letter, November, 1943.

being extended to Negroes through their schools. Just recently the Louisiana Library Commission has established a branch center at Southern University for the Negroes of the state. A competent staff is employed and the purchases of books are made as requests come from the field. A number of educational work conferences at colleges and at other centers in the state have received library services directly from the Louisiana Library Commission.

"Negro leaders in education, health, and home and farm extension service are cooperating with the white leaders of their state and local units in determining the needs of the Negro schools and population and in planning programs in accordance with the needs. In my judgment this is one of the most effective means in Louisiana today of bringing interracial cooperation; for example, the state department of health has employed a Negro doctor who works with local health units and local school officials in improving the health conditions of Negroes. The same may be said of home and farm agents. Gradually, we are employing more Negro nurses in connection with local health units. It is encouraging to find that local health directors and local home and farm agents work with the Negro assistants, determining their needs, planning programs for improvement, and in giving general administrative guidance and support."

MISSISSIPPI[7]

In Mississippi also there is no record of any general policy or practice of equalization, but there are a few hopeful developments. Within the last few years Mississippi has established a state college for the training of Negro teachers. The appropriations for this were made by the legislature after the regular appropriations for higher education for the year had been made and after the legislature had refused to increase these appropriations in general. During the same administration, the next session of the legislature doubled the appropriation.

"Recently the legislature increased the public school appropriation dividing the increase on a fifty-fifty basis between the white and Negro teachers of the state. This means that for the first time in the history of the state of Mississippi, the state board of education through the increase in school appropriations gave the same increase, per month,

[7] P. H. Easom, letter, March, 1943.

per teacher, to whites and Negroes alike. Should there be an extraordinary session of the legislature, the Governor and the State Board of Education are pledged to divide any increases on the same basis. It appears that a step has been taken in the direction of wiping out the differential between white and Negro teachers' salaries.

"Also, this year for the first time, the state board of education is granting funds to counties not having high school facilities for Negroes and an appropriation for the development of high school facilities, with an increase in the length of term."

MISSOURI[8]

"Our state is now in the process of equalizing the salaries of our teachers with that of white teachers with similar qualifications and experience. Court action to bring this about was begun by the Missouri State Association of Negro teachers with Miss Emma Jane Lee, the plaintiff on behalf of herself and others similarly situated, versus the Board of Education, Festus, Missouri. Federal Judge Richey M. Hulen decreed in favor of the plaintiff. Missouri school terms, per capita expenditures, transportation, equipment, while unequal because of local administration of funds, according to the state's plan would be equal. There is great difference in buildings for Negro children and those for white children.

"We have Negro curators of Lincoln University, our state school. In Kinlock, Missouri, with an all Negro population, there is a Negro Board of Education and Superintendent of Schools. We have a Negro Division of Education with offices in the Capitol along with the other divisions of education headed by a state supervisor of Negro schools, with an assistant, two area Jeanes teachers, and a secretary, all under the State Department of Education.

"There is a trend toward better equipped libraries in our schools. Our smaller schools receive assistance from the Rosenwald Fund. Lincoln University, our state school, has recently begun operating the rental system of the most current books, and the School of Journalism operates its own library.

"The Missouri State Constitutional Convention is now in session and attempts are to be made by the Missouri State Association of

[8] D. F. Martinez, letter, October 13, 1943.

Negro Teachers to remove from the constitution the mandatory clause on separate schools for Negro children."

It may be significant that not only the Negro teachers but the St. Louis Race Relations Committee, an interracial body appointed by the mayor and including some of the city's most distinguished white and Negro citizens, proposed that the new constitution should eliminate the mandatory segregation clause. In St. Louis, also, in 1944, St. Louis University, a private Catholic institution, opened its doors to Negro students for the first time.[9]

NORTH CAROLINA[10]

North Carolina has an outstanding record of progressive legislation and administration for all its citizens. Its record in the sphere of public education is therefore of special interest. In broad terms, it has already established absolute equality for whites and Negroes in length of school terms, teacher load, courses of study and requirements for accreditation, and program for training and certification of teachers; it is approaching equality with respect to average daily attendance, graduate training of teachers, average training of teachers, and salaries. The biggest remaining differential is in the school buildings, and steps are being taken to correct this.

Back of this record lies a long story of public concern and effort.[11]

"The State Department of Education, particularly since the beginning of this century, when Governor Charles B. Aycock gave such impetus to the cause of education for all people, has worked in the field of interracial cooperation, as a matter both of desire and necessity. Many specific illustrations could be given. Governor Aycock once threatened to resign his office as Governor and return to his home in Goldsboro to the practice of law if the legislature passed a bill that would have required the expenditure of all public tax money paid by the white people upon white children and left Negro children to be educated by the amount of school tax paid by Negroes. This threat by the Governor defeated a very determined effort to pass this law in the Legislature of 1903. About the same time, State Superintendent

[9] *Monthly Summary*, June, 1944, p. 25.
[10] Forrest interview with N. C. Newbold, 1943.
[11] N. C. Newbold, letter, December 18, 1943.

of Public Instruction, J. Y. Joyner, who held office for seventeen years, made the statement in his first Biennial Report that the obligation of the State for the education of the children was the same regardless of the color of the skin. Other leaders in education who added their voices and efforts to the movements which helped to lay the groundwork for whatever has taken place since then in better patterns of racial attitudes in North Carolina are: Dr. P. P. Claxton, later U. S. Commissioner of Education; Dr. Edwin A. Alderman, later President of the University of North Carolina and still later of the University of Virginia; Walter H. Page, who late in life became Ambassador to Great Britain; Josephus Daniels, former Secretary of the Navy and former Ambassador to Mexico; and there were many others who made real contributions to the causes of Education, Health, and Welfare." Mr. Newbold's own devoted and effective work for Negro education in the state over a more recent period of many years is a factor that should not be overlooked.

North Carolina also has recognized the right of its Negro citizens to share in the direction of educational institutions which serve their children. In 1933 Governor Ehringhaus appointed Dr. Robert R. Taylor, formerly vice-president of Tuskegee, to the Board of Trustees of the State Teachers College for Negroes at Fayetteville, in which capacity he served for ten years until his recent death. A few years ago the Governor appointed Mr. C. C. Spaulding of Durham to be a Trustee of the North Carolina College for Negroes in that city. Mr. Spaulding was also made a member of the Board of Morrison Training School, a correctional institution for delinquent Negro boys. Both of these Negro citizens have been cordially received by their white fellow board-members and have had the most cooperative relationships with them. More recently, two Negroes have been appointed to the Board of Trustees of the North Carolina Agricultural and Technical College for Negroes at Greensboro.

The whole problem of Negro education in North Carolina was studied in 1934 by a commission of fifty whites and fifty Negroes, appointed by Governor Ehringhaus. The commission's report, issued in January 1935, recommended in principle equal pay for equal training and equal service, and specifically that differentials in salary between white and Negro teachers be reduced 50 per cent in 1935 and eliminated as rapidly as possible within a period of three to five years. Governor Hoey then appointed a commission from the house and senate to review the subject. This committee reported in 1939, advocating immediate reductions in the differentials which still existed. Since a differential still remained in 1943, a committee representing the North Carolina Negro College Conference sent a representative to the Joint Appropriations Committee asking for final action. The legislature responded by appropriating $1,750,000 to be applied to the equalization program.[12] The differential is expected to be wiped out by 1945.

Meanwhile in 1939, the state legislature had moved to deal with the question of graduate and professional training for Negroes. First, for graduate work on the master's degree level, it provided for the establishment of training in the liberal arts and professions at the North Carolina College for Negroes in Durham; and for training in agriculture and technology at the Agricultural and Technical College in Greensboro. Second, for graduate programs above the master's degree level and for certain courses not yet available, it provided for fellowships to institutions in other states which admit Negroes. The program is now in its fourth year: schools of law and library science have been set up, and much of the training has been given by professors from the University of North Carolina and Duke University.

After a careful study made by another committee, the Governor has further recommended increased agricultural and vocational training for Negroes, further consolidation of Negro schools especially to provide more adequate buildings, and cooperation of agricultural and health agencies with those for education in working out long-time programs for the improvement of Negro community life.[13]

How these state policies work out at the local level is seen in the following report from Harnett County.[14]

"During the past eight years, the number of schools for Negroes has been reduced from thirty-nine smaller schools to eighteen larger

[12] *Observer*, Charlotte, N. C., April 29, 1943.
[13] This general account is drawn from interviews, letters, and materials supplied by Mr. N. C. Newbold, except where otherwise stated.
[14] J. S. Spivey, April 5, 1943.

ones. At present there are only two one-teacher schools in the county. Bus transportation is afforded practically all children not living within walking distance. This consolidated school program has improved in general the standard of education in Harnett County."

Another instance comes from Gaston County:[15]

"The Gaston County and city school systems under supervision of Superintendents Hunter Huss and K. G. Phillips offer equal opportunities for white and Negro citizens. All facilities and materials available for schools and teachers are allotted equally and at the same time.

"The county has complete high school consolidation for elementary graduates and partial elementary school consolidation. Two adequate buildings for training of boys and girls for life vocations have been erected at two of the large union schools. Three spacious gymnasiums were built by Superintendent Huss for the large union schools. These buildings are used for physical education and for educational and recreational programs.

"Last year the two superintendents provided a course in curriculum study under a professor from the University of North Carolina. White and Negro principals and teachers studied the new curriculum set-up together and planned for its adaptation to local needs. All other educators sent to discuss problems with teachers are available to both race groups."

OKLAHOMA[16]

Oklahoma has virtually wiped out all differentials in expenditures in the public schools within the last few years. In March, 1943, the legislature created the position of Negro High School Inspector in the State Department of Education, and J. H. Sanford, former president of Langston University, was appointed to the position. He is the first Negro to have an office in the State Capitol Building.

TENNESSEE

Tennessee, like Maryland, Oklahoma, North Carolina and Texas, has adopted a definite policy of equalization of educational opportunities. Control is not so completely centralized as in some states;

[15] Maude M. Jeffers, 1943.
[16] E. A. Duke, letter, October 8, 1943.

public policy is not so broadly liberal as in North Carolina; consequently there is a somewhat slower and more uneven progress and much greater need for the action of citizens through organized civic groups for the effective carrying out of this policy. But the adoption of the policy and the steps already taken are in themselves encouraging.

As far back as 1937, even before the Gaines case, the state of Tennessee had gone on record as intending to make good the "separate but equal" principle in public education by establishing a single state salary schedule for teachers based upon professional preparation, experience, and educational position without regard to race. State regulations pertaining to textbooks, course of study, length of school term, and teacher certification are already equal. In pursuance of this general policy, the state has since then been carrying forward a definite program of upgrading Negro secondary and elementary schools throughout the state. This upgrading has been carried on under the leadership of the city and county superintendents, the State Department of Education, the twenty-five or more Jeanes supervisors, and local leaders and groups both white and Negro.[17] By May, 1943, it was possible to report:

"The condition under which subventions are given to the eighty-four counties where the levelling up process is acted upon is that there shall be no discrimination in the salary scale on account of race, color, or any other thing. The four large cities of the state hitherto practiced discrimination, but Knoxville and Nashville both now pay the same scale, Chattanooga is stepping up within a three-year period, and Memphis alone remains on a discrimination basis."[18]

Here we see the differentials in response due to the degree of relative independence in the large city boards. In both Knoxville and Nashville, law suits were necessary to bring about the change. In Nashville, suit was brought by one of the public school teachers with the backing of the local and national N.A.A.C.P., after attempts at securing a voluntary change of policy had failed. It is interesting to note that when the local branch of the N.A.A.C.P. decided that a suit was the only way to obtain redress, some of its members were warned by alarmed "friends," both white and Negro, that it would

[17] Report of W. E. Turner, 1943.
[18] *Southern Frontier*, May, 1943.

be highly dangerous to bring suit. Even were the suit to be won, the reaction would, they warned, be dire. The N.A.A.C.P. pursued its course, suit was brought; the Board of Education contested the case, the plaintiff won. Aside from the Board of Education members and a half-dozen or so white citizens sympathetic with equalization, not a white person attended the case. It passed off without a ripple. Not a teacher who participated was penalized. The raised salaries were paid when due. White and Negro teachers have since continued in friendly cooperation, joining soon afterward in a common plea for a new salary scale for all teachers with a slightly more adequate minimum base and more regular advance with length of service.[19]

On the level of higher education, Tennessee is taking further steps. In 1937, in answer to petitions by Negro students, the General Assembly enacted a scholarship law "whereby qualified Tennessee Negroes were eligible to receive the difference between the cost of attending the University of Tennessee and the cost of attending the nearest university giving courses equal to the University of Tennessee, that admits Negroes." As we have seen, however, the United States Supreme Court ruled that such scholarships for out-of-state study did not constitute equal provision for Negroes by a state. So, in 1941, the General Assembly enacted a new law. This law authorized and directed the State Board of Education to make provision for Negro graduate and professional education within the state equivalent to that made for whites at the University of Tennessee. The costs were to be paid from appropriations made to the state board of education or from any other available funds.

In carrying out this mandate the state has now begun raising the level of opportunities, facilities, and standards at the Agricultural and Industrial College for Negroes at Nashville, at present the only state-supported college for Negroes in Tennessee. As of March 15, 1943, this college was officially reorganized into seven divisions corresponding to the seven colleges of the University of Tennessee at Knoxville; namely, the Graduate Division, the Division of Agriculture, the Division of Business Administration and Education, the Division of Engineering, the Division of Home Economics, and the Division of Liberal

[19] M. C. McCulloch, Field Report.

Arts. A general program of upgrading is being put into effect to insure that each division shall have personnel and facilities to make its work comparable to that of the University; and the salary schedule of the Southern Association of Colleges which is in use at the University is being applied. While these developments are taking place, only the first two years in engineering will be offered; for more advanced students in this field and for students in law, scholarships will be available for the present, but a law library is being purchased. For medicine, dentistry, and nursing, scholarships will be given to Meharry Medical College, a private college for Negroes located in Nashville and offering work equivalent to that at the University. In carrying out all these plans, administrative and instructional officers of the University are serving as consultants.[20]

In bringing this report up to date for 1944, the president of the college added the following statements:

"Fifteen new staff members have been added and negotiations are under way to add as many more by the beginning of 1944-45. Additions are being made to the library. Every effort is being made to develop and strengthen the offerings in agriculture, home economics, and business. A special gift of $35,000 has recently been made available to the division of agriculture so that the work of this division may be extended to all Negro rural families within the state. As now conceived the entire state is the college campus and all Negro citizens are its clientele.

"During the regular session graduate instruction is being given during the afternoon and evenings. At the 1944 commencement—twenty years after the graduation of the first bachelor's degree class—candidates are to be presented for the master's degree.

"A series of workshops are being planned for the summer of 1944 to assist in the in-service development of teachers and workers in the fields of agriculture, home economics, supervision, health and physical education and high school teaching subjects."[21]

In February, the State authorized the employment of an engineer to make a study and recommendations for such repairs and improve-

---

[20] Report of W. E. Turner, 1943.
[21] President W. B. Davis, letter, January 24, 1944.

ments as are needed on the buildings. The firm of McKissack and McKissack, Negro contracting builders, has been engaged to make the study.[22]

In the meantime the State Department of Education is planning for the future beyond these immediate developments. For 1943-44 it planned to add Jeanes supervisors in all remaining counties with a substantial Negro population. The commissioner of Education also has appointed four committees to study post-war needs of secondary school students and teacher education, one of which is specifically charged with the problems of Negro secondary school students and teachers. In addition study groups are being sponsored to consider these questions in connection with teachers' meetings and with the Tennessee Negro Education Association.

TEXAS

Texas also is on the march. In the summer of 1942 a Commission on the Improvement of Negro Education was organized. Back of this action lay a long story. In 1939 the legislature appropriated $50,000 for out-of-state aid to Negro students desiring to pursue studies which were not provided at Prairie View State College for Negroes but which were provided at the Agricultural and Mechanical State College for whites. Since the United States Supreme Court had already declared such scholarships not a substitute for equal educational opportunities within the state, this was to be only a temporary plan. Facilities within the state were to be made equal. However, nothing was done to accomplish this and for three years in succession, the scholarship appropriation was renewed. So in the summer of 1942 concerned Negro leaders of the state of Texas formed a council of Negro organizations devoted to improving the opportunities for Negroes in education and in other fields. Three committees were appointed: one to work for a university, one to work to bring Prairie View State College for Negroes to an equal footing with the Agricultural and Mechanical State College for whites, and one to work for equalization of educational opportunities and facilities in the elementary schools. This committee met with President Homer Rainey

[22] *Nashville Tennessean*, February 12, 1943.

of the University of Texas and discussed the whole study and project.[23]

President Rainey, President Walton of the Agricultural and Mechanical College, and Mr. Woods, state superintendent of Education, then suggested the organization of a bi-racial committee to pursue the matter further. This committee was organized and called the Commission on the Improvement of Negro Education.

The membership of the Commission included most of the leading white and Negro educators as well as Negroes leading in other fields. Meetings were held in the senate chamber, and the Hogg Foundation of Texas appropriated $1,000 for the work. The steering committee made a survey of thirteen counties, finding among other facts that the average salaries of teachers and principals in white schools was $1,244 and in Negro schools $760. It also made recommendations, among which were "that teacher-training colleges train teachers and superintendents to handle bi-racial school problems, that two Negroes be added to the supervisor staff of the State Board of Education, that adequate training for home-making for Negroes be set up." The Commission adopted a series of recommendations covering these and other points and laid them before the state legislature in March, 1943.[24]

In the meantime the struggle for equalization of salaries was being carried on. In February, 1943, in a case before the United States District Court of Dallas, agreement was reached that the salaries of Negro teachers in Dallas should be gradually equalized with those of whites in four successive steps over a period of three and a half years.[25] In Houston, Negro citizens appeared before the City Board, April 5-12, 1943, and the Board voted to equalize salaries by a series of steps beginning September, 1943, and completed by September, 1945. Wichita Falls voluntarily adjusted salaries. In Corpus Christi, Galveston, and Fort Worth, teachers had prepared by May, 1943, to enter suits for the same redress.[26]

Thus slowly, laboriously, yet irresistibly, sometimes by the collaboration of white and Negro citizens, sometimes by legal action in the face of determined resistance, progress is being made toward bringing

[23] Carter Wesley, letter, March, 1943.
[24] *Ibid., Southern Frontier*, February and March, 1943.
[25] *News*, Dallas, February 26, 1943.
[26] *Southern Frontier*, May, 1943.

the level of educational opportunities for southern Negro children up to those of southern white children. Some states, less hampered by the economic and social patterns of the Deep South, are far in advance. But the process is going on everywhere and cannot be reversed without denying one of the essential articles of the American Creed. We may therefore expect to see, not only in North Carolina and Tennessee but in every state in the South, the eventual provision of educational facilities for Negroes duplicating those made for whites in every respect from the lowest to the highest level. At the same time it is noteworthy that the excessive financial burden imposed upon the state by this procedure has already induced the state of Maryland to admit qualified Negroes to the school of law of its state university; and has moved leading white citizens of Missouri to suggest the removal of mandatory segregation provisions from its State Constitution.

CHAPTER V

AVENUES TO UNDERSTANDING

SOUTHERN COLLEGES

The south's colleges have for some years been making a growing contribution to understanding across racial lines. Before 1900 the Negro and Negro-white relations had not been thought of as objects of serious research, except by a few distinguished scholars. But since then there has come a tremendous interest in and development of the fields of sociology, social work, anthropology, and related social studies, all of which gave an important place to the study of differing cultures and the contacts between different races and cultures. In southern as in nothern colleges, these courses are elected by an increasingly large number of students, and they contribute an evergrowing mass of information to our knowledge about our many American stocks and ethnic groups.

Foundations for college study had to be laid first by pioneer scholars in the field. One thinks of such figures as Robert Park, a white American from the Middle West who spent seven years at Tuskegee Institute with Booker T. Washington, and in 1914 went from Tuskegee to the Department of Sociology at the University of Chicago where he established a point of view and a research interest that have influenced the entire literature on race in America. Negro and white southern scholars also pioneered in these fields. Among these were Carter G. Woodson, W. E. B. DuBois, and Benjamin G. Brawley in the Negro group, and Edgar Gardner Murphy, Theodore DuBose Bratton and Howard W. Odum in the southern white group—men who ventured to explore with an honest effort at understanding and scholarly objectivity a field so obscured by emotion that many feared to enter it. These men opened up the area of Negro life and history and Negro-white relationships to scholarly study. By

1915 it was possible to found an Association for the Study of Negro Life and History, now past its thirtieth birthday, and to launch the *Journal of Negro History,* a professional journal through which scholars, white and Negro, could publish the results of their researches. In the 1920's there began to appear numerous serious and objective studies of Negro history, Negro biography, Negro art, Negro churches, and many aspects of race relations; and in the 1930's sociological works on the Negro and race relations began to pour from the press. The subject had become an accepted part of our social studies.

Three agencies have hastened and strengthened this movement in the South: the Institute of Social Research of the University of North Carolina; research fellowships offered by the Rosenwald and Phelps-Stokes funds for southern students interested in race relations; and the work of the Commission on Interracial Cooperation in putting into readable pamphlet form the findings of scholarly research and in stimulating through correspondence and travelling secretaries the study of race relations in southern high schools and colleges.

As a result of all these activities, by 1931 Mr. N. C. Newbold of North Carolina was able to find 106 southern colleges for white students which were offering some work in this field. Of these, 39 offered a full course on the Negro or race relations. Ten years later, in 1941-42, Miss Margaret McCulloch found 187 colleges doing work in the same field, of which 53 offered at least one full course on the Negro or race relations. At 20 of these colleges research on the Negro was being carried on; 80 supplemented course instruction with programs such as lectures and concerts, while 58 carried on some type of interracial activities in most of which students participated.[1]

Negro colleges, too, with good reason, are keenly interested in the subject. We cannot expect the findings to compare numerically, as the number of accredited colleges is so much smaller. In 1941-42, for instance, there were listed 481 colleges for white students in fifteen southern states and the District of Columbia; while only 44 Negro colleges in this same area were given an "A" or "B" rating by

---

[1] Information from survey of southern white colleges, 1941-42, by M. C. McCulloch. Article based on this appeared in *Journal of Negro Education,* October, 1942, pp. 471-472.

the Southern Association of Colleges and Secondary Schools. However, a survey of these in 1942-43 brought replies from 22 and every one of these offered some work on the Negro or race relations; 21 of the 22 offer at least one full course. Many offer much more: 11 offer two courses each; 5 offer three courses each; one offers five; and one university offers eleven. These courses fall into three groups: courses on the American Negro, courses on the Negro in Africa, and courses on Negro-white adjustment or race relations. Interest in the subject is also shown by the fact that proportionally more students elect these courses, while in some cases one such course is required. Again about nine-tenths of these colleges carry on some type of program designed to further interracial understanding, and four-fifths of them sponsor some forms of interracial activity. Particularly at five strategic centers of Negro education—Hampton Institute, Virginia; Howard University in Washington, D. C.; Fisk University in Nashville; Dillard University in New Orleans; and Atlanta University—significant programs are being carried on designed to promote interracial understanding and cooperation.

There are, then, ever-increasing thousands of students in the South, Negro and white, learning to think straight and unemotionally about each other's cultures and problems, and many times with each other as individuals. It is a development full of promise for southern unity and progress. How is it being carried out?

HOW IT IS DONE: WHITE COLLEGES

Two hundred and fourteen white colleges answered this question in 1941, and reports on special programs in others have come in since. In singling out a few from among the many, there is no implication that other programs do not compare with them. But a choice must be made, and one of two in each state have been selected, closing with a few of particular interest.[2]

Alabama

Alabama College, in Montevalla, included work on the Negro in two sociology courses and three history courses, making use of Negro year-books, magazine articles, publications of the Conference on Edu-

[2] This information is pre-war, as of 1941. War changes have not been surveyed.

cation and Race Relations, books by Negro authors, and other books from a reading list supplied to students. The history courses which include work on the Negro are American History, History of the South, and History of Alabama. There is also a two-year social service training course in which students do field work in the Department of Public Welfare. Negro cases are always included in their field work, and they do school attendance work for both Negro and white schools. Thus the program includes not only sociological studies, but integration with history, and practical experience with the Negro community, under expert guidance, as a service to the community in which the college is located.

The University of Alabama offers similar courses, reaching an even larger number of students—345 in sociology and 68 in history. Researches in this general field have been published, and are in process. An instructor in English at the University received a Rosenwald Fellowship in 1943 "for the writing of a novel on race relations in the South."

Florida

Rollins College, in Winter Park, Florida, carries on a program of special interest. There is a sociology seminar devoted entirely to the Negro and Negro-white relations; there is a course in race relations, devoting about 30 sessions to the Negro; and there are four other courses in which study of Negroes is integrated: economic problems, social problems, international relations, and religion in modern life. Supplementing this academic program, the college has a "Race Relations Committee" open to any student who is interested and desires to participate. This committee arranges an annual trip to the Hungerford School (for Negroes) for discussion with the students. The course on social problems visited a housing project for Negroes and talked with the superintendent. A vital part of the program is the annual Florida Intercollegiate Interracial Conference at Bethune-Cookman College. About twenty-five students from Rollins go to this conference. Eight colleges, four Negro and four white, are members. Usually about six are represented at individual conferences. This experience of seeing a fine Negro college in action is particularly valuable. The Race Relations Committee usually brings one or two Negro speakers to address its group on the campus.

Georgia

Among the Georgia colleges, Georgia State College for Women has an especially well-balanced program. No whole course is devoted to the Negro; but parts of all the following courses deal with the Negro or race relations: Social Problems, Rural Sociology, Social Legislation, American History, American Government, American Literature, The School and Society, and Contemporary Georgia. Actually this pattern is considered by the wisest students of education in the field of race relations to be more effective as well as more realistic than the practice of devoting an entire course to the subject, which sets the Negro apart as special and exceptional, instead of treating his history, his achievements, and his problems as a part of the whole stream of American and southern development.

In the sociology and education courses at Georgia State, an effort is made to have the students study books and pamphlets on race relations, especially those of the Commission on Interracial Cooperation. The instructors find a good deal of deep-seated prejudice to be broken down at the outset before they can present the picture of some of the inequalities in our present practices; this they follow up by describing some of the cooperative methods that have been found most effective in correcting these inequalities. Every year at least one assembly program is given by or about Negroes. Almost every year some Negro artist or group of artists appears on the Artist Series programs. Several times each year the Y.W.C.A. or other student organizations invite Negro choirs or other entertainers to appear on their programs. More rarely, there is an interchange of lectures between presidents or faculty members of the Negro and white colleges. Some of the student organizations, notably the Sociology Club and the Y.W.C.A., take an interest in community services, especially the Negro WPA Nursing School.

Kentucky

Berea College in Kentucky, as befits an institution founded in the 1850's for the "co-education of the races,"[3] has a noteworthy program

[3] Edwin R. Embree, *Brown Americans*, p. 64.

in this field. Although the Kentucky segregation laws, passed in 1904, caused Berea to become a school for whites only, it has not lost its sense of social responsibility. The college offers one full course on race relations, three sociology courses including work on the Negro (Population Problems, Principles, and Rural Sociology), and three courses giving some attention to the Negro: Freshman Bible, American Literature, and Labor Problems. Readings, book reviews, short papers, term papers, addresses by Negro college professors and other methods are used to present material about Negroes. A Negro glee club sings at Sunday evening chapel services; and, more significantly, there is a bi-monthly meeting of Negro school superintendents and teachers with Berea faculty and student members to study various aspects of Negro life. Students also work with Negro school pupils in recreation, home economics, and woodwork. A labor conference was attended by students of both Negro and white colleges of the state.

Louisiana

A number of colleges in Louisiana are doing interesting work, curricular and extra-curricular, but particular interest is attached to the extensive programs of Louisiana State University and of Tulane University. Parts of three sociology courses at Louisiana State deal with the Negro, enrolling over eight hundred students; there are also two advanced courses, Race Relations, with eighteen students, and a seminar in Race Relations with seventeen. A master's thesis has been written in the field; and there is both faculty and student cooperation with Southern University, the state university for Negroes.

Tulane University offers a slightly less inclusive curricular set-up, enrolling fewer students; but Tulane students participate actively in an interracial forum in New Orleans, in which both whites and Negro colleges, Catholic and Protestant, are represented, and which had an attendance of sixty in 1940-1941.

Maryland

No Maryland college reported a program of special interest, but one feature of the Hood College program is appealing. In cooperation with the Baltimore Urban League, a field trip is arranged at times for interested classes through the Negro community of Baltimore.

Students visit "hospitals, businesses, housing projects, churches, newspapers and so forth, eat at a Negro restaurant, visit Urban League Headquarters." They prepare for the trip ahead of time by studying published materials on the Negro in Baltimore.

Mississippi

In Mississippi, likewise, no college reported a curricular program even reasonably adequate in this field; but work of interest and distinction in special ways is being done at Millsaps College in Jackson. A member of the faculty has published an article in *Phylon* (literary journal of Atlanta University) on "The Race Issue in the Overthrow of Reconstruction in Mississippi"; another faculty member is preparing for publication a dissertation on "The Negro in Mississippi, 1865-1890." Every year at least one college chapel program is devoted to the theme of Race Relations, and a program by the Tougaloo College (Negro) choir was "received with the most overwhelming acclaim." Y.M.C.A. and Y.W.C.A. programs are devoted to this theme and there are frequent exchange programs with Negro associations. Y.W.C.A. students "engage in directed work with Negroes at the William Johnson Bethlehem Center every week." Students of Millsaps' sociology classes and of two Negro institutions "have just finished a survey of the main Negro residential section under direction of the Bethlehem Center head resident." And there is a monthly meeting of the Jackson Area Intercollegiate Council, including Millsaps College students and students of several Negro institutions. Among all the small colleges reporting, this extra-curricular program at Millsaps seems perhaps the most alive and interesting.

Missouri

In Missouri, excellent courses seem to be offered both at Park College, Parksville, and the University of Missouri at Columbia. Park College offers one full course in Race Relations and a number of sociology courses which integrate work on the Negro. The University offers two full courses: Race and Race Relations, and the American Negro, the latter on the graduate level and one of the very few courses anywhere devoted wholly to the Negro. The courses on general sociology and cultural anthropology integrate work on the Negro.

At Park College, there are some interesting extra-curricular activities. Negro lecturers come out from Kansas City to address the sociology club and classes; an honor student in sociology "has organized a program on the local 'Negro town' in Parksville," students "went over and worked with Negroes in putting a new roof on a Negro church." These activities seem a bit random and disjointed, but suggest interest and a willingness to try new procedures.

North Carolina

Because the states of North Carolina and Tennessee lead in extra-curricular programs and student interracial activities, it is difficult not to do them an injustice through the omission of many promising programs. In North Carolina the entire system of state education has certain aspects that promote better understanding. A vigorous and progressive educational policy and strong leadership have resulted in the development of an influential university, an excellent system of state colleges for Negroes, state-wide, planned study of race relations, and cooperation between institutions. A "Division of Cooperation in Education and Race Relations" holds annual conferences and plans programs and cooperative activities. One of these activities might be termed undergraduate social research on the life of Negroes in North Carolina, conducted by a group of Negro and white colleges, each one selecting a specific unit of study and contributing its findings to the cumulative results of the cooperative study. The reports are mimeographed and made available to all North Carolina colleges desiring them.

The whole system of state colleges heads up in the University of North Carolina at Chapel Hill. Here is the most extensive academic program in the study of race relations and of the Negro reported by any southern university. One full course on the Negro enrolls sixty students. Practically every course in sociology integrates material on the Negro, especially the courses in social problems, social anthropology, race and culture contacts, population, southern regions, and criminology. In other fields the general courses frequently integrate material on the Negro. Extensive research is carried on by graduate students; and the Institute of Social Research has made and published, generally through the University of North Carolina Press, many studies in the field of Negro life.

This integration stems not from crusading zeal but from a frank recognition of the intellectual validity of including full and factual treatment of the Negro in any field of study where it is pertinent. As a consequence emphasis will vary from a maximum in such a field as sociology to zero or near zero in such a field as Greek or mathematics. Students with special social interests at the University of North Carolina can obtain both extensive and intensive work pertaining to the Negro and race relations, or they can complete their course practically untouched by study of this subject.

Outside the classroom, there are concerts, speakers, one to five annual conferences in which Negroes participate, a photographic exhibit of Negro art, an annual Negro football game for charity played in the University Bowl, and participation by Negroes in the annual Drama festival sponsored by the Carolina Playmakers. All these activities are carried out on the campus under the auspices of various groups—Y.M.C.A., Y.W.C.A., Carolina Playmakers, Sociology Department, and so forth. Students from Negro colleges have also been invited to occasional Sunday morning breakfasts and worship services, and to other meetings and services held by student religious groups. These activities will be spoken of in greater detail in the chapter on religion.

Members of the faculty of the University of North Carolina have taken an active part in getting "a large WPA Negro community house," and some of them now give graduate courses at the North Carolina College for Negroes in Durham. Sometimes there are joint meetings of graduate seminars.

This brief sketch of the University program is very incomplete and inadequate, based upon a modest statement by one of the professors. But it will serve to indicate in a general way the type of activity taking place, activity primarily intellectual and objective, but in some of its aspects infused with a strong sense of social responsibility and human fellowship.

Oklahoma

No one program in Oklahoma stands out, although several colleges seem to be doing good work in a rather limited way. One fact, however, is noteworthy for its implications. In every case where interracial activities or programs with Negro speakers are mentioned, the contact is with Langston University, a Negro institution. As one thinks over most of these colleges' reports, it is noticeable that Hampton, Fisk, Tougaloo, and Langston serve repeatedly as points of contact, while other Negro colleges fill the same function, though less often. Students all over the world, not to speak of teachers, have much in common. It is evident that the very existence of these Negro colleges in the South provides many opportunities for establishing contacts, and that more use could well be made of them as bridges between groups that are in some ways increasingly isolated from each other.

South Carolina

Furman University and Livingstone College in South Carolina each reported one full course on race relations, in addition to several sociology courses, parts of which deal with the Negro. Furman also reported that several students had attended an interracial conference at Winthrop College. However, the programs at these two colleges stand out rather by comparison with other South Carolina colleges than as distinguished in the total southern picture.

Tennessee

Tennessee ranks with North Carolina in the variety and vitality of activities in this field. For instance, Lambuth College and Union University in Jackson both report friendly cooperation and interchange with Lane College, the college for Negroes in the same city. Maryville College offers a full course in race problems, elected by seventeen students; Union University has a similar course elected by thirty-five, in addition to three sociology courses, parts of which deal with the Negro, elected by a total ninety-five students; and students and staff members of William Jennings Bryan University in Dayton hold Bible classes in the neighborhood Negro community, and at the reformatory for Negro boys at Pikeville.

Two other Tennessee institutions stand out, each in its own way; George Peabody College for Teachers and Scarritt College for Christian Workers, both in Nashville.

George Peabody College offers one summer course, and one fall term course in "Problems of Dual Education,"[4] aimed to open up and interpret the racial aspects of southern educational problems to teachers, prospective teachers, county supervisors, and others in the educational field. Students come from all over the South, and speakers from various state boards, educational funds, federal agencies, and the like, address them during the course. At least one Negro speaker generally appears before the class, and a trip to Tennessee State A. and I. College and Fisk University acquaints the students with the two leading Negro colleges in the city. During the 1941 summer session, a course called "Education and Culture in the South," but dealing largely with race relations was taught by Mr. R. B. Eleazer of the Commission on Interracial Cooperation. Sociology courses, notably "Southern Regional Problems" and "The American Community," deal with the Negro as an integral part of their subject matter. A course in southern literature includes books by and about Negroes. In several other fields, professors use the materials of the Commission on Interracial Cooperation.

During the summers, there are numerous South-wide educational conferences. The 1941 Curriculum Conference on Democratic Living in a Critical Time, for instance, drew educators from all over the South in addition to the summer school students. In almost every address delivered to the general meetings, the southern educational leaders who spoke stressed the absolute necessity for practicing democracy at home if we desire to maintain it at all; that this means, among other things, that every American shall have equal opportunity, educational, economic, civil and political, irrespective of race; and that we must not merely reluctantly permit this but honestly work for it.

The actual number of Peabody students devoting any serious study to the Negro is very small; the vast majority of students are untouched by it. Nevertheless the liberalized attitudes of even a few are significant because of their role in the communities from which

[4] Suspended during the war.

many of them come and to which they go as teachers, supervisors, social workers, and the like. Among students in these courses, prejudiced attitudes do give way to open-minded interest and desire for justice. And over and above this, the impact of the speakers at mass meetings must have some effect upon their larger audiences.

The second institution of special interest is Scarritt College for Christian Workers. This is a national Methodist training school for religious workers, a small specialized college offering the upper two years of college work and graduate courses leading to an M.A. degree. It is unique among the colleges discussed here in that its program is based upon a definitely Christian philosophy and directed to the training of Christian workers for the foreign and home fields. A number of missionaries on furlough and a number of foreign-born students are also among its students, with their wide experiences in race and culture contacts to contribute to what the college offers in formal training.

Scarritt College presupposes a Christian approach to all problems and activities. National, racial, and class barriers and prejudices are recognized as facts, but as social defects are to be transcended and as far as possible eradicated. This implies a more direct and less timid handling of social issues than in most "scientific" approaches whose advocates are generally very hesitant about touching the areas of emotional tension. Material on the Negro is thus integrated with practically all courses where it is pertinent, and for prospective religious workers—teachers, religious education experts, social workers, etc.—these are numerous. One course in sociology is entirely devoted to the subject, and chapel talks, classroom discussions, and informal student discussions often include reference to race, always with the implication that not merely justice but brotherhood is world-wide irrespective of nationality or race, and that personal and social conduct should be shaped accordingly. The result is a far more positive and dynamic response than is called forth by the timid and rather colorless approach in most institutions. Negro speakers are occasionally invited to speak at appropriate classes; Negro students often meet informally with individuals or groups of Scarritt students—sometimes for discussion of study material, sometimes for cooperation in the community, sometimes in organizations unrelated to the college in which both are interested. Scarritt College students work regularly at the Bethlehem Center, cooperating with Fisk University students there in serving the Negro community. The general reaction of Nashville Negroes to the college outlook and program is evidenced both in the fact that their leaders naturally turn to members of the Scarritt College faculty in matters of concern to both races, and in community comment. A group of Negro women, after discussing the various white colleges of Nashville, reverted to Scarritt with the satisfied remark, "Well, there's always *somebody* on the Lord's side, anyway."

Scarritt students are drawn from all over the South, to a lesser degree from all over the nation and the world. They include South American, European, and Oriental mission-school students as well as students from the United States. In turn Scarritt graduates go out all over the nation and the world as active workers, influential in the religious thinking and social action of the communities to which they go. It is therefore doubtful whether any other institution reporting, unless it be the University of North Carolina in its very different way, is as significant in this field.

Texas

In Texas only one program of unique interest appears. Sam Houston State Teachers College offers the best rounded program reported. It offers a three-hour race relations course, part-time work on the Negro in three sociology courses, still more time in each of four history courses; it uses extensive materials, carries on programs, discussions and conferences, and it has fifty to a hundred students participating in interracial activities with students of Prairie View College, Tillotson, and other Negro colleges. It was the pioneer college in the state in this field, and the work is well established and finds an active response among the students.

Virginia

Not a single college in Virginia reported even one full course on the Negro or race relations. Three colleges, however, reported a considerable amount of study and activity on related lines. Mary Washington College in Fredericksburg listed two sociology courses and three history courses in each of which from two to four weeks are devoted to the Negro with extensive reading material, class assignments, discussions, required readings, visitations, term papers, and outside speakers on the subject. There were numerous programs: Y.W.C.A. and International Relations Club programs, Hampton Quartet, visiting lecturers, trips to Negro schools, colleges, and churches, and delegates to an interracial conference. Students participated in programs at Negro schools and churches in the local community and student interest and response was high. The University of Richmond offers only incidental instruction about the Negro, but a number of its faculty members are actively associated with the work of the Committee on Interracial Cooperation; Hampton singers appear annually, speakers sometimes, and there is extensive interchange and cooperation by both faculty members and students with Union University, the local Negro college. Washington and Lee University, in Lexington, reports slightly more academic work.

On May 5, 1944, the Richmond, Virginia, *Times Dispatch,* published an account of the Richmond Inter-Collegiate Council, organized in the fall of 1943 "to promote better relations among the college students of Richmond, and to discuss and act upon the problems facing college youth." Its active membership includes 400 students from Westhampton College, Virginia Union University (Negro), Richmond Professional Institute, Virginia Union Theological Seminary (Negro), St. Philip Hospital, the Medical College of Virginia and the Assembly Training School. On May 10, 1944, the Council sponsored a public forum on race relations at the Virginia Medical Auditorium. A panel of two students and two faculty members, evenly divided between the races, discussed "The Negro's Contribution to America," "The Cure for Racial Problems," "The Causes of Racial Problems," and "The Myth of Race."

In addition to the colleges and programs mentioned, other confidential reports were received. These have not been included because sometimes illiberal individuals in a local community might make use of them against an institution. The story given here is, therefore, only partial, and an understatement of the heartening progress being made.

HOW IT IS DONE: NEGRO COLLEGES[5]

The leading Negro colleges, aside from the one federally supported university, Howard, are private institutions. While the equalizing process is rapidly raising some of the state colleges to a comparable level in plant equipment, personnel, and academic standards, the best private institutions are still in the lead.

In their whole history and in their present nature most of these private colleges for Negroes are already adventures in interracial cooperation and education. White churches and white teachers cooperated with ambitious Negro scholars, their families and friends in the founding of these colleges; and to a large extent this cooperation still continues. Hampton, Fisk, Dillard, Atlanta, for example, all belong in this family of the early mission schools grown into colleges, with a long tradition of white contributors, trustees and teachers gradually supplemented by Negro teachers, contributors and trustees until a genuinely interracial situation has been brought about. In some cases the pendulum has swung so far that there is now danger of these institutions completely Jim-Crowing themselves by the exclusion of whites from all participation save as contributors. But for generations every one of these colleges has been a living education in race relations for both students and faculty members, and to a lesser but real degree for its trustees and contributors.

An excellent example of this in terms of the completely southern scene is Paine College in Augusta, Georgia. Paine was founded, and has been supported and run throughout its history by white and Negro Southerners. It was founded in 1882 at a meeting held at St. John Methodist Episcopal Church in Augusta. Five white Southerners from the Methodist Episcopal Church South and five Negro Southerners from the Colored Methodist Episcopal Church met together in what must have been one of the earliest instances of interracial meeting and cooperation in the South. Their meeting was a response to the request of Bishop Lucius H. Holsey of the Colored Methodist Episcopal Church, a former slave, who saw the need for training leaders for that newly formed church. The governing boards

[5] Information based chiefly on a survey of Negro colleges, 1941-42, by M. C. McCulloch.

of both churches approved the request; and in 1834 Paine Institute was opened with a board of trustees equally divided between the two races, with a southern white faculty and a student body of southern Negroes. Five years later the first Negro member was added to the faculty, and both board and faculty have been interracial since. In 1902, southern Methodist women became interested in Paine and from that time have helped to support it. Through its student body of three hundred, through its bi-racial faculty and board of trustees, through its relationship with white and colored Methodist churches of the South, and through conferences and community contracts, Paine has served for sixty years as a living venture of education in race relations.[6]

The private church-supported schools and colleges for Negroes have in general followed this pattern, educating in race relations in a way in which southern schools and colleges for white students have not done; because of them numbers of educated Negroes have had contacts with white persons of culture and of good will, a factor which has contributed enormously to mutual understanding. Unfortunately the reverse has not been true, in that it is entirely possible and even probable for southern white students to complete their education without ever having had any direct contact with educated Negroes.

Under the rapidly changing conditions of modern times, however, new methods are needed and are being devised to fulfill this vital function. As the state schools and colleges, staffed wholly by Negroes, take over the responsibility for Negro students, and as trained Negro staffs and faculties largely replace whites in the church schools and colleges, a complete Jim-Crowing of the educational set-up threatens. Negro colleges in general today find themselves confronted with the same narrowing educational limitations of a uni-racial institution in a bi-racial society. They too must resort to some artificial means of compensating for this educational handicap.

Perhaps because of their tradition and heritage, perhaps because they are a part of a minority group life, the better Negro colleges are more active in one aspect or another of this field than the white colleges. Let us see what some of them are doing.

[6] E. C. Peters, letter, 1943.

1. *Academic Work*

Probably the most extensive academic program in the field is that of Howard University in Washington, D. C., a federal institution and one which has been offering graduate work for many years. Here is a list of courses offered:

A. Courses devoted exclusively to the Negro, race relations, or some aspects of Negro-white relations:

English 144. *American Prose and Poetry of Negro Life.* 5 quarter hours. 30 students.

Political Science 130. *Africa Today.*

Education 290. *Advanced Educational Psychology.*

Education 238. *History of Negro Education in the United States.*

Education 244. *Problems in Negro Education.*

Sociology 198. *The Negro in America.* 5 quarter hours. 43 students.

History 113. *The History of Ethiopia and Egypt in Ancient Times.* 5 quarter hours. 18 students.

History 130. *The Negro in American History.* 5 quarter hours. 13 students.

History 134. *West African Civilization in the Middle Ages.* 5 quarter hours. 13 students.

History 141. *The Peoples and Culture of Africa in the Old Stone Age.* 5 quarter hours. 21 students.

History 205. *Seminar on the Negro in American History.* 5 quarter hours. 12 students.

B. Sociology courses parts of which are devoted to the Negro or to aspects of Negro-white relations:

Sociology 136. *The City.* 5 quarter hours. 37 students.

Sociology 138. *Rural Sociology.* 5 quarter hours. 1 student.

Sociology 52. *Social Institutions.* 5 quarter hours. 33 students.

Sociology 125. *Introduction to Social Psychology.* 5 quarter hours. 39 students.

Sociology 141. *Criminology.* 5 quarter hours. 20 students.

Sociology 147. *Social Maladjustments.* 5 quarter hours. 65 students.

Sociology 180. *The Family.* 5 quarter hours. 30 students.

In addition to this, the University offers 21 quarter courses in history in which the subject of race relations in the more inclusive sense is dealt with incidentally.

The *Journal of Negro Education,* a professional quarterly magazine of high quality, is edited and published at Howard, and Howard faculty members and graduate students have made and published many studies in the field of Negro life and history, and race relations.

Tuskegee Institute has a Department of Research and Records, and for years the *Negro Year Book,* which has served both races as a handy encyclopedia of Negro life, was edited and published by Dr. Monroe Work of that department.

Atlanta University offers graduate study in the fields of anthropology, Negro life and history, and race relations, and publishes *Phylon,* a journal dealing with races and cultures in general, though emphasizing the Negro all over the world.

Fisk University has extensive general course offerings in the fields of sociology and anthropology dealing with the same theme. It supports a considerable program of research in social and economic problems in the south. It also often conducts through its Department of Social Sciences surveys requested by local health, welfare and other agencies as the basis of action programs. It has recently added several special features that are related to the understanding of race relations. One of these is a kind of "interneship" for graduate students in education who teach and work in a bi-racial rural community in Tennessee and report and analyze their findings. Another is the Institute of African Studies, with native African graduate students participating in the work. For its work in Races and Cultures, the Social Science Department has had as faculty members or graduate students natives of Hawaii, Haiti, Austria, England, Gold Coast, South Africa as well as white and Negro Americans—a veritable living laboratory in race and culture contacts. The headquarters of the newly organized Division of Race Relations of the American Missionary Association also are on the Fisk campus in close relationship with the Division of Social Sciences.

Most Negro colleges, of course, are just colleges. They do not offer graduate work, and their courses are therefore more limited in variety and more general in content. Some of these colleges offer two or more courses dealing exclusively with the Negro or race relations, among the most frequent being Negro History, Negro literature, and Race Relations; and in some colleges at least one of these is required for graduation. As all Negro students have to study white history, white literature, and white culture, they thus get in general a better basis for understanding a bi-racial society than white students do.

What is more, there is a different attitude on the part of administrative and academic officials towards such study. Commonly in white southern colleges, the study of the Negro is included only through the interest of some individual professor or professors, though there are noteworthy exceptions. In Negro colleges, however, the necessity for students living in a bi-racial society to study the cultures of both groups and their relationships is recognized by the administration and curriculum builders, and the academic program is more rationally and effectively planned in this respect.

II. *Programs and Projects*

But books are not enough. Lectures are not enough. As we have seen, white colleges conduct programs to reach a wider portion of the student body than may elect particular courses. Negro colleges do the same.

Dillard University, for instance, reported in a single year programs devoted to Negro life and race relations in the forms of speakers, debates, forums, concerts, art exhibits, etc. Over a five-year period, it reported the following as noteworthy:

"Dillard conducted (1936-1941) the only national competition for Negro artists; it organized and conducts a forum for study of local and national issues affecting Negroes; it brings to its forum platform speakers of every shade of opinion whether conservative, liberals, communists, or other. The attitude of the University is to expose students to every philosophy, while attempting to so discipline them that they can evolve philosophies for themselves."

From the other colleges and universities come reports of concerts, debates, forums, art exhibits, plays, chapel speakers, and social science classes devoted to this theme.

We have already seen that 90 per cent of the replying Negro colleges conduct some interracial activities.

In North Carolina there is, as we have seen, a state-wide intercollegiate organization for the study of Negro life and problems and race relations within the state. This is termed the Division of Cooperation and Race Relations and functions through the State Department of Public Instruction, the University of North Carolina, and Duke University. It has been supported financially by the two universities and the General Education Board. There are cooperating committees from each of the universities and the Department of Education, including such sociologists as Dr. Howard W. Odum of Chapel Hill, and H. E. Jenson of Duke University. These committees, together with the director, constitute the program and policy-making groups of the Division. The Division has successfully organized from twenty to thirty groups at both Negro and white colleges, whose members make studies of conditions existing in the areas where the colleges are located, and discuss their findings and conclusions at an all-day session at Duke or Chapel Hill. There are generally about 150 or more students and faculty representatives present at these annual meetings. Faculty members of the two universities have been invited to give lectures on the subject of race relations in many of the colleges. In 1942-43, Duke University freshmen invited Dr. Heningburg of North Carolina College for Negroes to deliver a series of lectures to freshmen on the general subject of race relations. The lectures, presented in the faculty apartments, generally lasted about forty minutes and were followed by a discussion period of twenty minutes. At the request of the director of Religious Activities, Dr. Heningburg was next invited to hold discussion groups with some twenty-five graduate students in the social sciences. Indication of the enlightened interest of these students is found in the second topic which was requested for discussion: "What does the American Negro expect of America." Dr. Heningburg also directed a study of "Attitudes of College Students in Matters of Race," and received cooperation from both Duke University and the University of North Carolina. Besides such inter-collegiate cooperation, the Negro colleges in North Carolina send delegates and materials to the annual meeting of the North Carolina Interracial Commission at the University of North Carolina.

In 1940, a plan was developed among students of the area around Durham for the study of problems of mutual interest. Representatives from North Carolina College for Negroes, Duke University, and the University of North Carolina met in the School of Religion at Duke University and formulated their program. General meetings are held three times each academic year, rotating from campus to campus. At present both chairman and vice-chairman are from North Carolina College for Negroes and the group is studying the findings of the Seminar on New Race Issues which were presented at a nation-wide conference March 10, 1943. These are some of the ways in which Negro and white colleges can collaborate in a well-planned state-wide program and in local, smaller-scale activities as well.

In Florida and in New Orleans, intercollegiate interracial conferences are well established. In Florida, four white and four Negro colleges participate. In New Orleans, there is an interracial youth forum in which students from Tulane University, Loyola, Ursuline Dominican, Xavier, and Dillard all take active part. Dillard University has also had part-time instructors from Tulane and Newcomb in New Orleans, chiefly in the field of art and for the purpose of improving race contacts in that field. It has cooperated actively with social studies groups at Tulane and Newcomb in making surveys, in arranging for lecturers and artists, and has shared with Newcomb College in art exhibits. Students from Dillard have shared experiences in discussion groups with students from Newcomb College and with other groups in local white colleges.

Bishop College in Marshall, Texas, reports that through the action of the Southwestern region of the Y.M.C.A. and the Y.W.C.A. there is an exchange of speakers between white and Negro groups, and students of both races attend conferences held at both Negro and white colleges of the area. This practice is becoming increasingly widespread. We have mentioned instances of it in North Carolina, Louisiana, and Texas, and Tennessee is also moving up into line.

White and Negro faculty members of Negro colleges also serve as race relations educators in many roles. They are called upon by other colleges, church groups, civic groups, and youth groups to give talks on race relations or to advise on community problems involving members of both groups. For instance, Shaw University in Raleigh, North Carolina, has had its teachers in social science serve as guest lecturers at the University of North Carolina, Wake Forest, Atlantic Christian College, and others. Members of the faculty of Fisk University in Nashville have been guest speakers at George Peabody College for Teachers, Scarritt College for Christian Workers, and Vanderbilt University in Nashville; they have also served on the Research and Planning Committee and Executive Committee of the Council of Community Agencies, on the newly-formed Council of Human Relations, in the local branch of the N.A.A.C.P., as consultants on municipal housing problems, on the Southern Executive Committee of the Fellowship of Reconciliation, and on the interracial boards of local welfare agencies. The director of the Department of Social Sciences also serves on the race relations programs of the Julius Rosenwald Fund and the American Missionary Association, has served for years on the Commission on Interracial Cooperation, and now is chairman of the Executive Committee of the newly organized Southern Regional Council.

At LeMoyne College in Memphis, Tennessee, members of the administration and faculty have served in many community relationships. The administration was active in securing a federal slum-clearing and housing project in a needy area near the college; members of the faculty enlisted qualified Negroes to take Civil Service examinations for the 1940 census, in which their average rating was higher than that of the white candidates. The Department of Sociology has made numbers of surveys of local conditions of Negro life at the request of agencies, federal and local, to be used as the basis of action programs, and its students have for years served as volunteer workers with the Memphis Family Welfare Society and other agencies. The head of the Department of Social Sciences at LeMoyne has been increasingly used by the Council of Social Agencies as a consultant on Negro Welfare and race relations, and through this beginning, there have grown up various interracial committees to deal with welfare programs among Negroes and a definite attempt has been launched to study the needs of the Negro community and to work out an adequate welfare program for them.

All too often in the Negro colleges this work is carried almost exclusively by a few members of the faculty who give themselves unstintingly to such services, just as it is a few individuals in the white colleges who serve as interracial interpreters. This results in an undue, almost a breaking, strain on a few persons, whereas a broader administrative and faculty policy of spreading the load could result in even more effective service without the exaggerated individual burden-bearing. But the services rendered by these individuals are among the vital contributions of Negro colleges to community life.

CHAPTER VI

MOULDING OF ATTITUDES

COLLEGES ARE EXPECTED TO PROVIDE LEADERSHIPS, but what actually takes place in the minds and hearts and lives of children is likely to be more decisive in shaping their attitudes than the later learning of college years.

It is important, therefore, to inquire whether there are any activities going on in the schools, the libraries, the scout troops, and settlement houses which are helping our children and youth to understand each other better and at the same time, to understand themselves and their relationship to the community and the region in which they live.

SCHOOLS

If it is true of Negro colleges that they are increasingly becoming uni-racial, it is even more universally true of the grade schools and high schools where our southern children are being educated.

Mission schools for Negroes with interracial boards and interracial faculties were first in the elementary as in the college field. But primary and secondary education for Negroes in the South have now been taken over almost one hundred per cent by the states themselves. Out of 500 elementary and secondary schools which the American Missionary Association opened and operated for shorter or longer periods, it now retains a connection with only ten. All of the 5,000 rural schools for Negro children which were built in the South with the help of the Julius Rosenwald Fund and with the support of both whites and Negroes have either been taken over by the state or replaced by public schools. All this, of course, is as it should be. It is also as it should be that Negroes trained as teachers, since they have no opportunities to teach elsewhere, should be employed in schools for Negro children. Yet the result is clearly to widen, in the most formative years, the gulf that separates one race from another, so that children of one race have no opportunity to establish contacts with the other race at the time when such contacts could most naturally and unselfconsciously be made.

A very few schools with church support, or recently taken over by the state, still have interracial boards and staffs. Lincoln Institute at Lincoln Ridge, Kentucky, for example, is a state high school for Negroes with an interracial board of trustees, a Negro director of Education, and a white business manager. The faculty is bi-racial and drawn from all parts of the country. Each year the Presbyterian Church conducts a special training school for Negro women at the Institute. In the ten years of its operation, it is believed to have contributed much toward better understanding in the state. Every year some of its students attend an interracial conference at Berea College, with discussion centering on economic problems.

Some of the church-supported schools, with their relatively broad contacts and philosophy, will be discussed later in the chapter on religion. It is enough to say here that with these significant but rare exceptions, elementary and secondary schools in the South re-inforce the isolation of the two groups. However, here and there groups and individuals and sometimes the students themselves have undertaken activities to counteract this, and to throw across the gulf some slender strands of common experience and mutual understanding.

The largest single undertaking of this nature through the school system has been the work of the Commission on Interracial Cooperation. Over a period of years the Commission sponsored a high school competition, in which over 1,000 southern white high schools participated, for the best posters, programs, and study units on Negro life and history and race relations.

Other such programs spring up locally in response to local initiative.[1] A few instances will serve as illustrations.

In 1942 white high school and college students in one southern community were holding joint assemblies, forums, and discussion groups at a local white college. To expand the scope of these they invited a Cuban, a Chinese, and the Negro students from the local Negro high school to participate. The assemblies were a success; din-

---

[1] As there is sometimes a local element which would use the information against the schools concerned, identities are being withheld.

ner was served to all the guests, and a spirit of good fellowship prevailed.

Because the Florida interracial intercollegiate conferences had to be suspended for the duration of the war due to gas rationing, the sponsors of the conference decided in 1943 to hold a high school interracial conference. The conference was well attended, and students of both races spoke and shared in the discussions on the theme, "The American Negro and the War."

In a North Carolina township the students of the white school sent to the superintendent of schools urgent and repeated requests for a chapel program to be given by the glee club of the local Negro high school. At last the request was granted, several programs were given, and the response was enthusiastic. As a return courtesy the band of the white high school gave a concert in the auditorium of the Negro high school, which was equally well received. A similar exchange of concerts has been going on for some years in a rural Tennessee county where the local Negro high school has a glee club and the local white school a band. This sort of exchange is rather frequent. One Negro school official reported: "We have been asked to sing in abundance, but rarely to speak."

From North Carolina and Tennessee come reports of white and Negro high school students sharing an athletic field. In one instance a barrier had for years separated the games of the Negro children from those of the white children, but two years ago the students, tiring of the restriction or simply wanting more space, shoved it aside and now play on the same field. On one of these playgrounds the white and Negro school teams play each other in football, baseball, and softball.

There are also reports from Tennessee of the interchange of student programs during Negro history week or on similar occasions. In one instance, Negro high school students were invited to give a program of spirituals, and classical music, interpreting Negro life to the white students in the white high school. In another the white students visited the Negro high school to attend a program on the accomplishments of the Negro in Africa and America. They were so well pleased with the program that they invited the Negro students to come to their school the following year and put on another program. This second presentation made use of the program suggestions of the the United States Office of Education in a pamphlet "National Unity Through Intercultural Education." Contributions of all the racial and nationality groups in the United States were touched upon to show how each had played its part in the building of one great American people and culture.

In addition to these very limited contacts between white and Negro school children, there are scattered instances of cooperation and joint discussion between white and Negro teachers and school administrators. Some white schools have invited the Negro Jeanes teacher to visit and observe, or to be present at special programs and conferences at the white schools. White and Negro teachers have sometimes joined with local citizens to help procure specially needed equipment in rural Negro schools; and there have been some friendly visiting and consulting between school librarians and teachers, with white and Negro teachers meeting sometimes in the white high school, sometimes in the Negro school, to hear special speakers or to discuss special problems of common interest. Exchange or sharing of visual aid materials, health materials, scientific equipment, and county circulating libraries, and regular conferences between white and Negro supervisors and other county officials to work out educational plans are among the other scattered instances of friendly cooperation reported from North Carolina, Tennessee, Georgia, Alabama, and Kentucky.

From Hamilton County, Tennessee, for example, comes a report of professional meetings set up on a professional basis in place of an earlier racial basis. The teachers of this county regularly held their professional meetings on the same day, but Negro teachers met at the Negro high school and white teachers met at the white high school. For the past two years a new type of professional meeting has been instituted, bringing white and Negro teachers together two or three times a year, usually in a large white church or in the white high school. One member of the planning committee is a Negro; and there is a discussion leader invited and selected by the Negro teachers, who is guest of the Negro teachers for the two-day period. This discussion leader serves on a panel to assist the director of the conference with the main discussions. Directors in recent years have come from Columbia University, the University of Oregon, and the University of Chicago. Both groups profit not only through increased understanding and good will, but through the improved programs made possible by pooling resources.

There is one other form of interracial contact experienced in some schools for Negro children which reflects credit on human kindliness at the same time that it points up a situation which is fundamentally out of balance. This includes those innumerable instances in which individual white citizens or groups make contributions of funds or materials to supplement the inadequacies of Negro schools with respect to equipment, services, or even the bare necessities of life for the pupils. Thus in De Kalb County, Georgia, the University of Georgia has contributed records to make possible a music appreciation program; a club of white women in Decatur pays the salary of a Negro dentist to conduct a dental clinic for the school; and the De Kalb County chapter of the American Red Cross contributes boxes of shoes and clothing for needy children, without which regular school attendance would often be impossible.

A situation in which children lack essential clothing and schools lack essential health facilities obviously calls for a concerted public policy to support the foundations of the school program and broaden the base of economic security; but these are developments calling for a long range program and, until they can be brought about, alleviating measures undertaken on private initiative are important and indeed indispensable.

Reviewing this section, it is clear that neither states nor counties nor city boards of education have yet accepted education for mutual understanding as an integral part of the publicly supported education of our boys and girls. But individual supervisors, principals, teachers, and groups of high school young people are making a beginning, and here and there organized groups of citizens outside the school system are lending a hand.

RURAL SCHOOL AND COMMUNITY

More than half the Negroes in the United States still live in the rural areas. What the country school does for the Negro child and his family consequently affects many more Negroes than all the pioneering, experimenting, and improvement in the city schools. We are therefore noting here some interesting things that are going on in a few rural communities. Others, undertaken with church sponsorship, are discussed in the chapter on religion.

In October, 1943, the *Nashville Tennessean* carried a little feature article on three Tennessee schools for Negroes. It ran thus: "Race Relations Aided by Schools. Three of State's Negro Institutions Declared Rendering Fine Service. 'Community service programs, ranging all the way from building houses to improving hog breeds are being carried on by three Negro schools in Tennessee in such a way as to do much towards improvement of race relations in the state,' W. E. Turner, head of the division of Negro education in the state department of education, said yesterday. The schools are Allen-White at Whiteville, Booker T. Washington in East Chattanooga, and Webb at McKenzie, and their contribution towards mutual understanding is accomplished by gradual heightening of Negro standards and sympathetic cooperation of white persons backing the work. . . . The schools have the usual agricultural and trade courses, but the students carry their activities far beyond them and into their communities.

"Allen-White has a truck garden providing food and free hot lunches for elementary grade children. Students in the wood-working department have built houses for faculty members and also go to the homes of students to help with repair work on houses, barns, and sheds. There is an annual dinner to which white leaders of the county are invited and at which students decorate the dining room, prepare, and serve the meal. A lending wardrobe for expectant mothers, providing clothing and other articles needed, is another project.

"Students at the Booker T. Washington school are participants in the Chattanooga Chamber of Commerce 'pig-chain'. Each is given a pure-bred pig, must breed it to the like, and give one pig each from the first litter to two other boys."

Such accounts, though necessarily incomplete, afford a glimpse of the kind of rural programs through which some of our southern schools serve to raise the whole level of community life for the Negroes in the area and to develop friendly cooperation with the white resi-

dents. Many schools are doing this all over the South in different
ways and in varying degrees. We will choose an example which is
certainly not typical but which, because of what it has accomplished
and the direction it has given to the thinking of many people
interested in rural life, is both significant and influential.

Penn Normal, Industrial and Agricultural School, St. Helena
Island, is located on one of the Sea Islands, just off the coast of Beaufort, South Carolina. St. Helena is a long, low island of soft silty land
with wide salt marshes, "tide rivers," and stretches of pine woods.
The population numbers around 4,000 people, the overwhelming
majority of whom are Negroes. Penn School, with its saying "The
Island is the School," is the life-center of the community. Its beginnings go back to 1861 when the Island was seized by northern
troops and declared free territory. Escaping slaves fled there by the
thousand, and out of the emergency relief work begun among them
grew a little school that has persisted and grown through the years.
For some twenty-five years past the school has sought to be a genuine
center of development for the whole island, and it has served increasingly also as a center of interracial cooperation and a demonstration for both whites and Negroes in rural education.

Starting with the elementary grades, Penn has increased its
curriculum gradually until it offers the full twelve-year program. At
the same time, it has increasingly tied in with the whole community
life, through the constant stream of visitors—trustees, educators,
students, sociologists, artists, health and agricultural workers, and
many others who visit Penn School from all over the South, the
nation, and the world, coming from as far as India and Africa for the
educational suggestions they can glean from its program.

A letter written in 1943 to the principal, asking to be brought up
to date on Penn's latest contributions to the field of better race relations in terms both of cooperation and of understanding, brought the
following reply:[2]

"As we have so few white people on the Islands, the question of

[2] Miss R. B. Cooley, letter, October 29, 1943. Miss Cooley retired December 31,
1943, after more than 25 years of service. The new principal is the Reverend Howard
T. Kester.

race relations does not loom so large as in most sections of the South. . . .

"1. There is an increasing contribution to current expense from the Negroes both in the North and in the South. On our Board of Trustees we have two Negroes, (24 members). On our faculty we have two whites, the Principal and the associate Principal, (26 members).

"2. There is close state and county cooperation. The Farm Demonstration Agent is a Penn School graduate whose home is on Ladies Island (between St. Helena and the mainland, connected by a bridge). He works directly with Penn School as well as with the county activities.

"The Home Demonstration Agent is located at Penn School and serves as Home Economics teacher in the school as well as Demonstration Agent in the community.

"The school and the Public Health Department work in close cooperation. Our school nurse serves in the clinic for venereal diseases. She serves with the county nurse in the midwives' class, she takes all the opportunities given for t.b. examinations and the prenatal clinic held in Beaufort. Vaccine points are provided by the state. Diphtheria anti-toxin is provided for pre-school children. The county has a fund for cancer treatment for whites and Negroes. There is also a well-baby clinic. Speakers and motion pictures are provided by the county for our Annual Baby Day.

"The St. Helena Cooperative Credit Union was organized in 1925 with its state charter. The St. Helena Consumer Cooperative was organized in 1942.

"There is a close relationship with State College for Negroes. The senior girls in the department of education are sent to the Island in groups during the year to have practical experience in our rural schools under a skilled critic teacher. They make a study of Penn School and its methods of community education.

"Groups of graduate students from Yale University, Duke University, and Scarritt College, and Negro teachers from high schools and colleges in the South have visited Penn School to make a study of its methods and results. Students in the sociology department of

Furman University, Greenville, South Carolina, have been brought to Penn School.

"3. There is close cooperation between the County Farm and Home Demonstration agents, white and Negroes. Speakers (state and county) respond to the invitation to speak at our Farmers Fair and these fairs are attended by the whites as well as the Negroes. Contributions are made for the fair by our white friends.

"Regular community sings are held in our Community House attended by both races."

In all of this, of course, no opportunity is given to tell the story of Penn's influence on the daily life of the community—of the transformation of crude, drab little cabins into neat, white-washed or white painted homes, the substitution of healthy, covered wells for shallow holes in the ground, the planting of trees, vegetables, flower gardens around each little home, the gradual diversification of cash crops from cotton alone to include sweet potatoes, Irish potatoes, peanuts, eggs, chickens, and turkeys for the market, and produce for canning the year round, the building of a Rosenwald school, and the improvement of the county schools round about, and all the other details which alone can give color and substance to the tale. Yet these things are happening, and make up the day-to-day life of the island, highlighted by such creative expression as the singing of the beautiful St. Helena Island spirituals, studied and recorded by scholars but still happily sung by the people in the old folk manner.

All this can be done. For, given the leadership and the will, it has been and is being done in the Deep South, in the tragic "Black Belt" that gives birth to Ku Klux Klans and white supremacy leagues. Whites and Negroes, private and public agencies, and individuals can make a single school a center that not only transforms its own community, but whose influence radiates out through the county, the state, the nation, and the world.

PRE-SCHOOL PROGRAMS

Of recent years the little children too young to go to our regular schools have claimed the attention of educators. For good or ill their education is increasingly passing out of the home into the nursery school. Indeed, where mothers must be away working all day, no one will question that children are better off in a nursery school than locked out in the alley for fear the house will burn down, or tied to the bed post lest they wander away and be lost. For many of these children, who formerly were necessarily uncared for and under-nourished, these day-care programs are an inestimable blessing. In the South they began largely under the WPA of a decade ago; after Pearl Harbor, they were transferred to the Lanham Act Administration with the idea of releasing mothers to work in defense industries or in any form of essential civilian labor. This program was under joint federal and local sponsorship on a fifty-fifty basis of support, with a division of authority between the Lanham Act Administration and the local Board of Education. Perhaps in part because it was semi-federal, perhaps in part because it was new and is beginning in a day of greater justice, the program was set up on a basis of industrial need and individual qualification rather than of race, although the schools are of legal necessity separate.

It will serve our turn to survey the program in a single locality and through it to conceive the whole, for, while there are variations, the general plan is uniform throughout the South.

In six states in the area around Tennessee, some 5,000 children were in attendance at Lanham Act nursery schools; more were, of course, enrolled. In Tennessee about 1,000 were in daily attendance. In the city of Nashville, there were seven such schools, four for white and three for Negro children. Owing to certain restrictions in Tennessee, while the Board of Education controlled the program locally, it did not operate it in public schools nor support it; the buildings and local funds were provided by local welfare agencies and were supplemented by fees from the parents. Thus, three of the four white nursery schools were run and supported by the McNeeley Day Home, the Fanny Battle Day Home (community agencies); and the Elliott School sponsored by the Council of Jewish Agencies. The fourth was in a Federal Housing project and was supported by the Nashville War Chest, an emergency supplement to the Nashville Community Chest. The three Negro nursery schools were operated in and supported by the Bethle-hem Center, Methodist; the Fisk University Social Center; and the South Street Community Center (Community Chest Agencies). The

Boards of the three Negro community centers are interracial. Thus, there were cooperating in the support and conduct of these programs the Federal Government agency, the Nashville Board of Education, which supplies a supervisor, the Nashville War Chest, the Nashville Community Chest, and six local boards (three white and three interracial), including one Jewish, one Methodist, and two on which local colleges were officially represented—Scarritt College (white) and Fisk University (Negro), on the Bethlehem Center Board, and Fisk University on the Fisk Social Center Board. In addition to this, a good deal of cooperation was required on the part of parents, and the health inspection and care were supplied by local physicians and hospital staffs of both races on a volunteer basis.

Qualifications for teachers, salary scales, and in-service training were uniform, irrespective of race, and in-service training was given by the director to the entire city staff without segregation. George Peabody College for Teachers operates a private demonstration nursery school, with special booths for observation, and teachers from any of the nursery schools, white or Negro, are welcome to come and observe freely at any time. Meetings of the entire staff are held in rotation at the different nursery schools.

There have been problems and rough spots, plenty of headaches for everyone concerned; but these have been community problems, not race problems—problems of changing administrative organizations and rulings, changing prices, securing qualified personnel, reconciling the conflicts of Federal, State, and City regulations with each other and with local community needs. They have been tackled cooperatively on a community basis, and, thanks to this, some thousands of Tennessee children have been getting much needed care, shelter, food, play, rest, and training on a sound community basis without discrimination by race.

LIBRARIES

What do our boys and girls (and our adults, too) have to read in the South? Do they have access to the books they need, and that will open to them the fascinating world of mind and imagination? Do whites and Negroes fare alike? Do they work together for these essential services? These are vital questions for the future of the region and the people of both races who live in it.

In general the answers are discouraging, though there are a few interesting things being done to change them.[3] In 1939 only 42.73 per cent of the white South and 21.39 per cent of the Negro South received any sort of library service. The service for Negroes, where it existed at all, was generally inferior to that for whites. The big urban centers, which had the best facilities, also as a rule gave the Negro the nearest to an equal chance. Small towns seldom supply any service to Negroes. Counties sometimes serve the rural Negro schools. Where the situation is distinctly better than average, we are told to look for two factors: a head librarian who is awake and at work, and the efforts of "crusading Negro women." Now and then there are other factors, always decidedly personal.

Those were the answers in 1939. Have four or five years brought any improvement? The following reply to that question was given in a letter from Dr. Eliza Adkins Gleason, director of the Atlanta University School of Library Science:

"There has been no widespread increase in total southern library facilities for Negroes. There has, however, been a decided increase in library school training for Negroes. Most state and some private colleges are now offering courses for teacher-librarians. North Carolina College for Negroes has established a library school leading toward the B.S. degree in Library Science. Students working towards that degree must have completed their college work before entrance. Atlanta University has established a professional library school leading to the B.S. degree in Library Science. This school is now accredited by the American Library Association as a Type II Library School.

"There seems to be little indication of better financing and staffing of existing public libraries. No outstanding exceptions in this area have come to our attention. With regard to membership in professional library associations, there is no discrimination by the American Library Association in regard to membership of Negroes. I have recently been elected to the American Library Association Council which is the policy-making body of the Association. The American

[3] The general description from here on, unless otherwise noted, is from Elizabeth A. Gleason, *The Southern Library and the Negro*, 1939.

Library Association has gone on record as not scheduling its conferences in any states which will not allow Negroes equal privileges in hotels housing the convention attendants. Southern states and regional library associations do not generally admit Negroes to membership. The Library Association of the state of Virginia is the one notable exception to this custom. There is some question in my own thinking as to how much effort Negroes have made to become members of these associations.

"Many southern states provide scholarships in the field of library service if the state college for Negroes does not include work in this field in its curriculum. So far we have had students from Kentucky, Arkansas, and Texas who have received scholarship assistance of this nature."

Trained librarians, though absolutely essential, are not very useful where there are no libraries. This denial of books on a racial basis appears as one of the most meaningless yet profoundly harmful discriminations. An example of the subterfuges to which it constrains those hungry minds whose natural food is books, is related by Richard Wright, the Negro novelist. As an eighteen-year-old in Memphis where Negroes were not allowed to take books from the public library, he persuaded a white man to sign a card asking that books listed from time to time on separate sheets be sent him "by this boy." He "wrote out long lists of books and carted them off to devour" in his room.[4]

Yet in the darkness of the general picture, some gleams may be observed. A small exception is the existence in two southern cities and three southern counties of "stations" of the general public library, rotating collections of books from the main library made available to readers at some special place, such as a Negro public school. Services at the main library are rendered to Negroes on the same basis as to whites in six southern communities: Covington, Kentucky; El Paso and Pecos, Texas; Boydtown, Charlottesville, and Halifax, Virginia. Main libraries offer limited service to Negroes in four other Kentucky libraries, four in Texas, one in Virginia, and one in Oklahoma. This is obviously the least expensive basis and affords citizens and taxpayers the maximum use of books.

[4] Edwin R. Embree, *13 Against the Odds*, p. 36.

A much more common pattern, however, is the Negro branch of the general public library. The number of such city branches by states is: Texas, 12; Virginia, 10; Florida, Kentucky, and North Carolina, 7 each; Tennessee, 6; Oklahoma, 5; Alabama, Georgia, and Mississippi, 3 each; South Carolina and Louisiana, 2 each. In addition the following states provide Negro branches in the counties: North Carolina 8, Texas, 7; Tennessee and South Carolina, 3 each; Alabama, Arkansas, Georgia, Kentucky, Louisiana, and Mississippi, 1 each. A relatively unusual form is the independent Negro public library. There are 13 of these in the South, 7 in North Carolina alone, 2 in Georgia, and 2 each in Florida and Oklahoma.

As yet Negroes are nowhere members of the governing boards of Negro branches of the public library; but sometimes they serve on advisory or supplementary boards. This is the case in Georgetown, Kentucky; Kinston, South Carolina; Memphis, Tennessee; and Pine Bluff, Arkansas. The functions of the advisory boards vary. In Pine Bluff, Negroes really support and run the branch. In Miami, Florida, a Negro branch of the general library was organized as such; it is still affiliated but has a separate board of trustees, five Negro and four white, appointed by a Negro who gave the site and hopes to erect a new building; the organization is that of a non-profit-making incorporated library.

This report, made in 1939, shows clearly that local initiative can change the general pattern for the better. Yet even more can be done. In March, 1943, a Virginian reports: "In Virginia, research barriers no longer exist: the state and city libraries can be used by Negroes, college and university libraries are open to them, and the very fertile city and county archives are wide open to every one. Aside from being merely 'open', the Negro investigator finds a friendly cooperative atmosphere." The writer is referring only to the mature scholar, the research worker; and this does not, of course, mean equal availability of all resources to the general reader, but it shows a spirit that cannot fail in time to transform the whole state picture. Several cities are reported also as having developed public libraries or branches lately. Negroes of Mexia, Texas, largely through their own efforts, had by December, 1943, secured a public library for themselves.[5] Negroes of

[5] *Southern Frontier,* December, 1943, p. 4.

Tyler, Texas, through their own efforts and the cooperation of a community council composed of both races, have similarly developed an excellent small public library.[6] In Raleigh in 1933 there was no public library for Negroes. The local interracial committee held several meetings with representatives of both groups and finally evolved a plan for establishing one. Members of the group attended meetings of the County Commissioners (the tax levying authorities of Wake County) and the City Commissioners. To these groups they made appeals for appropriations to support a Negro library. These requests met approval and now the Richard B. Harrison Library is a very useful and attractive institution in the city of Raleigh. It receives annual appropriations from the city and the county.[7]

Another interesting public service is the bookmobile service of Gaston County, North Carolina. This service has been made possible by the superintendent of schools and the Gastonia public library and is available for all white and Negro communities. The books are distributed to adults and children, read eagerly by both, and regular library rules are well observed. Several hundred dollars were recently spent to buy books pertaining to Negro life, which are to be read by both races, to reinforce self-respect among Negroes and to acquaint white people with Negro achievement. In the opinion of a local supervising teacher, both citizenship and general intelligence have been improved as a result of the bookmobile service. Meantime, Gastonia is at work on plans for a Negro public library; a local white citizen is ready to donate the site, and details are being worked out.[8]

Private agencies and individuals also lend a hand. Private secondary schools and colleges for Negroes, for instance, often supplement their services to their own students with service to the community. In 1939, Dr. Gleason found 32 of these institutions giving full library service free to both city and county residents of their area and 13 more serving local residents only. A few others gave some service on a free basis.

A small library was erected for the Negroes of Winter Park, Florida, as a memorial to one of the white winter residents who had

[6] Peck, Lillian, *Team Work on the Home Front.*
[7] N. C. Newbold, letter, December 18, 1943.
[8] Maude M. Jeffers, report in Newbold materials, 1943.

been interested in broadening cultural and educational opportunities for Negroes. Although more than half the sum needed to put up a small fireproof building was contributed by the family of this man, the winter residents and the students and faculty of Rollins College also contributed to the building fund, and to the furnishing and equipment. The land was given by the city. The members of the Student Interracial Committee of Rollins were especially active on this project. The first hundred books were purchased with what has been called "flower money." At the death of a wife of one of the professors, the money which would have been spent on funeral flowers was used for books for the Negro library.[9]

Of all library ventures the most picturesque and in many ways the most challenging and hopeful is that of the Faith Cabin Libraries in South Carolina. About 1930 Willie Lee Buffington, a young white man working in the cotton mills of Edgefield, South Carolina, wanted to return a kindness to a local Negro preacher. Buffington had spent one year at the Berry School in Georgia, and the Negro preacher, who had taken a friendly interest in the ambitious youngster, managed out of his own meagre salary to send him a much needed dollar a month to help him stay in school. Returning to South Carolina to work in the mills by day and attend high school courses at night, Willie Buffington sought some way to express his gratitude. The preacher suggested that he help find books for a recently built Rosenwald School in the nearby countryside at Saluda. Without money, without influence, without experience, and with almost no leisure time, the young man seemed to have little to go on. But he did have faith, vision, and determination. He started talking to local people and writing letters to others he had heard of in his quest for books. The response was amazing. In a short while he had not just the few shelves full of books he had hoped for, but some two thousand volumes, far too many to fit into the small space available. So he did some more thinking and some more talking. White and Negro neighbors agreed to contribute lumber from their pine-wooded farms, and labor for the erection of a building. More lumber than was needed was given, and the surplus was sold to buy cement, hardware

[9] Major Graham Aldis, letter, November 29, 1944; Elizabeth A. Gleason, *op. cit.*, p. 155.

and windows. So the community worked together and in 1932 the first Faith Cabin Library was opened—a neat sturdy log cabin on a pine-shaded hill near the little school house. The walls were lined with books, there were home-made tables and benches, and a pleasant open fire-place. The state sent a worker to train the teachers of the Rosenwald School in cataloguing and handling the books. White readers were welcomed to share the books with the Negro school children and their families. Even to those who helped in the labor, it seemed a miniature miracle that they who seemed at the outset to have nothing and to be nobody could have achieved this themselves in little more than two years.

The idea spread. Neighboring communities heard the story, sent members to see, and soon began to call on the young wonder-worker to help them too. Still working in the mill, putting himself through school and college at night, supporting a wife and in time two children, he yet found time to respond to these appeals. By 1943 twenty-eight little Faith Cabin Libraries had been built for the Negroes of twenty-eight rural South Carolina communities, with a total of over 100,000 volumes circulating through South Carolina's rural schools.

READING ABOUT EACH OTHER

Few white people ever stop to think that Negroes are always reading about them, almost never about themselves, while whites are forever reading about themselves and almost never about Negroes. Indeed it is hard for us, if we live in the South, to get books by or about Negroes, even though thousands have been written. The consequence is that while educated Negroes are pretty well informed about white people, most white people are ill informed about Negroes, and many Negroes know very little about their own people. This is true all over the South, indeed more or less all over the nation. Yet here and there in the South, whites and Negroes are beginning to do something about it.

In 1933 Miss Dorothy Porter, a librarian, made a study of "Library Sources for the Study of Negro Life and History" which was printed in the *Journal of Negro Education* the following April. In the southern area, Miss Porter found special collections of books by or about

Negroes in the Houston, Texas, public library (which had 1,390 volumes on Africa), and of course in the Library of Congress in Washington, D. C. Besides these, she found special university collections at Fisk University in Nashville, Howard University in Washington, D. C., Johns Hopkins University in Baltimore, and the University of Texas in Austin. There is also the Collis P. Huntington Collection in the Library of Hampton, Virginia; and the University of North Carolina has both a good general selection of books and the raw materials in old manuscript and document form for research into the history of the South, white and Negro. Some of the other southern universities and colleges have smaller selections, yet large enough to surprise their students or in some cases even their faculty members and to provide a fruitful field of reading once their presence is discovered.

On the level of the schools, still less has been done. Tennessee, however, offers at least a partial exception. In 1941 the Division of School Libraries of the State Department of Education issued a forty-page booklet entitled, *The Negro: A Selected Bibliography for School Libraries of Books by or about the Negro in Africa and America.* It is a good list, annotated with the age of child for whom the book is suited, the publisher, price, and brief descriptive notes. Some of the Negro schools in Tennessee now have these books in their libraries so that their children are getting a more balanced diet of reading; and the white schools can procure them if they will. The spreading of these little libraries through the white public schools and the children's reading rooms of white public libraries of the South would be a big contribution to the growth of mutual understanding and good will.

SCOUTING

Ten years ago in the South Scout troops for Negro boys and girls were almost non-existent. The development which has taken place in the last ten years has required and has called forth active practical cooperation between members of both races.

Taking the girls first, we find that as late as 1940 there were only 52 Negro Girl Scouts in the five states of Alabama, Arkansas, Louisiana, Mississippi and Tennessee (Region V of the National

Girl Scout organization). By the end of 1942 there were 497. In Region VI, which includes Florida, Georgia, North Carolina, and South Caorlina, there were just 604 Negro Girl Scouts in 1940. In December, 1942, there were 1,448 and new troops were rapidly being formed. To achieve this growth, whites and Negroes have worked together all along the line. A scout executive writes:[10]

"All of our employed personnel, white and Negro, have the same standards of experience and training, and their responsibilities in the local communities are the same. A number of Girl Scout councils in the southern states employ in addition to an executive secretary a number of what we term field secretaries. When there is a large enough Negro Girl Scout membership in the community and financial support to warrant it, a field secretary, who is a member of the Negro race, is employed to supervise the Negro troops. At present we have eight Negro field secretaries in the South—in Memphis, Tennessee; Jacksonville, Florida; Atlanta, Georgia; Charlotte, North Carolina; Greensboro, North Carolina; Richmond, Virginia; Dallas and Houston, Texas. A number of councils are in the process of employing Negro field secretaries.

"The National Girl Scout organization charters a local council to administer Girl Scouting in a certain local community. This local council has the responsibility of supervising all Girl Scouting under its jurisdiction. The Negro Girl Scout troops are organized and supervised by the local council just as are any other troops under the local council jurisdiction. There has been a marked growth in the number of local councils which have organized Girl Scout troops for Negroes in the past few years. In a number of these councils there is an interracial committee which is a subcommittee of the local council and has direct responsibility for advising on questions of organization in regard to the Negro Girl Scout troops. The chairman of this committee is a member of the Girl Scout council. In some communities the chairman of this committee is a Negro, in others white. . . ."

The story of Girl Scouting for Negroes in Memphis, Tennessee, illustrates this general history of progress. The development of recent

[10] Mrs. G. P. de Westfeld, letter, November 12, 1943.

years would seem even more impressive if it could be seen against the background of misunderstanding and lack of cooperation between the white and Negro communities in Memphis, which for a long time were stumbling blocks in the way of any constructive projects. But this tale is too long, too confused, and too depressing to relate. In any case, in 1939 there were no Negro Girl Scouts in Memphis. Of subsequent achievements, a local scout executive writes:[11]

"When I became active in Scouting a number of years ago, there were a few of us cn the Council who were interested in having Negro troops, but the organization was in a precarious condition. Financially we were in the 'red' for some thousands of dollars, and the Scout membership had fallen off alarmingly. It took some years to get on a sound basis. We were then asked to come into the Community Fund. It was after that that the question of Negro Scouting was discussed. The Council of Social Agencies favored it. The Council appointed a Committee to make a survey and see what was being done in other communities. A number of years ago an independent group of Negroes had set up a summer camp which they called a Girl Scout camp but it did not have the sanction of the National organization, nor was the local group aware of its existence.

"After the Committee brought in a report, it was voted to lay plans for Negro Scouting with some definite recommendations. I was made the Chairman. We called together representatives of various Negro groups—principals from some of the schools, preachers, and those interested in Social Service, together with some of the white groups who were interested. The project was very well received and plans were made to start with ten troops, spotted geographically throughout the city. Our white staff gave the training course to 88 prospective leaders and committee women. Out of this group, three committees were formed to take care of organization and training, camping, and program. The troops were organized and progressed for a year under the supervision of the white staff. We were even able to give the group a camping experience that summer, through the cooperation of the Boy Scouts.

"We realized that we could not progress without funds and with-

[11] Mrs. Abe D. Waldauer, letter, March 2, 1944.

out a Negro professional. Our staff was already carrying a very heavy case load. We appeared before the Community Fund and secured a budget that permitted us to secure the services of Mrs. V. Beauchamp. She took her training at Camp Edith Macey at her own expense. Our choice of her as a field secretary was a very fortunate one. She had had experience in group work before she came to us, and under the supervision of our Scout Executive, she has developed the project so that now we have 30 Intermediate troops. We voted at our last meeting to enter the field of Brownies and hope to start 10 troops of the younger girls shortly; then, after that is well established, proceed to the senior level. Mrs. Beauchamp has trained the adult group with the help of some of her Leaders.

"Our Branch Council is composed of the Chairman of the Standing Committees and the Advisors. Each committee has an adviser, who is the chairman of the corresponding committee of the larger group. In this way the work is coordinated. I, as chairman, represent the branch on the board.

"We feel that we have progressed and become well established with over 700 girls registered, and a large registration from the adult group. We have been organized only three years and had to start from scratch with no one in the group trained and no one having any experience in Scouting."

Easily understood, then, is the statement of a worker in a community center for Negroes: "It has been a thrilling experience to get the work going here."[12]

The growth of Boy Scouting among Negroes has been similarly stirring, although it began much earlier. Here is a brief account of Regions V and VI of the Boy Scout organization.

In two years, Negro Boy Scouts in Region V increased from 4,610 Scouts in 288 troops to 8,262 Scouts in 430 troops. Cubs increased from 92 in 6 packs, to 800 in 38 packs. The total number of Negro Cubs and Scouts was 9,062, an increase in two and one-half years of 92.7 per cent. The executive called attention to the fact that this rate compares with 27.4 per cent increase in the total membership, white and Negro, showing Negro membership, which started later, rapidly

---

[12] Mary Ora Durham, letter.

responding and overcoming its handicap. "I know of no movement," he writes, "with which there is more wholesome cooperation of both whites and Negroes, than the Boy Scout movement. Every Scout Council in the South has approved the program for Negro boys and has Negro units in various communities. The number of these communities is growing very rapidly. The cooperation—on the part of both Negroes and whites—is definitely on the increase. I am delighted with the way this program has been received both by the white people in our movement and the splendid Negro leaders who have been attracted to it as an opportunity to serve Negro youth."[13]

A similar story comes from Region VI. "Within the last ten years Boy Scout troops for Negro boys have been organized in every local Council or trade area in Region VI. . . . These troops are under the leadership of Negro men, especially trained in Scouting skills and techniques. Most of these troops are sponsored by churches, while others are sponsored by schools, lodges, and groups of citizens. . . . There is a registered adult volunteer for every three boys who participate in Scouting and Cubbing. These leaders attend courses of training which help them to develop skills and techniques in Scouting leadership and also provide fellowship and morale." Twenty-seven Negroes now serve as full-time Field Scout Executives in Region VI; contributions from Negroes for support of the program are increasing; camping sites are being bought, and from December, 1941, to March, 1943, the number of troops of Negro boys had risen from 392 with 6,980 members to 594 with 11,152 members.[14]

One of the national executives reports progress all over the nation and believes the present membership among Negro men and boys is rapidly approaching 100,000.[15]

Texas gives us a specific example of this work. Boy Scouting began among Negroes in Texas ten years ago, following repeated visits by Stanley Harris, interracial director of the National Boy Scout office. The Lone Star Area, comprising thirteen counties, now has 25 Negro troops with 392 Scouts and 70 leaders.

In the spring of 1943, Negro Scouts received as a gift a 25-acre

[13] Harold E. Erb, letter, 1943.
[14] *Southern Frontier,* October, 1943, p. 2.
[15] Stanley A. Harris, letter, November 8, 1943.

camp site near Paris, Tennessee. It is named Camp Musselman after the giver, a former president of the Paris and Lamar County Chamber of Commerce and Rotary Club. The site cost Mr. Musselman $3,500, and included a lake. To show their appreciation and response Negroes in the Paris area almost at once raised $600 among themselves to apply to the salary of a full-time Negro field executive.[16]

Another instance of such cooperative relationships is the support of the Negro Boy Scout Camp by the Piedmont Council of the Boy Scouts of America in North Carolina. The Scout executive and the editor of the *Gastonia Daily Gazette* got together to promote the program. The *Gazette* carried pictures of Eagle Scouts and Scout activities, information about the Scouts, and suggestions of how the program would build good citizens; it also promoted the idea of a camp. The Piedmont Council became interested and bought thirty acres of choice land and also contributed part of the equipment. Negroes raised the money for the camp building, and the camp is now in its third year. A part-time Negro Scout Executive has also been employed.[17]

PRESS, SCREEN, RADIO AND STAGE—REFLECTION OR CARICATURE?

"To see ourselves as others see us" may not be altogether the boon that Robert Burns thought it. In modern life other people see us and we see them through the daily paper, the comic strip, the movies, the radio. The less direct contact we have with any particular nationality or group or class, the sharper and more fixed becomes the composite which we make for ourselves out of the pictures presented to us by these media of mass communication. At best these images can hardly be more like the original than the screen version of a novel is like the novel as the author wrote it. And if there is added to these ordinary run-of-the-mill distortions the extra ones superimposed by prejudice and lack of knowledge, the result is something like the average white man's idea of the Negro. Even those who consciously seek a clearer picture have their thoughts and emotions affected more than they realize by the images and ideas which the majority have and

[16] *Southern Frontier,* October, 1943, p. 2.
[17] Maude Jeffers, in N. C. Newbold materials.

which they continually reinforce by passing them about to one another through newspapers, moving pictures, and radio programs.

It is perhaps even more damning to ignore than to distort. It is therefore a major obstacle to the development of genuine mutual acquaintance, and especially to white understanding of Negroes, that press, screen, and radio overwhelmingly give us racial rather than national or community news and portrayals. In the South, for example, we have not a southern press, southern drama, southern movies, or southern radio, but a white press with news about whites, white plays and movies about white people with white actors, and a white radio with white announcers and commentators and nearly all white performers sending out news and views of the white world. When Negroes do appear, it is still largely in the old distorting roles, as the "Ham Bones" in the comic strip, the criminals in the news stories headlined "Negro Kills," or at best the loyal but humble retainer. Consequently, the white South goes along for the most part wholly unacquainted with its Negro neighbors and fellow citizens save as objects of ridicule or fear. The traditional visitor from Mars reading our papers, attending our theatres and movies, or listening to our radios would never guess that one-tenth of the American people and nearly one-fourth of the people in the South are Negroes, engaged like whites in the ordinary daily occupations in church and home, in school and sports, in work and welfare, in civic and political activities, and in loyal and brave service to the nation on all its battle fronts.

Are there exceptions? Are there forward-looking editors and program managers who feel their responsibility to give the South a truer and more complete picture of itself? There are, and their numbers are growing, growing fast enough to make it impossible to give a complete list. Though they are as yet only a courageous minority, their existence is significant evidence that it is possible in the South to write and talk, read and hear, about people as they are and not as custom says they ought to be.

Press

In the first place, some Southerners do read magazines and newspapers as well as books from outside the South; a few here and there even read Negro publications and special southern publications which deal with the Negro.

In general the northern and western press are not much more American than the southern, but it does carry some discussion of outstanding developments or news items of Negro life and race relations. *PM* is exceptionally fair in this respect. National magazines such as *Time, News Week,* and the *New Yorker* have given increasing attention in their different ways to such developments. And even in the advertising columns, which are not news but which function just as effectively to mold the attitudes of the reader, there have been evidences of change. *The New York Times* of September 22, 1943, carried a full page advertisement of Emerson Electronic Radios with a picture of four American babies of Jewish, Irish, English, and Negro stock, captioned "Babies were not born to hate." *News Week* has carried a number of advertisements picturing Negro workers along with white. A Chicago baby foods corporation, the S.M.A., issues advertising pictures showing five charming American babies of varied racial and national stocks; and its products are used and advertisements appear in the South as well as the North.

Some Southerners who are especially interested subscribe to the *Interracial News Service* of the Federal Council of Churches or to the *Interracial Review* issued by the Catholic Interracial Council in New York. Occasionally, too, white Americans in the South read the Negro press. There are today over two hundred Negro newspapers in the United States, almost all of them weeklies, with a combined circulation of over a million and a quarter. Their chief function is to compensate for the appalling lack of Negro news in the white daily papers, but they are increasingly broadening their interests and improving the quality of journalism and editorial comment. In addition, there are excellent professional journals, the *Journal of Negro Education,* the *Journal of Negro History,* and *Phylon,* reaching a limited professional audience of both races. The *Negro Digest,* similar to *Reader's Digest* in form and plan, condenses magazine articles by or about Negroes or Negro-white relations. This is a recent publication of high quality and increasingly in demand.

Several publications issued by white Southerners, or by Southerners of both races, deal with race relations and are being read by a growing number of people in the South. Such are the *Southern Frontier*, a monthly news and feature sheet issued by the Southern Regional Council in Atlanta; the *Monthly Summary of Events and Trends in Race Relations* published by the Institute of Social Sciences at Fisk University under the auspices of the Rosenwald Fund; and *South Today*, a quarterly magazine dealing with many current southern problems, including those of race, issued at Clayton, Georgia, by Lillian Smith and Paula Snelling.[18]

All of these publications together reach only a handful of Southerners, and these chiefly persons already interested and desirous of knowing more; yet they do at least make it possible for such persons to keep up with what is going on in this area of our national life.

It is, however, the southern white newspapers that reach the masses of people in the South and influence beyond calculation their notions and emotions. Some encouragement can therefore be derived from the fact that some of these *white* newspapers are gradually becoming *southern* newspapers in a fuller sense of the word. The indications are small and tentative, but taken together they are not without significance.

In Georgia, for instance, the *Atlanta Constitution* of December 18, 1942, carried a report of the Durham Conference of Southern Negroes with the editorial comment: "If the southern Negro leaders asking for the cooperation of the majority race do not receive encouragement, then the South will have failed the first effort by southern Negro leadership along realistic lines." The *Daily News* of Macon, Georgia, in the fall of 1944 called editorially for equal opportunity for Negroes in education, health and recreation facilities, access to public utilities, and in the courts.[19] In the *Columbian Progress,* Columbia, Mississippi, July 8, 1943, an editorial protested that it is as stupid to "lump" all kinds of Negroes together in our thinking as it would be to lump all whites.

It would be a pleasant task, but one which would make for long and repetitious reading, to multiply the instances of fair-minded editorials which have appeared in certain southern papers in recent years.

[18] Publication suspended, 1945.
[19] Reported in *The Christian Century,* November 8, 1944.

They indicate clearly a recognition of the responsibility of the South to make good on its paper program of equal opportunity. Even more of significance, perhaps, is attached to new policies as distinct from editorial pronouncements, which indicate a disposition to report normal news of all Southerners. For example, the editor of the Louisville *Courier Journal* writes: "We try to carry the worthwhile news of the Negro community, just as we do with the white people. Until he resigned recently to go into the army, we had a Negro columnist who wrote once a week on the opposite editorial page. We haven't replaced him, for one thing because of newsprint rationing, and also because we haven't been able to find anybody as good as he is. We have a Negro sports reporter to cover the Negro colleges and schools."

The publisher of the *Courier Journal* also took a very progressive step by calling a meeting at Atlanta in December, 1944, of southern white and Negro editors and writers to consider restrictions on the suffrage in the southern states and possible reforms to be submitted for the consideration of southern legislatures. At this meeting, fifty newspaper editors and writers of both races conferred for two days and formulated a statement of needed election reforms (including abolition of the poll tax) which they proposed to distribute as widely as possible throughout the South and to bring to the attention of the law-makers in the different states by all possible means.

Several North Carolina papers handle Negro news in similar fashion. The *Durham Herald,* for example, in covering the community drive for welfare funds in 1943, treated Negro agencies in the same manner as those for whites. Its Sunday edition carried a long story on a Negro organization, John Avery Boys' Club, including a picture of the director and the club house. The titles "Mr." and "Mrs." were used for the Negro social workers and agency officers, as for the whites. The *Herald* also reported a strong speech on the need for interracial cooperation delivered in the Duke University Chapel, although the report omitted some of the more forthright statements. This paper also carries pictures of local soldiers, white and Negro alike, with their rank and their parents' names, courtesy titles included.[20] Standing solidly behind these good policies is the

[20] Wiley A. Hall, Field Report, October, 1943, with clipping.

Durham interracial council which seeks also to persuade the press to refrain from headlining "Negro" in crime reports, and to publish more news about cultural activities among Negroes.

The *Gastonia Daily Gazette,* another North Carolina newspaper, has been somewhat of a pioneer in giving fair news coverage to Negro activities. All aspects of Negro life are covered, with pictures where appropriate, as well as text. The paper carries frequent editorials dealing sympathetically with questions relating to Negroes, and it practices toward them the normal courtesies that it uses for any other citizens, including the use of appropriate titles. The *Gazette* having taken the lead, other white papers and magazines in the region are beginning to follow its example and are reported to be getting wider circulation because of increased interest among Negroes and liberal whites.[21] The *Greensboro Daily News,* in addition to editorializing in favor of justice to the Negro, has begun to use the titles "Mr." and "Mrs."; and following protests from its readers against the omission of pictures of Negroes in the armed forces, it printed these along with those of white servicemen on the page entitled "Tar Heel Fighting Men." The Raleigh *News and Observer* uses pictures of Negro notables in its regular columns, interviews such Negroes who come to the city, includes Negro football scores along with others, prints news supplied to it about Negroes, and included the pictures of Negro soldiers among "Tar Heels in the War Zone." Discussions of race relations questions appear in its "People's Forum." Its practices vary somewhat from time to time, reflecting in part changes in personnel and in part the extent to which interested persons make their wishes known and felt.[22]

From South Carolina, where customs are more rigid, we have only one report—that of the *Columbia Record* which has strongly advocated the equalization of salaries for Negro teachers and equal facilities in general. This paper, the largest afternoon newspaper in South Carolina, also is reported to have refused a political advertisement during the 1944 election campaign because it carried an appeal to race hatred.[23]

---

[21] Maude M. Jeffers, 1943, in Newbold materials.

[22] Unsigned report in files, plus clipping of November 17, 1943 and Forrest interview.

[23] *Monthly Summary,* November, 1944, p. 90.

Two daily newspapers of Chattanooga, Tennessee, the *News-Free Press* and the *Chattanooga Times,* are reported to handle news and announcements about Negroes in a fair-minded way, and to use pictures of Negroes freely. The *Nashville Tennessean* has several features indicating a desire to handle news on a genuine news basis, though it still hesitates to depart far from the customary racial taboos. It carries a regular Sunday column, "Happenings Among Colored People" prepared by a Negro and covering religious, civic, and welfare activities of Negroes, accompanied on at least two occasions by pictures. Although the *Tennessean* still plays up "Negro" in crime headlines, it occasionally offsets this by headlining "white" in connection with crimes committed by whites. It carries occasional news items about the Negro community and now and then a picture, and during the Institute of Race Relations held at Fisk University in the summer of 1944, it published almost daily articles about the conference, and reports of the lectures. Editorially it has consistently championed a more democratic suffrage, including voting by Negroes, the soldier vote and abolition of the poll tax.[24]

Of all the papers in Virginia, perhaps in the South, the *Richmond Times-Dispatch* makes the most constructive contribution to race relations through its handling of news and its editorial policies. Its editor, Virginius Dabney, has consistently urged a new and better understanding between the races in the South, pointing out the necessity for the white South to abandon paternalism in favor of justice and cooperation. He has not hesitated to be specific about some of the implications of this philosophy, even where it involved him in highly controversial issues, such as the inclusion of Negroes in local post-war planning projects and the repeal of the now unworkable laws governing segregation in transportation. The *Times-Dispatch* also gives recognition to Negroes of distinction, annually including a Negro in its "Virginia Honor Roll" of persons "who have reflected credit upon the state through the display of courage, ability, intelligence, tenacity, generosity, and unselfishness."

It is not alone the big city papers with the big circulations that are progressive in Virginia. The *Orange Review,* published in a relatively

[24] Files examined by M. C. McCulloch.

small and conservative community, carried its front page pictures and
write-ups of Orange men in the armed forces, including all without
regard to race. A typical write-up says: "Andrew Maples, colored, son
of Andrew and Julia Maples of Orange, was awarded wings and commissioned a second lieutenant in the Army Air Corps on January 14
at the Flying School at Tuskegee, Alabama. He was one of a class
of 43. The group included the first men from the school to complete
work at the aerial school in Florida where they made 100 per cent
records in firing of the new aerial combat system and received medals
for same.

"He volunteered for service in the Air Corps in the summer of
1941. His father and mother are well and favorably known in Orange.
His father is also a veteran of World War I and saw active service
overseas in the 92nd Division."

Thus, here and there, windows are opened in the wall of silence
and wilful ignorance, and signs appear of a new readiness to let the
Negro move out into the main stream of southern news as he is doing
in the other areas of southern life. It cannot yet be said that the
southern white press is playing the creative and constructive role that
it could play in the South's struggle for greater justice, democracy and
unity, but it is beginning to reflect, if rather timidly, the increasing
demand of intelligent southern leadership for abandonment of the
policies of deliberate news suppression that have so long kept the
majority of the South in ignorance of the minority.

Screen

The movies reach a far wider audience than the editorial pages
of the daily papers, and they add to the appeal of mere words the
persuasiveness of picture, motion, and sound. Yet there has been little
evidence, until very recently, of any sense of responsibility on the part
of producers of moving pictures as to what sort of ideas and emotions
were being disseminated through this powerful medium. "Box office"
has been by all the odds the most powerful censor and guide.

In the field of race relations, the overwhelming evidence is that in
general moving pictures have reinforced the stereotyped and prejudiced conception of the Negro. One scholar has listed these popularly
accepted stereotypes as follows: (1) the savage African, (2) the happy

slave, (3) the devoted servant, (4) the corrupt politician, (5) the
irresponsible citizen, (6) the petty thief, (7) the social delinquent,
(8) the vicious criminal, (9) the sexual superman, (10) the superior
athlete, (11) the unhappy non-white, (12) the natural-born cook, (13)
the natural-born musician, (14) the perfect entertainer, (15) the super-
stitious church-goer, (16) the chicken-and-watermelon-eater, (17) the
razor-and-knife "toter," (18) the uninhibited expressionist, and (19)
the mental inferior. A check of one hundred films shown in the
United States which included Negro themes or Negro characters of
more than passing importance showed that seventy-five of them
limited the Negro elements to one or more of these stereotypes, while
only twelve presented Negroes in roles of manliness and dignity.[25]

The movies are not southern or northern productions, but are
national in composition and distribution. The practices of motion
picture producers cannot therefore be classified as southern practices.
However, the South does play a part and an important one in fixing
these practices. As long as producers continue to believe that the
movie-going public in the South will not accept Negroes in other
than the stereotyped roles, it is doubtful whether there will be much
change for the better. In fact, one producer stated in an interview:
"In order to realize adequate profits on a production, distribution
must be nation-wide. It does not suffice that the East, West and North
accept Negro pictures, and the South refuses to accept pictures
wherein Negroes are starred."[26]

In recent years there has been an increasing number of sequences
involving Negroes which deserve commendation. L. D. Reddick men-
tions especially *In This Our Life* (Warner Brothers), in which a
young Negro law student is pictured as truthful, courageous, and dignified; *Bataan,* in which a Negro soldier "is drawn as naturally and
sympathetically as are any of his half-dozen companions," and *Sahara,*
wherein a brave and handsome French Negro soldier plays a leading
victorious role. There have also been special features such as the War
Department film, *The Negro Soldier,* and a "March of Time" dedicated to unity among racial and religious groups, which have presented
Negro achievements fairly. Unfortunately that part of southern opinion

[25] L. D. Reddick in the *Journal of Negro Education,* Summer, 1944, pp. 367-389.
[26] The *Afro-American,* May 17, 1930, quoted in L. D. Reddick, *op. cit.*

which wants to maintain the wall of ignorance and prejudice has managed to prevent most southern movie goers from even having a chance to see these pictures.

There also has been an increase in the number of non-commercial films which treat the Negro fairly and realistically and which are being shown more frequently before church groups, Y.W.C.A.'s, union groups, schools and so forth. A wider distribution of such films in the South could well be promoted by Southerners who are working for the improvement of race relations.

Radio

Although radio, like the movies, has often reflected the prejudices and preconceptions of the majority, most people agree that on the whole the large radio networks have consciously tried to be fair to the Negro population in their portrayals of Negro characters and in the presentation of Negro celebrities. Negroes of distinction are probably referred to as "Mr." and "Mrs." about as often as white notables in similar positions, the informality of radio making it almost impossible for any radio announcer to get through a program without calling the most distinguished guest by his first name at least once. As the war progressed and the need for national unity became increasingly evident, the networks gave more and more attention to the part being played by Negroes in the armed services and on the home front. Typical of these are *America's Negro Soldiers* (NBC), *This Is Our War* (WOR and Mutual), *Unity at Home, Victory Abroad* over various New York stations, *These Are Americans* (CBS), and *Democracy at Work* (NBC). It is, of course, in the comedy programs, such as *Amos 'n Andy,* and in the soap-dramas and other fictional presentations that the stereotypes tend to crop up, when the importance of democratic unity is not consciously in mind and, unfortunately, just when the audience is largest. News programs also tend to be restricted to news about white people presented by white people, for white people. But here also there are the beginnings of a broader viewpoint. Walter Winchell, addressing his enormous and diverse following, has on several occasions forcibly attacked instances of prejudice and discrimination.

Coming to specifically southern practices in the radio field, there are a number of instances where southern initiative and southern liberalism have opened radio channels to Negroes, and where good use has been made of these opportunities. Negro musical programs, of course, are not uncommon over southern radio stations. Another of the fairly common uses of the radio in this field is in connection with Community Fund drives, when the work of Negro agencies is presented over the air along with white agencies. Sometimes the talks are given by white social workers, and sometimes by Negroes.

There are some individual radio programs in the South worthy of special note. From Tuskegee Institute Chapel in Alabama, for instance, there is a regular half-hour broadcast on the theme "The Community and Leadership System in Action." On this program, Negro farm demonstration agents and successful farmers working under the United States Department of Agriculture Extension Service describe the system and tell how it has worked out in the case of some of the individual farmers. Music for these broadcasts, which are carried by two local stations, WAPI and WCOV, is furnished by the Tuskegee Choir.

Atlanta University has sponsored a very interesting program related to its People's College. The People's College is itself an interesting venture in adult education by the university in cooperation with other schools and social agencies. In 1942 there were over 400 persons enrolled in it and constituting 35 classes meeting at the university, Y.M.C.A., Y.W.C.A., public library, and the high school. It offered technical and social studies and general studies, "ranging from the a b c's of daily living to the philosophies of religion, arts and crafts, and leisure-time resources. It used classroom teaching, radio, moving picture, laboratory, forums, workshops, and simple association." In 1943 a series of broadcasts was given on "Freedom in the Modern World." This dealt with freedom in Russia, Africa, Germany, France, and the United States. No serious difficulty was confronted in arranging for these broadcasts. No Atlanta station, it is true, would sell time to the People's College, but any one of them would give it, and no segregation of any kind was attempted in the studio arrangements for broadcasting. Radio has proved so effective an instrument in the People's College program that the university is now introducing into the program a Radio Workshop where materials for use on these programs can be prepared.[27]

In Gastonia, North Carolina, while no one program of special distinction has been noted, a particular station, WGNC, is owned and operated by "a Christian philanthropist and business man, F. C. Todd," and it welcomes and encourages programs pertaining to all phases of Negro life. Church programs of both races have been sponsored and through these the station has helped to remove the indebtedness of four Negro churches and several white churches.[28]

A similar instance comes from Greensboro, North Carolina. Here fine cooperation has developed between station WBIG and Bennett College, a Methodist college for Negroes. Bennett College has conducted all the phases of preparing and rendering a daily broadcast, from writing the scripts to operating the controls. There have been five fifteen-minute programs a week running Monday through Friday. A faculty-student staff has prepared and conducted the programs and taken care of all the announcements and station identification. For one year, a student trained by one of the technicians at the station operated the controls. This was successful, but no trained student is at present available. The programs have included such themes as a series on "Safeguarding Your Health," another on "Dusky Poems" by the Dramatics Art Department, "An Afternoon of Talent" by students and faculty, song programs, and "Your Consumer Reporter," a program by one of the students. The song programs appear to have been most popular and "Your Consumer Reporter," next, but the entire program has been well received.[29]

From Livingstone College, Salisbury, North Carolina, a series of radio shows, bringing the college twenty dollars a week profit, has been broadcast, the script being written by a member of the faculty.[30]

Radio Station WBT in Charlotte, North Carolina, has received awards for its "civic enterprise in behalf of racial amity."[31] On Decem-

[27] *Phylon*, Supplement, 2nd quarter, Vol. IV, 1943; letter of Ira DeA. Reid with enclosures, November 4, 1943.

[28] Maude M. Jeffers in Newbold materials.

[29] Albert N. Whiting and Edney Ridge, letter. Unsigned field report, and Calendar of Bennett College on the Air.

[30] Unsigned and undated field report.

[31] ANP report, December 20, 1944.

ber 16, 1944, the CBS network program "The People's Platform" originated from this station, with a discussion on the topic "Is the South Solving the Race Problem?" Participants on this nation-wide broadcast were the Governor of North Carolina, the editor of the *Asheville Citizen* (a white newspaper) and the presidents, both Negroes, of two North Carolina colleges for Negro students.

In Chattanooga, Tennessee, local stations broadcast three radio programs each week with all-Negro participants and narrators. One of these programs, "Crossing the Waters," opens with the statement: "This program serves to acquaint our listeners with the accomplishments of the Negro and the contribution he is making to the war effort."

So the radio is becoming increasingly the voice and instrument of the people of democracy. Even more than the moving pictures, radio offers an opportunity for interracial committees and groups with similar interests to work for presentation of Negroes and Negro problems in a fair and sympathetic manner, and for the correction of programs which help to keep old prejudices alive.

Stage

Older than the movies, the radio, or even the press is the legitimate stage. What has it to express, to contribute in this area of our life? Until a few years ago, the drama, too, was almost wholly racialist, in the nation as a whole as well as the South. Aside from burlesque or comedian roles and the Negro minstrel show, only a very rare production—perhaps of Shakespeare's *Othello,* or of O'Neill's *Emperor Jones*—includes a significant Negro role. Even these played generally in the North only. In the 1930's the drama began to move. Paul Green's play *In Abraham's Bosom* led off. It was followed by a number of plays by white writers dealing with Negro life, most notably perhaps, Dorothy and DuBose Heyward's *Porgy* and Roark Bradford's stories of *Green Pastures* which became a great spiritual folk play with Richard B. Harrison in the leading role. In 1933 a Negro folk play, *Run Little Chillen,* written by a Negro, was given in the New York season. By 1934 there had begun "a dramatic awakening among the young people of our Negro colleges and universities in the South," looking towards a theater and drama of their own people.

In the decade since, dramatic departments in many of the southern colleges for Negroes have been developing Negro folk plays, of ever increasing variety; some of them of considerable merit. Inter-collegiate drama tournaments have also been held at Union University, Richmond; Hampton Institute, Hampton, Virginia; North Carolina College for Negroes, Durham; Dillard University, New Orleans, and elsewhere. Meantime, southern white drama has been similarly developing in the southern colleges for whites.

Each of these parallel developments holds promise for the eventual development of a genuine southern drama which will have adequate range and depth to express the life of a society composed of two major racial groups. But each tends as yet to suffer from isolation, and from the danger of weakness growing out of that isolation, in its portrayal of the other race. The gradual growth of contacts tending towards better mutual insight is therefore significant.

As far back as 1919, Paul Green, then a student of drama at the University of North Carolina, wrote a Negro play, *White Dresses,* which the new head of the department of drama, Dr. Koch, wished to present, but members of the university faculty advised against it. Sentiment in the university and the state was not ready for it. As Negro drama developed, however, sentiment became modified. Dr. Koch interested himself in stimulating and encouraging this movement in the Negro colleges; he was invited to serve as critic-judge in many of their drama festivals and has given addresses and Shakespearean recitals at Negro colleges in the region. It became possible to invite one or another of the dramatic groups from the Negro colleges of North Carolina to attend the Annual Spring Festival of the statewide Carolina Dramatic Association. The Negro groups invited are not yet participants in the tournament, but each brings a one-act play as a guest performance. In 1934 the St. Augustine College Players of Raleigh brought to the Carolina Playmakers' stage Paul Green's *White Dresses.* "They gave a fine performance of it and were enthusiastically received." In return the Carolina Playmakers of the University of North Carolina have been guest performers at North Carolina College for Negroes in Durham and at Hampton Institute in Virginia. When at last Richard B. Harrison came to Chapel Hill with *Green Pastures,* the big Memorial Hall was crowded to the rafters.[32]

Such things do not just happen; they are brought to pass out of the vision, the enthusiasm, and the long patient toil of artists and students with faith in their art and in human nature; but that they can be achieved gives us increasing hope for the future, a future in which the drama may give us a genuine medium for expression of southern and of American life.

MISCELLANY

In the field of the arts, now and then, there occur also significant developments which contribute to our mutual understanding and respect. There is, for instance, the recognition of scholars. The recent election of Dr. W. E. B. DuBois to the National Institute of Arts and Letters was such an event. Membership in this society, limited to 250 scholars in art, literature, and music, is drawn from all over the nation. Dr. DuBois was the first Negro ever elected to membership.[33] This honor was national. More distinctively southern was the award of the Mayflower Cup for 1943 to J. Saunders Redding, a Negro. The Mayflower Cup is an award made annually for the past thirteen years by the North Carolina Society of Mayflower Descendants in conjunction with the State Literary and Historical Association; it honors the best book published by a North Carolinian during the year. J. Saunders Redding had written *No Day of Triumph,* while he was a teacher at Elizabeth City State Teachers College in North Carolina, and this book was selected from among thirty-two considered by the committee of five critics. Such a recognition shows that in North Carolina, at least, southern literature also is shedding its shackles of fear and prejudice and growing up into a full-fledged art in which all who have gifts to make are welcomed and judged according to their performance.

In the field of music Negroes have long been accepted as artists, especially in song. It is noteworthy, however, that in January, 1943, Marian Anderson gave a concert for the benefit of the Chinese War Relief in Constitution Hall in Washington, D. C., the very hall for

[32] Letter and material supplied by Dr. Koch.
[33] Raleigh, North Carolina, *News and Observer,* December 3, 1943.

the use of which her contract with the D.A.R. had been cancelled just a few years before; and this time, for the first time in the history of the Hall, there was no discrimination.[34] In the same month, Harold Ickes accepted for the nation a Marian Anderson mural commemorating the Easter Sunday concert of 1939 when Marian Anderson had sung at the Lincoln Memorial before 75,000 persons.

Here, too, in the nation's capital, another mural is nearing completion, representing the Negro's contributions to American life. This one, in the Recorder of Deeds Building, contains several separate pictures, each showing a particular episode in Negro life: (1) Crispus Attucks in the Boston Massacre; (2) Benjamin Banneker, surveyor, inventor, astronomer, with the map of Washington which he helped lay out; (3) the death of Colonel Shaw at Fort Wagner; (4) Andrew Jackson at New Orleans with slaves building bulwarks; (5) Cyrus Tiffany saving the life of Commodore Perry in the Battle of Lake Erie; (6) Frederick Douglass appealing to Lincoln and the cabinet to enlist Negro soldiers; and (7) Mathew Henson planting the American flag at the North Pole under the supervision of Commodore Perry. Of the seven artists designing the seven scenes, four are men, three women; six are white, one a Negro. So the artists move out of the stagnant pools of racial inhibition, white and Negro artists joining together to contribute to the main stream of American culture.

[34] It is one of those strange anomalies arising out of racial taboos that Negroes are often excluded from performances by Negro artists in southern cities, or in any case restricted to inferior seats. Thus it was a source of municipal self-congratulation when Negroes for the first time were permitted to buy seats on the main floor of the municipal auditorium for a Marian Anderson recital in Louisville, Kentucky, in 1944.

CHAPTER VII

HOUSING

"BE IT EVER SO HUMBLE, there's no place like home." The familiar line evokes the picture of a neat little country cottage, whose humble owners dwell there in peace and contentment. For them, the sentiment may well be true. But for the tuberculous tenant in a city slum, the words have little meaning.

North, South, East and West, our cities have blighted areas where human beings exist in cellars and attics and in condemned buildings with rotting walls and falling plaster, without a place for garbage or ashes. These conditions are not confined to any region or race; but the worst sufferers are our "ethnic minorities"—the families of most recent immigrant stock, and those whose skin color and appearance make them easily distinguishable from other Americans: Mexicans, Orientals, and Negroes. This is partly because they are relatively poor and experience special difficulties in getting good jobs. But it is also because of "restrictive covenants," agreements among home owners, landlords and real estate agents not to sell or rent residential property in certain areas to members of this or that "race." This practice, common all over the United States, has never been declared unconstitutional, although any law or city ordinance restricting a citizen's choice of residence on the basis of race is unconstitutional. By this extra-legal device, Negroes and similar groups are commonly restricted to the least desirable sections of our cities, sections often doomed to disintegration before these groups are permitted to occupy them. Though a Negro may be able to afford a better home in a pleasanter neighborhood, he is not allowed to buy or occupy it, while the many whose incomes are small are forced to pay high rents for miserable accommodations, since they have to compete in a restricted area for an insufficient number of dwellings.

It is worth noting that these covenants are in the long run ineffective instruments even for the purpose for which they are intended, since they serve to dam up natural residential expansion long enough to create problems of sanitation, health, overcrowding, and delinquency which necessarily affect the city as a whole, but cannot permanently prevent that expansion, nor prevent the deterioration of property in areas adjacent to the ghetto they have produced.

For the future healthy development of our communities, it is vital that restrictive covenants as a means of residential control be replaced by intelligent municipal planning in which all groups participate. Although almost nothing has yet been done to this end, certain developments of recent years have in some respect both alleviated the present situation and foreshadowed possibilities for the future.

Because almost no new homes were built during the depression, a serious situation developed. A federal government survey in 1936 demonstrated statistically what nearly every city dweller knew from sad experience, that there was an over-all housing shortage in the United States, especially for low-income groups. To meet this situation, the Federal Public Housing Authority was set up in 1937 to assist cities in the development of public housing projects. The federal government would not engage in construction, but would make loans to local authorities on the following terms:[1]

1. Ninety per cent of the cost of development, including the land, would be lent for a period of not over sixty years at a low rate of interest.

2. After the units were built, the FPHA would grant a limited yearly subsidy to bridge the gap between costs and receipts from rent.

3. The local community must establish a local housing authority to build and manage the projects.

4. It must prove the need and the fitness of the project to meet it.

5. It must raise 10 per cent of costs.

6. It must make an annual contribution to help reduce rents.

7. It must retire from use an equal number of slum dwellings.

[1] U. S. Housing Authority. *What the Housing Act Can Do for Your City,* 1938.

8. It must keep costs and rents down in accordance with a specific schedule.

9. It must pay the prevailing wage for all work.

It is clear that although the federal government lends most of the money under this plan, local communities must take the initiative, tackle their own problems and make their own plans.

The Act met an immediate response: scores of cities in all parts of the nation set up local housing authorities, planned projects, and applied for federal aid. At first, however, almost 100 per cent of the planners were white and most of the projects were planned for whites, although the need of Negroes and other minorities was generally greater. Some authorities even proposed to tear down slum homes in which Negro families were living and take the land for housing projects for whites, with no new provision for the displaced Negroes. Fortunately, plans such as these were not approved; and to prevent such mistakes in the future, certain principles were laid down. Authorities were not to tear down more dwelling units for a racial minority group than they would build for the same group under the new program, unless sufficient safe and sanitary dwellings were available in decent neighborhoods at rents which the evicted tenants could pay. In general, moreover, the FPHA advised against building units for whites in former Negro areas. If any exceptions were sought by the local authorities, they must get the consent of representative local Negroes. This was the first step: it prevented the housing program from being used to hurt Negroes; while at the same time, it fathered the thought that, since Negroes are concerned, they should have some voice in the matter, if only to say "no" to a bad plan.

Another principle was set up and on the whole readily accepted: that the management "reflect the racial composition of the project." This means white management of white projects, Negro management of Negro projects, and bi-racial management of bi-racial projects.

Finally, the principle was developed that wherever Negroes were concerned in the housing needs, they should be included in the planning groups.

The acceptance and carrying out of these principles have brought the local authorities a long way towards an all-American viewpoint which calls for the cooperation of all groups to serve the needs of all the citizens. The results can be partially seen from the following report, published in the *Southern Frontier* for May, 1943:

"Negroes will be living in 88,000 low-rent public housing units, twelve per cent of the total, when the current program of the FPHA is completed. . . . This is only part of the story. In building these projects, Negro workers had earned more than $33,000,000 by the end of 1942 and in their management and maintenance 1,000 Negroes now find employment. The FPHA has 1940 Negroes working on its departmental staff with forty more in the regional offices. Altogether Negroes comprise approximately ten per cent of all those employed in the Federal Public Housing Agency."

A number of southern cities, in cooperation with the federal government, have set up particularly large programs. Among these are Atlanta and Augusta, Georgia; Memphis and Nashville, Tennessee; Wilmington and Raleigh, North Carolina; Louisville, Kentucky; New Orleans, Louisiana; Jacksonville, Florida; St. Louis, Missouri; Corpus Christi, Texas; Columbia, South Carolina; and Washington, D. C. "Many southern communities, recognizing the acute need of housing for Negroes, voluntarily submitted applications for projects to meet this need, prior to their application for other projects." Some of these cities, notably Atlanta, Memphis, and Washington, have led in extending responsibility to Negro staff members, and in the good results achieved.

The South has also responded to the evident justice of the principle that all citizens concerned should be represented in housing plans. At first many local authorities, ready to work *for* Negroes but without experience in working *with* them, were hesitant. Some took a first step by setting up "advisory committees" on Negro housing, sometimes bi-racial, sometimes all-Negro. These committees had no authority but could make suggestions. Gradually other cities went further. Here and there a Negro was appointed to full membership in a local housing authority. The Federal Housing Authority and the National Association of Housing Officials welcomed such appointments, and others followed. Today Negroes are serving on at least eleven city housing authorities in the South: Winston-Salem, North

Carolina; Daytona Beach and Panama City, Florida; Charleston, West
Virginia; Nashville, Tennessee; Louisville, Kentucky; Richmond and
Newport News, Virginia; Baltimore, Maryland; Kansas City and St.
Louis, Missouri. The same practice is increasingly common outside
the South. In a number of cities the Negro members serve as officers—
secretaries, treasurers, and acting chairmen—while in Chicago, Illinois,
and Newark, New Jersey, they serve as chairmen.[2]

In all of these respects, the public housing program has gone forward in very much the same way in all regions of the country. Outside the area of mandatory segregation, however, there are a number
of unsegregated projects with tenants of different racial backgrounds
living together harmoniously. In the South, of course, this does not
occur. Yet of forty-eight projects which have dwelling units for two
races, three are located in the South, two in South Carolina and one in
Kentucky. These projects are divided roughly down the middle according to race, and it is reported that good feeling has prevailed
among the tenants and between tenants and management. To an out-
sider this might seem surprising, but anyone long familiar with the
South knows that in its cities there are often mixed neighborhoods
where whites and Negroes of limited means have lived side by side
as friendly neighbors for generations.

SAMPLE PROJECTS

From among all the housing projects in the South only a few can
be selected as illustrations. Many features are essentially alike in them
all. All replace slums; all are at low-rentals for low-income (the rental
features have been somewhat modified by war housing requirements);
all are of modern, fireproof construction, with modern heating, light-
ing and plumbing, modern laundry equipment, and some provision
for community activities—a social hall, reading room or the like. Most
of the projects are of one or two story brick construction, with small
separate buildings each housing two or more apartments. There are
grass and air space around the buildings; streets are paved and lighted;
and generally some play place is set aside for children. Tenants must
not only meet their payments promptly, but must be decent and
orderly in behavior. The managements makes an effort to see that

[2] Frank S. Horne, letter.

wholesome relationships and group activities develop among the tenants.

It would be tedious to repeat these features with each instance. The following brief reports, therefore, have been selected as examples of good practices:

Winston-Salem, North Carolina

One of the five members of the Housing Commission, appointed by the Mayor in July, 1941, is a Negro, Mr. Jack Atkins, executive secretary of Winston-Salem Teachers College. Each member of the Commission has identical powers and responsibilities.[3]

Louisville, Kentucky[4]

"Mr. J. Everett, a Negro, is one of the five members of the Louisville Municipal Housing Commission and has equal power with the others in shaping the program under which the city government has joined with the U. S. Housing Authority and the Federal Works Agency in creating six low-rent slum-clearance projects that involve a total outlay of nearly $15,000,000. Two of the projects already completed provide housing for Negro residents."

Lakeland, Florida

This city was reported to have a Negro on its Housing Authority, but inquiry made directly to the Housing Authority brought the reply that there has never been a Negro as a member of the Authority. The Negro manager of the housing project for Negroes is a member of an interracial committee. The white chairman of this committee is a member of the Housing Commission.[5] Thus, in a roundabout way, the Lakeland Housing Authority is in touch with the Negro community.

Nashville, Tennessee

Public housing plans were begun in 1935. The first two projects, Cheatham Place for whites and Andrew Jackson Courts for Negroes, were built by the Federal government under the PWA program, with a group of citizens serving first as a local advisory committee and later

[3] John R. Wright, letter, February 7, 1944.
[4] Grady Farley, letter.
[5] J. C. Whitaker, letter, February 7, 1944.

as the initial administrative committee. On this committee, President Thomas E. Jones of Fisk University served "primarily in the interest of the Negro race," and there was also a Negro member, Mr. J. C. Napier. In 1938 the present Nashville Housing Authority was established; it consists of five commissioners appointed by the Mayor, including one Negro attorney. Negroes, especially through Fisk University, have given extensive assistance in conducting surveys and in other aspects of planning. There are now two Negro projects with all-Negro personnel.[6]

Charleston, South Carolina

Mr. L. Howard Bennett's letter telling of the struggle for a sound housing program in Charleston is worth quoting in full:

"Early in the fall of 1941 Avery Institute (an American Missionary Association school for Negroes), in cooperation with the Negro community council, began laying plans for a city-wide survey to ascertain the needs for housing among Negro war workers. The survey was carried out in February under the direction of Avery with the use of its faculty and student body. When the survey was completed, a memorandum on the findings with suggestions as to how the need could be met was forwarded to Mr. Robert Taylor and Dr. Booker McGraw of the National Housing Agency. To further the action, a small committee was appointed, consisting of the following Negro citizens: the Reverend C. S. Ledbetter, Dr. W. H. Miller, Mrs. S. D. Butler, the Reverend R. I. Lemon and L. Howard Bennett.

"The National Housing Agency sent Dr. McGraw to Charleston to confer with local city, housing, Army, Navy and industrial officials relative to housing needs for Negro war workers. A considerable amount of lobbying had to be done during the months prior to the programming of houses for Negro war workers. The Committee carried its concern to Henry W. Lockwood, the Mayor of Charleston; General James T. Duke, Commanding Officer, Charleston Port of Embarkation; Admiral William T. Glassford, Commandant, Sixth Naval District and Charleston Navy Yard; and to Mr. E. D. Clement, Executive Secretary, Charleston Housing Authority.

"All of these individuals were interested and willing to cooperate.

[6] Charles W. Hawkins, letter, February, 1944.

Several trips were made by me, as a representative of the Committee and as Executive Secretary of the Negro Community Council, to Washington, D. C., and to Atlanta, Georgia, to confer with national and regional housing officials.

"We encountered considerable difficulty because private real estate interests in the Charleston area were desirous of erecting sub-standard and segregated housing units for Negro war workers, and for many months they effectively thwarted the erection of government housing for these workers. Several sites were considered, but each time the issue was raised that the proposed site was in a white neighborhood, although actually Negroes in Charleston have never lived in segregated areas.

"Two of the steps taken to overcome this resistance were: (1) the sending of carefully formulated memoranda by the Negro Community Council to the Federal Housing Authority, and (2) the sending of night letters urging the crying need of such housing by a group of Charleston organizations: The Negro Community Council, International Laborers and Hodcarriers Union, Interdenominational Ministers Union, Cosmopolitan Civic League, Charleston County Medical Association, Charleston County Tuberculosis Association, Charleston Congress of Negro P. T. A.'s, Ministers' Wives Alliance, Brick Masons Union No. 1, Pan Hellenic Council, National Association for the Advancement of Colored People, and the Carpenters' Union.

"Seven hundred and fifty units were finally programmed for Charleston to be erected on two sites, one to contain 550 units and the other 200 units. The 200 units are completed, and the 550 will be ready for occupancy within sixty days.

"White citizens of Charleston worked with the Negro citizens to bring about this success. An active interest was taken by (1) city, Army, Navy, and housing officials; (2) a committee appointed by the Citizens' Bi-Racial Committee to work with all interested parties and agencies, and (3) several labor unions and the Building Trades Council of the A. F. of L. which made representations to Washington and to local, regional, and national housing officials in behalf of the projects.

"The question of the use of Negro personnel on the staff of the projects is still unsettled. The low cost housing program and the slum clearance program started out by using Negro managers, but this was soon abandoned when the Negro manager had his status, authority, and position systematically reduced to that of a maintenance man. Since then, white managers have been used for Negro projects.

"Relative to the use and integration of Negroes in the planning agencies and the Housing Authority, no Negroes have yet been appointed to membership on the Housing Authority. The Negro Community Council is sometimes consulted by the local Housing Authority. The Federal Agencies, NHA and FPHA, have dealt directly and frequently with the Negro Community Council on questions of need and site selection.

"About a year ago a Community Development Council was organized in Charleston, which received some measure of support from the Rockefeller Foundation. At the suggestion of the Negro Community Council, three Negroes were invited to be members of the Council. This Council did much to assist in securing the housing project."[7]

Memphis, Tennessee

Although the Memphis Housing Authority is all white, it has built excellent and extensive Negro projects employing all Negro personnel, and has been especially commended by the National Housing Authority for its relations with these housing project staffs. The first housing project for Negroes, Dixie Homes, was opened February, 1938, with 636 apartments for Negro families; the second, William H. Foote Homes, was opened March, 1941, with apartments for 900 Negro families; the third, LeMoyne Gardens, opened November, 1941, with apartments for 500 Negro families; an addition to it was opened September, 1943, with apartments for 342 Negro war workers' families. In all these units, the entire personnel is Negro. The three Negro managers and the two white managers of the two white projects meet each month with the head of the Memphis Housing Authority to discuss problems of maintenance and operation. The Negro managers are consulted before any new Negro personnel is appointed. Thus, although the Authority itself is white and the Negro Advisory Committee does little, there is a good deal of opportunity for the expres-

[7] L. Howard Bennett, letter, February 25, 1944.

sion of Negro opinion. Moreover, these housing projects, like those in other cities, give the tenants training and experience in citizenship. Each project has a monthly newspaper, a credit union, social gatherings, child care organizations, Girl Scouts, Boy Scouts, pre-school clinics, and a tenants' association. Juvenile delinquency, which used to be very high in these areas, is now less than in almost any other part of the city, white or Negro.[8] One of the projects, LeMoyne Gardens, is named for LeMoyne College, an American Missionary Association College for Negroes, which played a part first in securing this development in a slum area near the college, and subsequently in services to it.[9]

Augusta, Georgia

"The erection of two low-cost housing projects in recent years under the Federal Housing Administration has provided excellent housing conditions at reasonable cost for 446 Negro families, or approximately 2,000 persons. Each project has a playground with splendid equipment. Approximately 70 per cent of the $1,800,000 available through the federal government for low-cost housing projects in Augusta was used for Negroes. Augusta was the first city in the deep South to build two housing projects for Negroes and just one for whites."[10]

Wilmington, Delaware

The city reports instances both of effective Negro action and of cooperation by citizens of both races:[11]

"When the Delaware legislature passed the original housing enabling act, it was defective in its tax exemption features. Despite the fact that funds had been allocated to the Housing Authority of Wilmington in 1938, the Delaware legislature persisted in its refusal to make the necessary amendments to the law.

"Finally the Authority appealed to the Negro leaders in Wilmington for their help and with their effective work the amendments were passed.

"The Wilmington Housing Authority then sought and secured another allocation of $1,000,000, intending to recognize the help of

[8] Annual Report of the Memphis Housing Authority, *Housing in War Time,* 1942-43; Cecil Thomas, Field Report, 1944.

[9] M. C. McCulloch, formerly at LeMoyne College, Report.

[10] E. C. Peters, letter.

[11] Oliver C. Winston, Region II, letter to Frank S. Horne.

the Negro citizens by making the first project a Negro project. At that time, however, there was tendered to the Authority the Price's Run Park site, at a favorable figure. With the acquiescence of the Negro leaders, this site was purchased for a white project. The Authority immediately applied for and received another ear-marking of $1,000,000 for a Negro project. This was located adjacent to a fine junior high high school, in close proximity to churches, Negro Y.M.C.A., and bordering on the new park the city is building, providing swimming pool, baseball and football fields, tennis courts and other recreational facilities. The Authority has two representative advisory sub-committees, one on Negro projects and one on white projects, which together constitute its advisory committee on over-all housing projects."

Spartanburg, South Carolina

This report typifies the remarkable reduction in delinquency and crime which these housing projects bring about. A small project of 150 units was built in 1941 in an area where there had been almost no decent homes for Negroes. The director reports:

"The tenants seem to appreciate their homes and generally take a good deal of pride in residing therein. We seldom find any of the tenants abusing the property, and such cases are found to be caused by a lack of knowledge of how to keep house properly. The locality has been changed from a slum area of bad repute into a community of self-respecting citizens.

"The small community hall affords facilities for community work in which children's work, clinics, etc., have been conducted. Although there is no social worker, the tenants themselves carry out a well-rounded program of community activities. They have organized two very good choirs and sing weekly over the local radio and at various other places in this locality.

"We are proud to boast that it has been necessary for the local police to visit the project only once during the twenty-one months of operation."[12]

Columbia, South Carolina

This city has both a bi-racial housing project and an Advisory Committee which functions successfully.

[12] Correspondence.

"The Housing Authority is composed of five influential citizens, representing education, finance, insurance, manufacturing, and the press. Associated with the Housing Authority are three Negro citizens of high caliber, acting in an advisory capacity. This Advisory Committee works closely with the Authority in formulating policies affecting the housing program in Columbia. These policies have met with the approval of all the citizens of Columbia.

"Of the four projects operated by the Housing Authority, one houses white army personnel and defense workers; another project houses army personnel, defense workers and low-income white citizens; another, low-income Negro citizens; and still another, both white and Negro low-income citizens. The mixed project has a white manager and bookkeeper, Negro Management Aide and maintenance personnel. There are five buildings housing seventy-four Negro families, and three buildings housing forty-eight white families. The project was opened on August 16, 1937, and to date there has been no friction between the races, not even the children, despite the fact that there is nothing to keep them from coming in contact with each other. The relationship between the management and Negro tenants and personnel has been extremely satisfactory."[13]

The all-Negro project, housing two hundred and forty-four families, is managed by Negroes. There is no difference in the rents paid by Negroes, nor in salaries received for equal duties, nor in the policies and management practices.

Columbus, Georgia

The private businessmen of the city set a precedent by raising among themselves $52,500 to apply against the purchase of a site for a housing project for Negro war workers. This sum, reported to be the only instance of a cash contribution by local businessmen to public housing, will make up the difference between the cost of the site inside the city and a less expensive one outside. Use of the close-in site will eliminate some of Columbus' worst housing and will contribute to the progress of the city plan, since it involves the straightening of a creek and the development of a bordering parkway. The 160-family

---

[13] M. M. A. Entzminger, letter.

war housing project will revert to low rental housing after the war.[14]

These Columbus businessmen are giving concrete recognition to the fact that good housing and slum clearance bring new life not only to the tenants but to the community as a whole. They are making sound investments in a city's future.

Newport News, Virginia

Newport News has a distinguished record in this field, but one detail only will be quoted:

"Residents of the Douglas Park housing project for Negro war workers have had an absenteeism record of a fraction of 1 per cent. This record gives some indication of the connection between good housing and efficiency."[15]

Because of this revitalizing power of housing projects, one is tempted to prolong the list of illustrations. Realization of what good housing can do, however, should not obscure the fact that public housing projects are, and probably will continue to be, only a drop in the bucket of housing needs. Up to now the field of privately financed housing for Negroes has been almost completely neglected. Such ventures have been discouraged by stereotyped opinions about deteriorating effects of Negro occupancy on property, difficulties of rent collection, etc. It is significant, therefore, that real estate men, both North and South, are suddenly awakening to the fact that they may have been missing a good thing. The National Association of Real Estate Boards issued a report in November, 1944, summarizing the results of a survey undertaken in cities representing all parts of the country. Southern as well as northern real estate men not only expressed the opinion that Negroes took good care of property when they had a chance to do so, made payments promptly, and offered a substantial market for private housing, but also declared their intention to do something about it.

Not much could be done in this field during the war. However, some private home construction for Negro war workers was undertaken. In Washington, D. C., although more than 14,000 priorities were made available by the NHA for privately financed housing, less

[14] Bulletin of Public Administration Clearing House, November 9, 1944.
[15] From an OWI release cited in *Monthly Summary*, September, 1943, p. 7.

than 1,000 such houses had been completed by October, 1944. One hundred more were under construction, and final commitments had been made on 1,200 more.[16]

In the Cherry Hill development in Baltimore, 600 privately financed homes are being constructed alongside of 600 publicly financed units. Another 500 units will be constructed in Day Village, which will also provide community and commercial facilities. Other southern cities which have made a beginning on privately financed housing for Negroes are Jacksonville, Florida; Atlanta, Georgia; Memphis, Tennessee; Norfolk, Virginia; Dallas and Houston, Texas.

The postwar period offers to southern cities tremendous opportunities for community reconstruction through both public and private housing. A nation-wide survey has shown that two out of three homes now occupied by non-whites are substandard. What is needed in each city is a housing inventory in which all groups of the city can participate. The facts about their own city can then be put before the citizens and whites and Negroes, working together, can plan a community development and housing construction which will serve the needs of all.

A TRANSFORMATION

An illustration of what good housing has done in one city to transform a blighted area and its inhabitants may serve as a stimulus to action. The following account of what has happened in New Orleans was written by Dr. Horace Mann Bond, formerly of Fort Valley College in Georgia and now president of Lincoln University, Oxford, Pennsylvania:

"In the not-so-long ago, curious tourists always listed in their 'must' items such monuments to the historical past of New Orleans as the Cabildo, the Cathedral, and the Old French Quarter. When these had been exclaimed over, the visitor was not yet content; he (and even sometimes she) simply must *see* that perfectly dreadful section where organized vice was as open and unashamed in its way, as the placid Cathedral, a few blocks away. And so the guide would conduct the visitor through Storyville: a scant ten years ago you could still see the crib-houses and the latticed blinds and the painted faces

[16] Talk by John Blandford, Jr., administrator National Housing Agency, October 2, 1944.

of lost women, while half naked little children scurried by the dozen from beneath the wheels of the cab, and the hideous faces of diseased old men and women, habituated to filth and misery, taught a lesson in human degradation not to be duplicated, perhaps, anywhere in America. Here the 'blues' had been born; here back of Basin Street, were old and new dives and Lulu White's establishment—worse, so travelers said, than anything in their experience except, perhaps, the bordellos and slums of Marseilles.

"Even the most curious of tourists usually got his fill of seeing the man lower down in Storyville. He had no curiosity left for the other sections where there was only human wretchedness, unrelieved even by painted vice. In these were square after square of little hovels, criss-crossed with unpaved streets and alleys, where houses had been crowded upon the precious land without regard for living space and air. For land in New Orleans is precious; what there is of it has been recaptured from the unwilling river through centuries of toil. In each generation poor people drifted into the city from the Mississippi Delta and the sugar plantations of the West, to work as stevedores or in kitchens, or to look for work but not to find it. Within the Crescent formed by the river there seemed no choice, short of the tremendous job of reclaiming the swamps beyond, but to house the very poor in the already congested living space. So now shotgun houses were tacked together, sometimes in the fantastic disorder dictated by early deeds and property holdings.

"This was the story of housing in Old New Orleans for the very poor, a story that might also be told with few variations of Yamacraw in Savannah, and Catfish Row in Charleston.

"Charleston and Savannah and New Orleans have alike been proud of their tradition of gentility. They have not been proud of the housing which the new hovels and the rotting mansions provided for the very poor white, and the very poor Negro populations. But at last, when the opportunity came, something was done about it. As New Orleans had perhaps the worst housing, the story of what was done there, though long, may be worth the telling.

"Visit the Magnolia project, one of six low rent housing projects now being operated by the New Orleans Housing Authority. Here is efficiency, order and cleanliness—these tenants, like their fellows in dozens of communities throughout America, evidently use their bath-tubs for purposes other than coal storage. Here children laugh, and of an evening, groups of their elders take their ease in a quiet dignity possible for men and women who live in homes, not in rabbit-warrens.

"But there is more to see in the Magnolia project. Men of vision have planned not merely for the ordinary beauty that lies in serving human convenience, but for that higher form and function in which may lie an extraordinary human convenience, and an extraordinary beauty.

"The land on which the Magnolia project is established was held at a high figure; and this was so of the other areas designed for slum clearance in New Orleans. As a result it was necessary to plan the project with a greater density of population than, ideally, might have been desirable. To meet this situation and to preserve functional beauty, some of the buildings were made three stories high. Frequently access to the living room was made from the first to the second floor, and within the living room, access was provided to the quarters on the third floor. A rear stair was planned so that delivery of supplies and garbage disposal would be separated from the main living quarters.

"The work of drawing the plans for this and other New Orleans projects was a labor of love. Not only interior design but site planning, arrangement of buildings and landscaping, were studied by the architects in the greatest detail. There is one beautiful tree that was grow-ing in the mind of the artist before a brick had been laid in the project; and even now he visits the project from time to time to see how that particular tree is faring. Every person who worked on the plans tried to create a homelike atmosphere, in spite of the large scale of the project.

"Perhaps only a southern city like New Orleans, with a warm tra-dition of beauty and friendliness in the midst of its diverse cultures, could have achieved this perfection in low cost housing. Yet it is pos-sible to trace—perhaps to follow—the steps that led to the final creation.

"Many years ago a young student from New Orleans travelled in Europe, as for centuries past the cultivated sons of the city have been drawn to a foreign culture of which, in their own city, they find so many evidences. This young man—Moise M. Goldstein—visited in England the Letchworth Village and Port Sunlight, fine examples of community housing, erected by industrialists for the workers in their plants. These housing projects are completely self-contained villages not far from the factories, with one-story row houses—two, four or six units in one group—in fine architectural tradition, facing upon winding lanes, without formal sidewalks or curbs.

"In 1929 Moise Goldstein, now an established architect in New Orleans, drew up plans for a housing development on two squares in one of the worst areas in the Negro section of the city. This was long before federal government funds were in sight. In Chicago, Julius Rosenwald had begun planning for privately financed housing; Alfred Stern, his associate, liked the New Orleans plans of Mr. Goldstein. Henry Wright, brilliant planner and writer on housing, saw the plans and liked them too. But, for a few more years, nothing came of them.

"Then the New Orleans Council of Social Agencies developed an interest. The leader was Miss Elizabeth Wisner, head of the Tulane School of Social Work; her students surveyed housing in New Orleans, and brought the rabbit-warrens, the human pigsties, the rot and stench of New Orleans slums to public attention. The report showed a need for housing for white and black; but it was clear that the need of New Orleans' Negroes was by far the greater.

"In October, 1933, the Council of Social Agencies sponsored a Committee on Housing to study two such projects, one for whites and one for Negroes. For the latter project the plan proposed several years before by Moise Goldstein was accepted; and he became the chief architect of a group associated on the Magnolia Street Housing Project.

"The architects received the heartiest support from every agency in the city. Social workers, businessmen, whites and Negroes—all agreed that the clearing of the horrible living conditions in this area was a cause worth working for. The New Orleans Housing Authority, made up of substantial businessmen, showed by their cooperation that they, too, shared the civic tradition of good taste and love of beauty.

"The personnel of the Board has changed since its inception, but the policy has not: the Authority continues to manage and plan for public housing, both for whites and Negroes, worthy of this tradition.

There are now six low-rent housing projects in the city, each distinguished for its architectural form and planning. There are 3,050 units for Negroes, and 2,400 for whites. In the Negro units, such an efficient manager as George Washington of the Magnolia Project takes pride, with his tenants, in living up to the gracious traditions of their city and the new standards of its modern housing.

"Where, little more than a decade ago, the painted ladies peered from latticed doorways just a step below Canal—there stretch today the handsome homes of the poor, who have taken on from their new surroundings a new dignity and a new self-respect. Not far away, the Lafitte Homes, named for a pirate, shelter in solid beauty a new generation of an old city. Uptown, the magnolia tree placed in a certain spot by a sensitive architect serves as a symbol of an old culture out of which is growing, through the common efforts of its people, a new and satisfactory one."

CHAPTER VIII

HEALTH FACILITIES AND TRAINING

WE ARE ALL AWARE that in the South as a whole the health of Negroes has been, in general, far below that of whites. Yet this group that has had the greatest need of medical, dental, nursing and hospital care, and health education has received the least of all these things. In general Negroes are poorer than whites; more of them live in substandard houses; and they are exposed to greater physical risks in their work. These conditions of their life largely explain why tuberculosis, syphilis, and infant mortality rates for Negroes are relatively high. At the same time hospital facilities for Negroes are segregated and in general inferior to those for whites; there are fewer Negro nurses and doctors in proportion to their numbers in our population, and fewer opportunities for Negro men and women to train for these professions.

Within the last two decades, however, through the cooperative efforts of white and Negro Americans, North and South, forward strides have been made in all these respects.

TOWARD BETTER HEALTH

An excellent brief account of this progress is given in the Julius Rosenwald Fund Review for the two-year period, 1940-42, in summarizing its own fifteen years of work in this field. In part, the report states:

"When the work was undertaken in 1928, there was little in the way of hospital facilities for Negroes. While there were a few institutions of acceptable standard and some beds in white hospitals set aside for colored patients, the vast majority of Negroes, even if they could afford it, either had no hospital to enter or could not hope to find one with facilities comparable to those available for white persons. There was only one colored physician to every 3,125 Negroes compared to one physician to every 805 of the general population. Since nearly 40 per cent of the doctors were concentrated in seven northern states which had less than 19 per cent of the total Negro population, many large and heavily populated areas in the rural South had no medical service available other than the charity of their white neighbors. While there were two excellent Negro medical schools—Meharry in Nashville and Howard in Washington, D. C.—colored graduates could find few hospitals approved for interne training and special experience. There were about 5,700 colored nurses in the country, one to every 2,076 Negroes, and the majority of them found it neither profitable nor desirable, because of the lack of hospital facilities, to work in the South where they were most needed.

"The public health authorities in city, county, and state, both North and South, showed little interest in their Negro populations. In fourteen southern states there was a total of twenty-nine public health nurses employed by county health units, eight states having none. No department of health in the southern states had ever employed a Negro officer in special charge of Negro health.

"The Negro death rate reported in 1924 was 17.6 per cent, while that for the rest of the population was 11.8 per cent. Chief scourges then, as now, were tuberculosis, syphilis, and infant mortality, and little was being done toward reduction of the high death rates, and the even higher rates of crippling diseases. . . .

"The picture in Negro health is brighter today than it was fifteen years ago. There are 110 Negro hospitals in the United States, of which some twenty-five have been accredited, thirteen of them approved for the full training of internes by the Council on Medical Education and Hospitals of the American Hospital Association. These hospitals show increasingly high standards of service and of opportunities for Negro professional personnel. There are 4,000 Negro physicians with several excellent centers for their advanced training and practice, and 6,000 colored nurses. Today in the South alone there are 341 public health nurses, officially appointed and publicly supported. Negro doctors and nurses in increasing numbers are finding important parts in the public service. The Negro death rate has dropped to fourteen per thousand. The campaigns against tuberculosis and syphilis have proved that it is possible and financially feasible to control these plagues. In a single decade the intensive campaign in Macon County, Alabama, reduced the syphilis rate from 40 per cent to 10 per cent, and public authorities have taken over responsibility for its control among Negroes as among the rest of the population. The tuberculosis mortality rate has dropped from about 235 per 100,000 in 1920 to an estimated 120 per 100,000 at present. The United States Public Health Service under Dr. Parran, the National Tuberculosis Association through its Committee on Tuberculosis among Negroes, the National Organization of Public Health Nursing, state and county authorities, and the public generally are showing an interest in the health needs of Negroes not found in 1926.

"Credit for the progress in Negro health does not, of course, belong to this Fund. This foundation was only one of many private and public agencies whose combined efforts have produced a measure of success."[1]

It is not an easy task to unravel the fabric of these combined efforts and to find what threads of struggle and achievement went into them. In the following pages, however, we shall try to look more closely into the progress which has been made in (1) establishing hospital facilities for Negro patients; (2) opening of training opportunities to Negro nurses; (3) provision for training Negro doctors; (4) public health services; and (5) special services and programs. All of these services are so interrelated that clear lines cannot be drawn between topics, but an effort has been made to point out important developments in each of these fields in turn.

BEDS FOR NEGRO PATIENTS

Answering an inquiry in regard to hospital facilities for Negroes in the South, Lieutenant Colonel M. O. Bousfield, formerly with the Rosenwald Fund, reports:

"There is no state in the South where a distinct effort is made to reach Negroes with health facilities comparable to that directed towards whites. As regards municipalities, in New Orleans the great Charity Hospital is about equally divided for Negroes and whites. I have not been in the hospital, but it is my understanding that equal

[1] Julius Rosenwald Fund, Biennial Review, 1940-1942.

facilities are offered. This is perhaps the most outstanding job of equalization during recent years in the South.

". . . Practically every white hospital in the South offers some kind of facilities for Negroes. There has been a tendency under federal government grants to take colored patients out of basements and give them equal facilities in all new buildings. . . . The most notable expansions of this kind have occurred in Norfolk and Newport News, Virginia, where increased facilities were made necessary by war conditions. Wilmington, North Carolina, may be included.

"One of the best examples of municipal interest in a Negro hospital is perhaps to be found in Durham, North Carolina, where Lincoln Hospital has frequently been editorialized in the white press and where generous official support is given. The State of Alabama (when its health department was under the direction of the late Dr. J. M. Baker) moved more rapidly than any other state toward equalization. It would be fair to count North Carolina next under the direction of state health officer Dr. Carl V. Reynolds. After that Louisiana, Texas, and even Tennessee took nibbles but didn't go very far."

It would be tedious even to begin to enumerate the southern hospitals which have in recent years added improved facilities for the care of Negro patients. Some of the best examples will be discussed below in relation to medical and nursing education. Each week brings the report of some hospital, large or small, which through a federal grant, state or municipal appropriation, or private subscription has established modern facilities for Negroes. A letter from Muskogee, Oklahoma, for example, reports the renovation of a Negro hospital at a cost of $20,000, the raising of standards, and securing of a trained staff.[2]

In Newport News, Virginia, a group of Negro citizens saw the need for greatly increased hospital facilities as a result of war-time increases in the population. They first raised $20,000 among themselves, and then appealed to the city. In response the city is spending approximately $70,000 and has secured a federal grant of $210,000, a total of $300,000 to improve hospital facilities for Negroes.[3]

Columbia, South Carolina, recently reported the results of a cam-

[2] W. J. Trent, letter.   [3] LeRoy Ridley, letter.

paign to raise money for the expansion and improvement of the Good Samaritan-Waverly Hospital, a hospital for Negroes with an inter-racial board of trustees. A total of $100,000 was raised of which $25,000 was contributed by members of the Negro community, $35,000 by individual white contributors, and $40,000 by large donors. Members of the Columbia Junior League worked under the direction of the executive secretary of the Community Chest in the fund-raising campaign.[4]

More significant than the provision of beds for Negro patients, however, are the indications that Southerners are beginning to recognize the importance of training Negro men and women as nurses and doctors. Such sharing of responsibility by Negroes for health services seems an indispensable condition of real progress in raising health standards among southern Negroes.

TRAINING FOR NEGRO NURSES

The National Association of Colored Graduate Nurses, a professional organization of Negroes working for better health among Negroes, sends this list of hospitals in the South which offer nurses' training to Negro students.

Stillman Institute, Tuscaloosa, Alabama (Church).

John A. Andrew Memorial Hospital, Tuskegee Institute, Ala. (Federal).

Freedman's Hospital, Washington, D. C. (Federal).

Brewster Hospital, Jacksonville, Florida (Church).

Florida A. & M. College, Tallahassee, Florida (State).

Grady Hospital, Atlanta, Georgia (Municipal).

University Hospital, Augusta, Georgia (State).

City Hospital, Columbus, Georgia (Municipal).

Provident Hospital, Baltimore, Maryland.

Municipal Hospital No. 2, Kansas City, Missouri (Municipal).

Homer G. Phillips Hospital, St. Louis, Missouri (Municipal).

St. Mary's Infirmary, St. Louis, Missouri.

Good Shepherd Hospital, Charlotte, North Carolina.

Lincoln Hospital, Durham, North Carolina.

L. Richardson Memorial Hospital, Greensboro, North Carolina.

St. Agnes Memorial Hospital, Raleigh, North Carolina (Church).

[4] ANP report, September, 1944.

Kate Biting Reynolds Memorial Hospital, Winston-Salem, North Carolina (Municipal).

Columbia Hospital, Columbia, South Carolina (Municipal).

Meharry Medical College, George W. Hubbard Hospital, Nashville, Tennessee.

Prairie View State College Hospital, Prairie View, Texas.

St. Philip Hospital, Richmond, Virginia (State).

Dillard University (5-year course leading to a B.S. degree in nursing), New Orleans, Louisiana.

One interesting thing about this list is its variety. Some of the hospitals are state and municipal institutions, some are under church sponsorship, others are private hospitals. To establish these facilities and make them available for the training of Negro nurses, municipalities, states, the federal government, churches with nationwide membership of both races, and philanthropic foundations have contributed. Many individual donors and small groups also have played a part in bringing about the final result. Commenting further on the list, the Association of Colored Graduate Nurses states:

"During the ten years that our Office has been functioning we have seen many improvements in the field of nursing, both in the basic training and in employment.

"The University of Georgia school, the St. Philip school, and the school at Meharry Medical College are all accredited in the State of New York. The Dillard school is recognized by the Association of Collegiate Schools of Nursing.

"The school at Kate Biting Reynolds Memorial Hospital is an excellent example of what can be done if the municipality is interested. The hospital buildings were donated by the Reynolds Tobacco interests. . . .

"Of the schools sponsored by religious denominations, Stillman Institute is operated by the Presbyterian Church and Brewster Hospital by the Methodist Episcopal Church. Both are private hospitals with small schools of nursing. St. Mary's Infirmary in St. Louis is operated by the Catholic Church. St. Agnes Hospital in Raleigh is operated by the Episcopal Church.

"Good Shepherd, Lincoln Hospital, and the L. Richardson Memorial Hospital, all three in North Carolina, are private hospitals, not under church sponsorship, operated by Negro and white Boards. The Hubbard Hospital at Meharry Medical College in Nashville is also operated by a Negro and white Board. The Hampton Institute-Dixie Hospital is operated jointly by Hampton Institute and the municipality of Hampton; and Dillard University Hospital School of Nursing is operated jointly by Dillard University, the Julius Rosenwald Fund, and the Federal Government. This institution also operates a school for nurse-midwives."

Citizens of southern communities where adequate facilities are not available for colored patients, and where Negro girls do not have an opportunity to train as nurses, may find in the examples given below indications of how these things can be accomplished.

Grady Hospital, Atlanta, Georgia

This municipal hospital of 720 beds, affiliated with the medical school of Emory University (an institution for white students), has always admitted both white and Negro patients. The present numbers of whites and Negroes are about equal; the facilities are separate. The resident and visiting physicians are all white. Until 1917, the nurses also were all white. In 1917 a school of nursing for colored girls was transferred to Grady from another municipal hospital which was closing. In 1921, because of the need for more space, adjacent land and buildings were loaned to the city by Emory University, and the buildings were converted into a hospital and out-patient department and a residence for Negro nurses, roughly doubling the capacity of the hospital. One administration and staff is responsible for the training of both white and Negro nurses, and standards are uniform.[5]

Grady Hospital was among the earlier hospitals to train and employ Negro nurses, but in recent years the municipality's interest, or perhaps that of the citizens, appears to have lagged. The building which had been remodeled for a nurses' home became so inadequate that in the summer of 1944 the Georgia Board of Nurse Examiners, acting under orders of officials of the U. S. Cadet Nurse corps, ruled that the city of Atlanta could not accept any more new Negro student nurses until adequate living facilities were provided. Spurred to action

[5] Fred M. Walker, letter, and Russell H. Oppenheimer, letter, February, 1944.

by this ruling, city officials and Georgia legislators got busy. In September, Mayor William B. Hartsfield and Frank Wilson, superintendent of the hospital, announced that they had been informed by Congressman Robert Ramspeck and Senator Walter George that the Federal Works Agency had allocated $400,000 for a new nurses' home. The new structure, under government requirements, was to be completed and ready for occupancy within six months.[6]

Homer C. Phillips Hospital, St. Louis, Missouri

The report from this institution depicts a more dynamic situation. Negro physicians as well as Negro nurses are working and training here and, despite opposition and delays, sufficient funds were finally appropriated by the city to provide adequate modern facilities. The efforts of a single Negro lawyer were so decisive in bringing this about that the new hospital was given his name.

"Homer G. Phillips Hospital is a municipal institution, dedicated to the hospitalization of indigent colored patients. It is a large hospital (765 beds) with a staff of both white and colored physicians, the medical service being directed by the two medical schools located in St. Louis which rotate in period of service.

"The staff of the hospital includes colored physicians integrated into the universities' organizations and serving as associate and assistant directors of services, visiting physicians, and associate visiting physicians.

"The hospital is well-organized with ten services or departments accredited by the American College of Surgeons. It is also accredited for the training of internes and residents. Average patient population for the past year was 570. In the present nurses' training classes there are 130 student nurses and a full corps of full-time instructors.

"The building occupies more than six acres. The cost of the present building was $3,165,000, and the budget for last year was $766,865.

"In 1915 a group of physicians and laymen demanded that the authorities of the City of St. Louis make some provision for the training of Negro internes and nurses in the City Hospital which hospitalized both white and colored patients. After a series of conferences the city organized City Hospital No. 2 for the accommoda-

[6] ANP news release, September, 1944.

tion of Negro patients and provided a vacant hospital structure at 2935 Lawton Avenue for that purpose. It was dedicated in 1919 and continued to be used for that purpose until the present Homer G. Phillips Hospital was opened in 1937.

"The present building and equipment was partially provided for in a Bond Issue of 1923, but after the passage of the bond issue actual construction of the new hospital was delayed by powerful antagonistic political interests for more than eight years.

"Homer G. Phillips, a civic-minded lawyer, led the fight in overcoming the opposition, hence the name Homer G. Phillips Hospital, given posthumously in recognition of his services. The amount of $1,200,000 appropriated in the Bond Issue was supplemented by other city funds, by the transfer of other funds in the Bond Issue through a referendum, and by a PWA grant."[7]

St. Philip and Dooley Hospitals, Richmond, Virginia

These two hospitals and a rented building used for crippled children are units of the hospital division of the Medical College of Virginia, a state institution. The college has two divisions: a hospital division serving both whites and Negroes, including clinics; and a college division conducting schools of medicine, dentistry, pharmacy, and nursing. The nursing schools are under the joint administration of both divisions.

"St. Philip proper was completed in 1920, financed by a local campaign for $254,000, without equipment; its bed capacity of 200 is sometimes exceeded. Dooley Hospital, with sixty beds and built at a cost of $75,000, was given to the state in 1920 by James H. Dooley of Richmond as a hospital for white patients; but since early in 1941 it has been used for Negro patients 'for which it is well located and suited.' Maintenance and operating funds are from state, city, endowment, gifts, etc.

"The college also maintains a large outpatient clinic most attractively housed; two-thirds to three-fourths of the patients of the clinic are Negroes.

"When the St. Philip Hospital was opened in 1920 a school of nursing for Negro women was established. This has developed into

[7] Wallace B. Chivers, letter, February, 1944.

a large institution, housed in a combination dormitory and teaching unit, which has cost something like $300,000. More recently we inaugurated a course for public health nursing, the only course of the kind for Negro women thus far established. For twelve years we have conducted a clinic for Negro physicians here in the summer for a two weeks period, until the summer of 1942 when the length of the course was reduced on account of the war.

"These advances in the care of Negro patients have come about gradually, initiated entirely by the Medical College of Virginia. Local support has been admirable. . . ."[8]

Dillard University, New Orleans, Louisiana

Flint-Goodridge Hospital is a unit of Dillard University for Negroes. A school of nursing operated in connection with the hospital had to be closed in 1934. On the other hand, there was and still is no really good school of nursing in Louisiana, Texas, Oklahoma, Arkansas or Mississippi. There are approximately three and a half million Negroes living in this area. From its beginning, Dillard University recognized the great need for training nurses. In 1942, it established a Division of Nursing in the regular college curriculum. The course takes five years and leads to a degree from the college and a diploma in nursing. Besides the training and facilities of Flint-Goodridge Hospital and Dillard University, students receive instruction and experience by a special arrangement at New Orleans Charity Hospital, a local state institution.[9]

University Hospital, Augusta, Georgia

The Dean of the State Medical College reports that there are in training 90 white and 50 Negro nurses. They take the same course. Negro nurses have been trained in the hospital since 1894 with continuing success, and on graduation some are employed in the hospital on general duty, others in charge of ward units.

Macon Municipal Hospital, Macon, Georgia

This hospital is not yet on the list of those which train Negro nurses, but it is working toward that end. The steady progress which

[8] William T. Sanger, letter, February, 1944.
[9] Dr. Horace M. Bond, Report.

has been made in offering constantly improved facilities for Negro patients make its report worthy of consideration. It appears to be a case in which the improvement has come about through the determination of the hospital and municipal authorities alone, rather than in response to the interest of the citizens, white or Negro. Mr. William C. Turpin writes:

"Some two years ago the Macon Hospital applied to the Federal Works Administration for funds to provide additional facilities made necessary by the normal growth of the community plus an influx of war workers into the area. After considerable negotiation, a substantial grant was made for an addition to the Negro wing of our institution. The grant was intended to be large enough to cover the addition and its equipment and at the same time to provide funds for the complete renovation of the existing facilities. When bids were secured, we found that the amount of the grant was not sufficient to do more than complete the addition to the present wing. We therefore let the contract and have just completed a substantial and attractive addition which makes these facilities amply large to meet the current need. We contemplate furnishing this addition and doing some of the necessary renovation from our own funds, though this presents many problems to us because the additional operating load occasioned by the additional facilities will place a heavy strain on our budget.

"The Federal Works Administration has been most cooperative with us, and we are most appreciative of the help they have given us. Without this assistance this Institution could not have met the demands which have been placed on us during the present emergency.

" . . . The much improved economic status of the Negroes in the community has made necessary and proper the provision of private rooms for those of them who could pay for such facilities rather than use the charity facilities which had already been provided for them. The new wing will supply these rooms together with other adequate means of taking care of this part of our problem. I do not think there is any inequality as between the races and certainly there is not, so far as medical treatment is concerned. Both races have the same doctors, the same nurses, the same operating room and X-ray treatment, the same food and the same care. In the Negro wing we use Negro registered nurses so far as we can get them. The new wing will mean the addition of some forty beds, a modern and well-equipped delivery room, additional clinical facilities and private rooms for pay patients who want them. I believe it fair to say that this addition gives us adequate and equal facilities for white and Negro alike.

"We are now working on a plan for the erection of a nurses' home for Negro nurses. If we can get this built, we plan to open a training school for Negro nurses, which, in the writer's opinion, is a much needed addition to the service we are now rendering the community. The fact that it has not already been done is due to lack of money rather than lack of desire.

"When the new wing was almost completed the Macon Hospital Commission requested a committee of representative Negroes to select a name for it so that we might pay tribute to some outstanding member of the Negro race who had been of service to the community at large. This committee took its appointment very seriously and recommended the name of Marie Rhone Ragan, who was a registered nurse and who did a fine work in years gone by. The wing has been given that name and the members of the committee seemed to appreciate the recognition which this action of our Commission showed. I might add, however, that so far as I know or have heard, there has been no particular civic interest expressed by any group from either race as to the effort we are making. We are not particularly disappointed that this is true, since our object is to run a hospital for the benefit of those who need it, and while the writer personally would be delighted to hear of any expression or interest, we are not seeking anything of that kind, but simply trying to provide the best possible hospital facilities for everybody in this community. I am happy to say that we are meeting with success in this effort."[10]

MEDICAL TRAINING FOR NEGROES—A CRYING NEED

There is little to give satisfaction in the provision for the training of Negro doctors. Dr. John A. Kenney, of the National Medical Association, reports that only around ten or twelve Negro doctors are

[10] William C. Turpin, letter, January 21, 1944.

trained annually in the predominantly white medical schools of the nation, and there are only two schools of medicine for Negroes in the South. One of these is federal and one is private. Not a single southern state provides a medical college to train its Negro citizens as doctors; and until recently it has been very difficult for even the small number of Negro medical graduates to obtain interneships or hospital staff positions. Yet the need for trained Negro physicians is acute. Dr. Bousfield estimates: "During the past eighteen months at least one-third of the Negroes in the seventeen southern states are continuing to die without a doctor."

In spite of this dark picture, one cannot read of the work of the two fully accredited medical colleges for Negroes without feeling stimulated by the example of what can be done. The following reports are summarized from letters received from the Dean of Howard University and the President of Meharry Medical College, respectively.

Howard University Medical School, Washington, D. C.

The Medical School of Howard University was established by an Act of Congress soon after the establishment of the University in 1867 and classes were begun in 1868. It developed in connection with the Freedmen's Hospital, and the history of the two is very closely interrelated. The faculty of the College of Medicine has always served as the attending staff of the hospital. The support of the hospital is wholly by congressional appropriation. The support of the medical school is partly federal, partly private. The Medical College is a class "A" medical school, approved by the Council on Medical Education of the American Medical Association and is a charter member of the Association of American Colleges. The board of trustees of the university is composed of both Negroes and whites. The medical faculty of the college is largely Negro, though there are three white professors. Students are drawn from many parts of the world. Last year they came from thirty states, three foreign countries, and one United States territorial possession. Some of them coming from the southern states receive scholarship aid from their states.

North and South, Negro and white American citizens support this medical college and hospital through their government and through the annual vote of their representatives in Congress. Negro and white serve on its board, and on its faculty. Its students come from all over the United States and scatter again to serve all over the United States.

Meharry Medical College, Nashville, Tennessee

Meharry, like Howard, is fully accredited by the Association of American Medical Colleges and the Council on Medical Education of the American Medical Association, with a class "A" rating. Hubbard Hospital, which is an integral part of its program, is similarly accredited.

The information which follows is largely taken from a letter received from the president of the College.

The Medical School enrolls some 400 students: 67 in nursing; 4 as Clinical Laboratory Technicians; 77 in Dentistry; 252 in Medicine. Of these about 33 per cent are from the North, 62 per cent from the South, 5 per cent from the West, U. S. Possessions, and foreign countries. From almost the beginning Meharry has been a cooperative venture of whites and Negroes. Starting with white instructors and white support, it has become increasingly an interracial project. George Hubbard, its first president, was a northern white man and his first associate teacher was Colonel Sneed, a white Southerner who had been a surgeon during the Civil War. Negro faculty members were trained at first largely at Meharry and later had additional training in special fields at recognized centers in the North.

Today most of the full-time faculty members at Meharry are Negroes; but there is a large group of part-time white faculty members, mostly local southern men who give their services with little or no remuneration as clinicians and dentists.

In the support of the institution all the large grants have come from foundations such as the General Education Board, the Rockefeller Foundation, the Carnegie Corporation of New York, the Julius Rosenwald Fund, the W. K. Kellogg Foundation; and from individual northern whites such as Mr. George Eastman, Mr. Edward Harkness, and others. But of late years both southern whites and Negro graduates of Meharry have begun to contribute to the institution as their own. The board of trustees is also bi-racial, and there is cooperation with the state, and with private institutions in the city.

"Meharry now has a contract with the State of Tennessee to furnish professional educational services in medicine, dentistry, nursing, and medical technology to 'bona-fide' residents of the State of Tennessee. Students pay the same tuition here that is required at the professional schools of the University of Tennessee, and the State Department of Education then pays the differential unit cost factor per student to Meharry Medical College."[11]

In September, 1944, the State of Virginia authorized the payment of $500 a year to Negro residents of Virginia who wished to study medicine, to enable them to attend Meharry.[12]

An important aspect of Meharry's work which the president omitted from his report is the service which it renders to the citizens of Nashville, both through the Hubbard Hospital with its services to Negro patients, and through the work of the Meharry faculty on committees and boards and in clinics throughout the city.

Concluding his letter, the president writes hopefully of the future:

"Public hospitals in the South are not yet utilizing Negro physicians as staff members . . . but it is my opinion that there is a greatly increased interest in improving race situations in the South. There is a very real interest and honest effort being made in a number of southern states to solve some of the problems of professional training for Negro youth. The question in the minds of many is just what the best solution is to be."

There is no ready made answer to this question. Any attempt to set up dual medical colleges, one for whites and one for Negroes, in every southern state would be so impractical financially that the schools could only be a farce. To send every young Negro in the South who wishes to study medicine to Howard or Meharry would also be expensive and impractical. Yet the Supreme Court decision in the Gaines case and the rising determination of responsible Southerners to deal fairly with their Negro citizens make it unmistakably clear that southern states must soon make available to Negro students facilities for professional training that are equal in every respect to those available to white youth.

[11] Dr. E. L. Turner, letter, October 14, 1943.
[12] ANP News Report, September, 1944.

NEGRO DOCTORS IN SOUTHERN HOSPITALS

It is appropriate to start this section with the best work that is being done in this field. It seems fair to say that the organization of medical and health services at Flint-Goodridge Hospital, affiliated with Dillard University in New Orleans, constitutes the greatest advance in service to the community and in the integration of Negro doctors. The following report was prepared by Dr. Horace Mann Bond on the basis of a first-hand study:

"First under the leadership of Albert W. Dent, more recently under that of Superintendent John L. Procope, the Flint-Goodridge Hospital has since 1932 reached enough high-water marks of medical and hospital achievement to fill a book of best practices in this field.

"It is in its demonstration of how white and Negro physicians can work together, however, that the example has particular value here. This contribution of the hospital to the great problem in the South as to how Negro physicians might be given opportunities for continuing professional growth, and how medical leaders of the two races can cooperate on the highest level of professional achievement, is exceptional and exemplary.

"The Flint-Goodridge Hospital is a unit of Dillard University for Negroes, in the city of New Orleans. The Hospital was the first branch of the University to open, in 1932. The Board of Trustees of the University from the beginning was planned, in its makeup, to give a demonstration of united planning by southern and northern white and Negro leadership for joint service to a people. The Board included representatives of mission groups responsible for two former Negro colleges in the city, merged to form Dillard University, and southern white and Negro men of substance and vision.

"Before the new Flint-Goodridge opened, the picture of the professional problems of Negro physicians in New Orleans was typical of that of any large southern city. In an older hospital of the same name, they had carried on in a poorly equipped, understaffed hospital in isolation from the leaders of the medical profession in this great center of medicine.

"In the organization of the new hospital every emphasis was made on the planned function of the institution as a teaching hospital for

Negro physicians in service; and all responsible for it conceived as one of its principal goals the growth of the Negro physicians of the city to the point where they could take their places professionally with the best men of any race in New Orleans, or indeed in any great medical center.

"To achieve this end, the hospital was organized with an active staff composed of paid personnel, entirely Negro; and a voluntary staff made up of the most distinguished medical men in New Orleans, all with extensive connections with the Louisiana State University and Tulane Medical Schools. The following services were established in the hospitals: Medicine, Surgery, Gynecology and Obstetrics, Pediatrics, Urology, Otolaryngology, Opthalmology, X-ray, Pathology, Psychiatry, Anaesthesia, and Dentistry. Each service is designed eventually to have an Active Chief of the Service who will be a Negro. Successive ranks provide for promotion with development from the lowest level of the Clinical Assistant, through the ranks of Junior Associate, Senior Associate, to that of Chief of Service. Three Negro physicians at present hold rank as Chiefs of Service: Rivers Frederick in Surgery, N. R. Davidson in Gynecology, and L. W. Horton in Otolaryngology and Opthalmology. Dr. C. H. Bowers is an Associate Chief in Medicine. In those services where Negroes have not yet gone through the development process necessary to attain the post of Chief of Service, a Negro serves as a senior associate. Leading white physicians serve as consultants in each of the services for which, as yet, there is no Negro chief.

"Under this arrangement, the senior associate is held competent to handle all cases in his service; other physicians can bring their own cases into the hospital under the 'open staff' arrangement, but where clinical cases are concerned, the order of precedence is maintained.

"From the beginning the process of education has been a feature of this organization. In addition to the invaluable stimulation derived from personal contact with the white consultants in clinical cases, the Negro physicians have had the advantage of regular monthly staff meetings. In these staff meetings, half of the session is given over to the reading and discussion of papers by staff members or consultants, in which hospital cases are discussed, and operative techniques dealt with. The other half of the meeting is given over to a business meeting.

"This system in effect has the value of a continuous post-graduate course for the Negro physicians, and the constant stimulation of contact with some of the great men of the medical profession in the United States. In addition, each year a post-graduate course is held for Negro physicians; this course typically enrolls 40 to 50 men from six or more states. Negro and white medical leaders participate in these courses, to the end of mutual respect and a united effort toward achieving professional growth and ability. Among the faculty members of the 1943 course were listed in the department of medicine, Dr. M. O. Bousfield, noted Negro physician now serving as commanding officer of Station Hospital No. 1, at Fort Huachuca, Arizona; four members of the Tulane University Medical School Faculty, and one from the Louisiana State University Medical School. The faculties in Surgery, Gynecology, Orthopedics, Urology, Eye, Ear, Nose and Throat, likewise included Negro physicians of national distinction, the Negro chiefs of service in the Flint-Goodridge Hospital, and the members of the Tulane and L. S. U. medical faculties.

"This plan for the in-service medical education of Negro physicians, which has now been operating for ten years, has paid off in increased professional skill and knowledge and self-respect of Negro physicians; in mutual respect between leaders of the medical profession in the city; in greatly increased health services for the Negro population of the city. In 1942, by the Superintendent's Report, the hospital served 3,150 patients in the hospital, 10,590 in clinics, 2,262 in the accident room, and 560 babies were born in the hospital. The school of nursing has already been mentioned. The Rosenwald Fund states that 'in addition to the care of the sick it (Flint-Goodridge) is a center for the professional developing of Negro doctors and nurses, the spread of health education throughout the New Orleans Community, and is the birthplace of the penny-a-day hospital insurance plan which has brought hospitalization within the easy reach of the Negro population of the South.'

"In its support, Flint-Goodridge again reflects the cooperation of many elements. Large grants have come from the Julius Rosenwald Fund and the General Education Board; but support also comes from southern sources. Recently the white and Negro employees of the Frieburg Mahogany Company of New Orleans jointly contributed to the hospital $2,000 which was used to rebuild and renovate the sterilizing room in the operating suite. 'The Women's Societies of the Congregational Christian Churches throughout the country very generously sent the hospital 17,457 pieces of surgical and hospital supplies, 526 articles of bedding, linen, and clothing, 391 pieces of infants' wear, and many miscellaneous articles. In addition to these gifts we received $454.32 from these Friendly Service organizations.' There is also a Women's Auxiliary to the hospital with 400 members. This auxiliary takes charge of various annual projects such as the Hospital Day celebration, annual children's Christmas party, and a lawn party for visiting physicians. It gives money each year to the Social Service Department and its members make layettes for the maternity department."

ON A SMALLER SCALE

Although there are few rivals to such a program as has been developed at Flint-Goodridge, public and private hospitals all over the South are making constant advances in the use of Negro personnel. Dr. Bousfield lists seventeen general hospitals in the United States, all fully accredited by the American College of Surgeons, which serve Negro patients and employ Negro doctors and nurses. Of these, twelve are in the South. Four others, of which three are in the South, are listed as conditionally approved.

North Carolina, as might be expected, sends in the greatest number of reports of hospitals in which Negro physicians are practicing. One reporter writes: "Municipal hospitals are extending facilities for the full participation of Negro personnel. Winston-Salem is an example."[13] From Craven County, North Carolina, comes the report:[14]

"We have a colored hospital, the Good Shepherd, which is modern in every way and was built through white and colored cooperation under the direction of the Reverend R. I. Johnson. The staff is bi-

[13] F. D. Patterson, letter.   [14] N. C. Newbold materials.

racial and in every department white and colored physicians and surgeons work together. They even use the same dressing room and shower."

Another report states that in the Negro hospital at Gastonia, North Carolina, purchased by the County Commissioners with the cooperation of the B. N. Duke Foundation, the best physicians of both races attend the patients.[15] The Greensboro hospital has a separate building for colored patients and employs Negroes as internes and on the staff. A more detailed account comes from Durham:

"Lincoln Hospital, Durham, North Carolina, is a community institution controlled by a board of trustees of both white and colored members. It is supported by donations from the city and county of Durham and the Duke endowment, and by fees charged to patients who are able to pay. All reputable physicians in the city are granted courtesy privileges of treating their patients in the hospital."[16]

The active or attending staff is composed of both Negro and white physicians, six Negro and eleven white. There are nine graduate nurses and fifty student nurses, all Negroes. The hospital was established in 1901 and Negroes have been on the staff since then, but the present teaching arrangement has been in effect since 1934. This policy was brought about by the effort of the trustees in conference with Dr. M. O. Bousfield, then on the staff of the Rosenwald Fund, Dr. W. S. Rankin of the Duke Endowment, and Dr. W. C. Davidson, Dean of the Medical School of Duke University.

Although North Carolina is outstanding, other southern states are recognizing the advantages of giving Negro doctors a chance to practice in hospitals which serve Negro patients. In Columbia, South Carolina, "it has been the policy of the Columbia Hospital for some years to provide adequate facilities for both races, especially for that group without means to pay for hospitalization. Negro physicians, members of the local medical society, are privileged to practice at the institution and they are doing so."[17]

In Birmingham, Alabama, Negroes themselves have organized to meet this need. There is at present "no adequate hospital in

---

[15] *Initial Survey of Best Practices.* March, 1943.
[16] *Ibid.,* also 38th Annual Report.
[17] W. S. Hendley, letter.

Birmingham in which a Negro patient can be treated by a physician of his own race." To correct this situation Negroes have organized the Birmingham and Jefferson County Negro hospital Association. The Association's goal is to raise $300,000 to purchase a lot and erect a hospital building. A white group has offered to contribute $150,000 if Negroes raise the other $150,000. In March, 1944, $50,000 had already been raised and the Association was hoping to raise the balance by May 1. The plan is for a hospital of one hundred beds, with Negroes eligible to the nursing and medical staffs. The annual operating cost is estimated at $164,250. Raising this will be another problem, but the Association recognizes this and is laying plans accordingly. It hopes to obtain a good part of the money from patients' and clinical fees, and to have this supplemented, as in the case of another hospital, by the Community Chest. However, it is recognized that these resources alone will not be adequate, and the Association is at work on a hospital insurance plan to enable Negro citizens to take advantage of such services.[18]

A word might be said here about the well-organized medical societies which Negro physicians are developing both in the South and in the North. In the interest of professional advancement and cooperation on health problems, it is still more significant that here and there a local southern medical society is inviting Negro physicians to membership.[19] Nurses, too, are beginning to see the value of joint effort and organization. At the biennial meeting of the American Nurses' Association in 1942 southern nurses joined other delegates in working for the removal of barriers against Negro nurses in the organization. In the American Social Hygiene Association membership is open to all citizens without respect to race; for twenty-five years the Association has had both white and Negro staff members, men and women, and has carried on health projects cooperatively with groups and organizations of both races, North and South.[20]

POST-GRADUATE CLINICS

In connection with Flint-Goodridge Hospital, mention has already been made of one of these clinics. There, and at the institutions dis-

[18] Bishop Shaw, letter; Cecil Thomas, Field Report.
[19] Walter J. Hughes, letter.
[20] *Opportunity*, November, 1942, p. 352.

cussed below, such clinics offer fine examples of interracial cooperation in hospital work and medical education.

John A. Andrew Hospital, Tuskegee Institute, Tuskegee, Alabama

This hospital is a "center for health work among the 23,000 rural Negroes in the surrounding country." It is "the product of the cooperative efforts of Tuskegee Institute, the United States Public Health Service, the Federal Children's Bureau, the Alabama State Department of Health" and the Julius Rosenwald Fund. Every year since 1912 there have been held at this hospital annual clinics in which white and Negro doctors worked together, treating in all nearly 20,000 Negro patients. In 1918 the John A. Andrew Clinical Society was formed composed of both white and Negro physicians from all parts of the country. White physicians have attended from Atlanta, Birmingham, Montgomery, St. Louis, from New York, Pennsylvania, Ohio, from Washington, D. C., and all the southern states. Negro physicians have attended from West Virginia, Missouri, Illinois, Kentucky, and Washington, D. C., besides those from nearer by. The State Department of Health of Alabama has sent a representative for some years past.[21]

Medical College of Virginia, Richmond, Virginia

"Some thirteen years ago the Medical College of Virginia, under its present President, Dr. William T. Sanger, secured a grant from the General Education Board to conduct a clinic for Negro physicians, using the faculty of the college, and the facilities of St. Philip Hospital, which treated Negro patients exclusively. The announced plan was widely heralded, both because the Medical College was a state supported institution for whites only, and because Negro physicians had been denied the privilege of attending patients, or even attending clinics, at St. Philip Hospital.

"The experiment proved a success from the point of view of the college and the Negro physicians who attended, and it has been continued each summer thereafter for a two-week period. The College subsequently included the conduct of the clinic in the budget submitted to the state. . . . The authorities soon began the practice of

[21] Julius Rosenwald Fund Biennial Report 1940-42, and enclosures from John A. Kenney, A. C. Terence.

inviting each year, for a single lecture, an outstanding Negro physician.

"Due to the pressure of its war program together with its regular program the College was unable to conduct the clinic at its regular time this summer. Conferences between some of the former 'pupil-physicians' and the Old Dominion Medical Society (Negro) on the one hand, and the Medical College authorities on the other resulted in the decision to hold a two-day clinic in September, at the time when the College was having a brief vacation, and to invite the Howard Medical faculty to conduct the clinic. Dean Lawlah of Howard accepted the invitation, outlined the plans, and brought to Richmond and the college ten of his department heads to carry out the project.

Comments from those who attended have been to the effect that, though brief, this year's clinic was the most successful; that both the College and the persons attending (one of the largest registrations) profited greatly; and that (as was expected) the Howard faculty acquitted themselves "more than well."

This summary of hospital services for Negroes in the South demonstrates again that where men recognize a basic human need, they move forward to meet it, not uniformly but in a variety of ways as great as is the variety of local communities with their local needs and local resources and their varying individual personal responses. Much remains to be done; but in different ways each institution cited is marking out new paths which others can follow and extend.

CHAPTER IX

HEALTH: SOME SPECIAL PROGRAMS

PUBLIC HEALTH PROGRAMS

SICKNESS IS NO respector of persons, nor do the problems of health consent to follow racial lines. As a consequence, governments and progressive communities have long recognized that the health of all the people is their concern. Not until recently, however, has recognition been given to the fact that the cure, like the disease, does not rest with the members of any one race and that we need the best that every group can contribute to solve common problems and meet common dangers.

In the nation at large there are evidences of this recognition. When representatives from the entire Western Hemisphere were called to a conference on post-war medical planning held in New York in March, 1943, by the Carlos-Finlay Institute, the National Medical Association, composed of Negro doctors, was asked to send representatives. Increasingly, Negro physicians are being given opportunities to serve the health of the community as a whole, as demonstrated by a list supplied by Dr. A. C. Terrence, recording secretary of the National Medical Association:

Dr. F. D. Stubbs—in charge of a chest clinic at Philadelphia General Hospital.

Dr. Charles Drew—examiner of American Board of Surgery for the District of Columbia.

Dr. P. M. Murray—member of the Academy of Medicine of New York.

Dr. Paul Cornely—member of the American Public Health Association.

Dr. Laurie Allen—member of the staff of Tuberculosis Sanitarium in Milwaukee.

Dr. Clarence Payne—member of the staff of the Chicago Municipal Tuberculosis Sanitarium.

Dr. Ralph Skull—instructor of nurses in dermatology at the Presbyterian Hospital in Chicago.

Dr. C. Leon Wilson—member of the staff of Michael Reese Hospital, Chicago.

Dr. George Shropshear—instructor in proctology at Northwestern University, Chicago.

Dr. William S. Quinland—member of the American Association of Pathologists.

In the South, the obstacles to full utilization of all resources of professional skill are much greater even than in the North, where they are great enough. But there has been increased willingness, particularly in the public health movement, to enlist the whole community in an effort to meet what is so obviously an interracial problem. *The National Negro Health News* of September, 1943, reports the following State and County Health Departments as among those taking part in Negro Health Week programs in 1943: Alabama, Arkansas, District of Columbia, Florida, Georgia, Louisiana, Maryland, Mississippi, Missouri, Oklahoma, South Carolina, Tennessee, Texas, Virginia, and West Virginia. Every one of these programs required cooperation between federal and local health authorities and between local white and Negro citizens, both public and private.

This National Negro Health Movement, supported by citizens of both races all over the United States and conducted by both white and Negro officials, has been throughout an outstanding example of interracial cooperation. It issues the *National Negro Health News* which, by its reports and illustrations of Negro health problems and progress, demonstrates to citizens of both races what can be and is being done. Through National Negro Health Week, with its poster competition in which hundreds of local schools participate, it stimulates the cooperation of thousands of individuals in tackling Negro health problems all over the United States.

Negro nurses are finding increasing opportunities to serve the public health. Well qualified Negro public health nurses have been employed by the United States Public Health Service from Arizona to New Jersey, from Louisiana to Michigan. Twenty-seven per cent of Negro graduate nurses are in public health services, a much higher proportion than the 10 per cent of graduate nurses in the United States as a whole who are public health nurses. The number of Negro public health nurses has increased over 50 per cent within the last few years[1] and is still increasing. Aside from these, about two-thirds of the Negro graduate nurses are engaged in hospital or institutional work, some in public and some in private institutions; and about one-third of those employed in institutions hold administrative, supervisory, or teaching positions.

The war gave to Negro nurses new opportunities of service. Ten Negro schools of nursing are today receiving federal aid through the Training for Nurses (national defense) Act; and the National Association of Colored Graduate Nurses has full voting membership in the Council for War Service. "Thirty-four hundred Negro registered nurses responded to the National Inventory of Registered Nurses and indicated their willingness to serve their country where needed throughout the war emergency."[2]

Today in practically all of the southern states Negro nurses are employed in public health work by state, county, and municipal health departments. Four southern states—Alabama, Louisiana, Texas, and North Carolina—also have full-time Negro physicians working in the state health departments.[3] The first-hand reports which follow, gleaned from all over the South, give a clearer picture of how these Negro public servants are working with other officials and with the people to raise the level of community health and well-being.

ALABAMA

The state health department employs Negro public health nurses, social workers, and physicians "as a matter of unquestioned common sense that their approach to Negro patients would be easier and more natural." "There never has seemed to me," writes the supervisor of a health center for Negro patients, "to be any reason why relationships with colored personnel there should be any different from relationships with white personnel elsewhere." At other public health centers

[1] Mrs. Mabel Staupers, letter.
[2] *National Negro Health News*, September, 1943.
[3] Dr. Walter J. Hughes, letter.

where white and Negro nurses and white and Negro physicians work in the same clinic, the procedures run smoothly and naturally. At those centers where there is only one social worker to serve both white and Negro patients, she is white, and all workers cooperate with her.[4]

Macon County

The program in this Black Belt county is a well developed demonstration of interracial cooperation.

"Since 80 per cent of the population of Macon County is Negro, you can readily see that most of our problems must be handled through this channel.

"The most unique feature of our program is that through cooperation with the United States Children's Bureau, U.S.P.H.S., Alabama State Department of Public Health, and the Tuskegee Institute, we are conducting the only school in this country for training Negro nurses in midwifery.[5] This project had to be approved by the Macon County Medical Society which is composed entirely of white doctors. At its inception the maternity service, which was developed for field experience for the nurse-midwifery trainees, was not to minister to patients within a specified area around the county seat (Tuskegee) since the doctors claimed that they had taken care of these people in the past and would continue to do so. After it was proven statistically that there were many women in this area who were dependent on the services of the granny midwife, they decided that the nurses should take such cases provided they were referred through a special system which was set up.

"The school itself is located on the campus of Tuskegee Institute, is staffed by a Negro obstetrician and five Negro certified nurse-midwives. While the director is white, she works in close cooperation with the County Health Officer and nurses of the County Health Department.

"The Negro obstetrician is a member of the Health Department staff and thereby works under the supervision of the Obstetrical Consultant Staff of the State Health Department. At the same time, he is responsible for the maternity service at the John A. Andrew Memorial Hospital at Tuskegee Institute where abnormal cases from Macon

---

[4] Miss Elizabeth Sessons, letter, April, 1943.
[5] Possibly the only accredited school.

and other surrounding counties are sent at the expense of the Health Department under their Maternal and Child Hygiene Program.

"Interracial cooperation has extended into the community especially in the organization of clinics. On a recent visit by Miss Morton, field representative of the American Missionary Association, permission was granted the Health Department to use a building at the Cotton Valley School for clinic purposes. A clinic had been conducted at Cotton Valley for five years and Miss Morton seemed delighted that it had outgrown its original quarters. (Note:[6] In 1945, not a single infant in the Cotton Valley community was lost—a record for this rural settlement.)

"Another clinic is held in the Masonic Lodge owned by the Negro Masons who are allowing us to use it gratis. The building was in poor condition and really unsuitable for service to patients. After struggling for a year under adverse conditions, the Negro men of the community agreed to repair the building and the Health Department to furnish the material. The use of still another building has been donated by a white group. This building was repaired by the Health Department and so far has been used exclusively by Negro patients.

"The white landowners throughout the county have again and again expressed their appreciation of the fact that the nurse-midwives are now available to take care of their tenants at time of confinement.

"A Negro private practitioner is paid by the Health Department to conduct four maternity clinics, four venereal disease clinics, and five infant and preschool clinics each month. A Negro dentist conducts eight dental clinics in the schools monthly at which he not only examines but repairs the children's teeth. At the same time, local white physicians are conducting venereal disease clinics attended solely by Negro patients.

"These are brief facts which serve to show you to what extent interracial cooperation must exist in a county of this kind."[7]

Wilcox County

The program here is less extensive and more typical.[8]

[6] Biennial Report of the American Missionary Association, Division of the Board of Home Missions of the Congregational and Christian Churches for 1942-44.
[7] Margaret W. Thomas, letter, January 28, 1944.
[8] E. L. McIntosh, letter, January, 1944.

"Wilcox is a rural county situated in the so-called Black Belt of Alabama and has a population of 26,279 of whom 5,255 are white and 21,350 are Negroes.

"The Health Department of the county is composed of a full-time Health Officer, one white and one colored public health nurse, and two clerks. The several physicians of the county serve as clinicians in the 7 V.D. clinics and 2 maternity and child health clinics which are conducted over the county weekly.

"While the services of the Health Department are made available to all persons in the county, 99.9 per cent of patients attending V.D. clinics are colored, and 100 per cent of maternity and child health clinic patients are colored.

"There are 65 colored midwives practicing in the county—of a total of 832 live births delivered in 1945, 716 were attended by midwives. The major number of these births were colored, but about a dozen were white.

"Clinics are conducted yearly in different sections of the county for giving typhoid serum and diphtheria and small pox vaccine. Both of the races avail themselves of these opportunities.

"Wilcox County has just completed the blood testing for syphilis of all ages between the ages of 14 and 50. This is the first county in the state to have this done under a recent bill passed by the State Legislature which makes it compulsory in the entire state.

"There are no obstacles to be overcome between the races. In conducting clinics at strategic places over the county, separate clinics for white and colored are conducted in larger places, but at smaller, the white are served and then the colored."

Birmingham and Jefferson County

"The growing interest of the Negro race in matters of public health, essential to 'Better Living' has given the utmost satisfaction to the Committee on the Negro program of the National Tuberculosis Association. . . . The increasing responsibilities being assumed by Negro leaders is encouraging and assumes further strides toward the goal of a well-rounded public health program for the whole community"—so states the foreword to a pamphlet published for the

Birmingham Health Association by the Alabama Tuberculosis Association.

"The Jefferson County Board of Health, with headquarters in Birmingham, has long been moving in the direction of a genuine total community health program with services for all and participation by all. Negro nurses were first employed in the control of a typhoid epidemic in 1917 under Dr. J. W. Dowling. Since then the public health nursing staff has grown to 26 in the county. Gradually a community health education program among white and colored has convinced many persons of the value of health services for all groups. Negro physicians have been asked to participate increasingly in the program. Despite some obstacles of initial suspicion and wariness, which have caused transient delays, the program has in the main moved steadily forward. The department feels it still has a long way to go but has 'covered the first quarter mile.'[9]

One of the most significant ventures in this field has been the establishment of the Slossfield Community Health Center. This Center, now about five years old, was first projected by a southern white employer, Mr. W. D. Moore, of the American Cast Iron and Pipe Company. But back of Mr. Moore stands another personality, Mr. John J. Eagan, who died in 1924. Mr. Eagan was a Georgian whose father left him a considerable fortune which he used to establish the American Cast Iron Pipe Company in Birmingham. Superintendent of a Presbyterian Sunday School for 30 years, active in Y.M.C.A. work, and interested in such movements as the Inter-Church World Movement and Federal Council of Churches, Mr. Eagan sought to put his religion into practice in all phases of his work. To him, his employees were individual men and women worthy of full consideration as persons in their own right. During his lifetime he tried to make the conditions of work in his plant such as to give them the best possible life, and at his death, he left the company to all the workers under what was termed the Eagan Plan of Industrial Cooperation. It may be that this plan has not in all respects been fulfilled as Mr. Eagan would have desired or achieved had he lived longer; nevertheless, this unusual tradition is a part of the whole train of personalities, plans, and events

[9] Elizabeth LaForge, letter, January 20, 1944.

that led up to the establishment of the Center, for the housing, recreation, and health of all the workers were among Mr. Eagan's concerns during his life and those of the company after his death.[10]

Among the employees of the American Cast Iron Pipe Company there have long been many Negroes. A good many of them lived in an area of extremely adverse housing and health conditions. A survey made in 1936 brought this to light, and Mr. W. S. Moore, president of the Company, became interested in meeting the problems. Working with the Board of Health of Jefferson County, he developed the plan of the Slossfield Community Center. The Center was designed to provide a program of recreation, education, health, and welfare for Negroes, not alone for employees of ACIPCO but also for residents of the blighted areas.

Because one of the most acute problems was the high rate of maternal and neonatal deaths, much of the Center program has developed around this program, and a maternity service was begun in 1940. It had a three-fold purpose: (1) to develop a teaching center and area for Negro physicians and nurses; (2) to raise the standards of obstetrical and neonatal care given by these two professional groups; (3) to show that adequate maternity care will reduce maternal and infant death rates and disease.

Today the Center is known as Slossfield Health Center. It gives services as follows: maternity, venereal diseases, child health, chest including tuberculosis, dental, medical diagnostic, laboratory, and X-ray. The medical director has been a Negro physician. Consultants are generally outstanding white physicians of Birmingham. Negroes serve as junior consultants and members of the visiting staff. In the maternity field alone in the little over three and a half years after the hospital and home delivery service had been in operation, there were almost fifteen hundred deliveries without the loss of a single mother.

The extent of cooperation is further shown by a list of agencies and groups coordinating their efforts in the program. The Federal Children's Bureau lent Dr. Walter H. Maddux to the Center to organize it and integrate the sponsoring groups. When he had completed this work in 1942, Dr. W. B. Perry of the United States Public

[10] John J. Eagan, *His Business Practice and Philosophy*, A.C.I.P. Co., 1941.

Health Service succeeded him. These two agencies work through the Alabama State Department of Health. During their brief period of life the National Youth Administration and Works Progress Administration helped. The Birmingham Health Association, Negro Auxiliary of the Anti-Tuberculosis Association of Jefferson County, the Maternal Welfare Association, and the Jefferson County Board of Health also aid. Among these agencies, medical and dental services are sponsored and provided for the low-income members of the group of 50,000 Negroes who live within a radius of two and one-half miles of the health center.

The interest of the white community in the center is increasing. Many groups of white persons such as the Junior League, Red Cross, and women's clubs visit the Center; and on Armistice Day, 1943, a group of white women of the First Methodist Church of Birmingham held a special service there as part of their program of interracial cooperation.[11]

Meanwhile, the scope and effectiveness of the work is constantly growing. A large building formerly used by the N. Y. A. is now being remodelled for a hospital annex; death rates from tuberculosis and venereal disease in the area are being reduced; and plans are being formulated to develop the Center increasingly as a training center for young Negro doctors who plan to practice in the South. Because Slossfield is as yet the only center of its kind in the South, many eyes are upon it and its growth.[12]

OTHER STATES IN BRIEF

No effort has been made in the following summaries to give a comprehensive survey of what the southern states are doing in the field of public health. An effort has been made, rather, to pick out a few examples to illustrate the new patterns which are being put into practice and the various and spontaneous approaches which are being made more or less independently in many different places.

Arkansas

The Department of Public Health at Hot Springs employs a Negro

[11] *1942 Annual Report* of Jefferson County Board of Health; William B. Perry, letter, January 30, 1944.
[12] Cecil Thomas, Field Report, 1944, based on conference with the director.

obstetrician and a Negro school nurse to attend Negroes. A white dentist serves patients of both races. The staff pharmacist is a Negro woman who has had three years of college medicine and is a registered pharmacist. A joint waiting room at the health department's offices is used by both Negro and white clients.

Under the state program, where study groups for public health nurses are held in various towns, the nurses of both races attend; classes for midwives are also attended by women of both races jointly. At the maternity clinic held as a part of the prenatal clinic each month, expectant mothers similarly attend together, regardless of race. After instruction there is free discussion in which all take part. The white instructress' comment was, "If you set Negro and white mothers down together and expect no friction, there is none."

The public officials responsible for the program feel that not only a sense of justice but the most practical common sense considerations make this community basis for handling community health the only sound procedure. This program, originating from the concern of a few good citizens for community health, and spreading through others who came in contact with them, has worked so well as to receive general community acceptance and approval.[13]

Louisiana

A report from the State Supervisor of Negro Education gives us the best over-all picture of progress in Louisiana.

"Louisiana has a centralized State Department of Health in New Orleans, and most of the parishes and a few of the cities have local health units which operate under the supervision of the State Department of Health. It is very encouraging to note that within the last few years both state and local health organizations have taken decided interest in Negro schools, and Negro adults are improving very rapidly. Dr. Fred B. Brown, a Negro who is highly trained in medicine and public health service and education, is assigned to the Negro public schools of the state, and his services are utilized through the cooperation of the Negro Education Division of the Department of Education and parish school officials. It is very encouraging to note that he receives the finest type of cooperation from white school offi-

[13] Carrie Lou Rilchie and Mrs. James A. Chestnutt, letters, 1943.

cials and citizens. In fact, Dr. Brown's attitude and his program of work are considered basic factors in the promotion of interracial cooperation.

"In addition to Dr. Brown's services, many of the parishes employ Negro nurses in connection with the parish health units. As much can be said of their services and their promotion of interracial cooperation in their local areas as has been said of Dr. Brown. In both cases white leaders in various professions and vocations are generally ready to cooperate with these health people. In addition, white state and local health officials and workers are showing a great deal of interest in the health of the Negro and are giving increasingly more of their time to the problems of Negro health.

"In several parishes in Louisiana, local school and health officials have organized parish-wide health committees, composed of white and Negro leaders in both health and extension work, for the promotion of health among Negroes."

This growing state-wide interest furnishes the background for fine achievement in some of the local programs. Following is a summary of a report on Roberson community in Bienville Parish, Louisiana, which appeared in the *American Journal of Public Health and the Nation's Health* for November, 1943:

Roberson community is a "typical rural Negro settlement" in Bienville, Louisiana. It has 45 to 50 families, about 300 people. Until April of 1942 it had but few and random contacts with the Parish Health Office, 40 clay-road miles distant. There was a part-time suboffice about six miles away. By April, 1943, it had built its own health building; someone in every family was actively engaged in health work; and the former "Roberson Colored School" had been changed to "Roberson Consolidated School and Health Clinic." This remarkable change began with the initiative of Dr. A. Oppenheim, Director of the Bienville Parish health unit, in Arcadia. He used National Negro Health Week in April, 1942, as a taking-off point. Every family and every school in every Negro community in the parish was reached. Response came from 10 communities, 40 of the 56 Negro schools, and 78 families. Assemblies, discussions, prizes, exhibits, playlets, health sermons, launched the move. The director himself proposed the clinic in a health sermon. The principal of Roberson Colored School and a committee of five undertook the designing of the Center and raising of funds. The director of Health Education of the State Department checked the plans. Volunteer workers in the commmunity erected the building. Negroes of the community contributed $75; sympathetic whites in the parish contributed $25. By March, 1943, the building was completed and in active service, offering general and special examinations, immunizations, and maternity and infant check-up. These services were rendered by the health unit personnel, two nurses, one sanitarian, and one secretary. For two weeks the State Department of Health supplied a doctor and a mobile dental unit. The Shreveport Charity Hospital, on recommendation from the new Center, performed 28 tonsillectomies and appendectomies free and cleared up three hearing defects. White citizens, the local white paper, the school board, the governing body of the parish, and the local Red Cross, Negro families, schools, and churches all participated, and among them are planning a continuation program.

Mississippi

Mississippi, like other states, finds that among the most widespread and persistent threats to the health and lives of its Negro citizens are venereal diseases, tuberculosis, and maternal and infant mortality. To conquer these, the State Board of Health, the United States Public Health Service, and the county health departments are working together. They are attacking the venereal diseases among citizens of both races through 287 venereal disease clinics, twenty-two of which are in counties without any full-time health department. At the same time the state is conducting an educational program on venereal disease. Similarly, working largely through the county health offices and their nurses, the state has reduced the Negro death rate from tuberculosis by 60 per cent. Attacking the third evil, that of maternal and infant mortality, the state brought under supervision and training the nearly 3,000 midwives who attend 81 per cent of Negro mothers at child birth. As a result, in ten years maternal mortality among Negroes was reduced from 12.1 per cent in 1930 to 7 per cent in 1940.[14]

North Carolina

Dr. Walter J. Hughes of Raleigh reports: "In North Carolina

[14] *National Negro Health News*, July-September, 1943, pp. 17-18.

several Negroes are employed by the State Board of Health including one physician, one public health nurse, and a health educator. In addition to this, there are 39 part-time Negro physicians working in the various clinics throughout the state, and approximately 40 nurses are paid from state funds and are assigned to various county and city health departments. The state also employs seven full-time dentists."

These workers are state employees and work out of the state office. Their offices, like those of white health officials, are in the departments where they work. "The racial relations in this state with these workers have gone on without friction and have been carried on in a cooperative and sympathetic manner."

With its usual progressive and cooperative approach, North Carolina has sought to work out better coordination of educational and health services. A five-year experiment begun in 1939 was carried out with the financial assistance of the General Education Board. In this the State Department of Public Instruction and the State Board of Health worked to develop "a joint organization to carry on all the health phases of social work." These include in-service training for teachers, summer conferences, and instruction in health education at the teacher training institutions of the state. Under the director or coordinator is "a field working force of one doctor, three public health nurses, and one nutritionist, and three health and physical education workers. Of this group one doctor and one health and physical education worker and one public health nurse worked exclusively in the Negro schools." Additional workers were supplied by the Department of Public Instruction and the State Board of Health. One of the main endeavors of the coordinating experiment has been to develop coordination at the county level also. Cooperation has been sought not only from school and health departments but also from each county medical society and Parent-Teacher Association, from farm and home demonstration agencies, county nutrition committees, federal security organizations, business and professional women's clubs, and such civic clubs as Rotary, Kiwanis, Lions, as well as many others similar in organization and purpose. To prevent the natural lapse into disjointedness as the coordinators depart, they recommended that each county or city employ a "local coordinator."

The influence of this program reaches beyond the state. At the 1943 summer conference, 48 white and 85 Negro teachers were in attendance from North Carolina, 17 white and 18 Negro from other states. In the child health conference for Negroes held at North Carolina College for Negroes in Durham and at Bennett College in Greensboro during the four years, there was an aggregate of members as follows: at North Carolina College, 121 in-state, 32 out-state, representing 11 southern states; at Bennett (1942 and 1943), 80 in-state, 8 out-state, representing 6 states. These members were teachers, nurses, dentists, and physicians from Alabama, Florida, Georgia, Kentucky, Mississippi, North Carolina, Oklahoma, South Carolina, Tennessee, and Texas.[15]

Instances of good local practices in North Carolina are also significant and deserve description. But we can only touch briefly on two of these. In Cumberland County there is a Health Center with a staff of thirty workers. Eleven of these are nurses, of whom three are Negroes. Each has a desk in the common office, and to prevent any possible partiality they drew lots for desks. All work together with the finest kind of cooperative spirit. In the Venereal Disease Department, a colored nurse serves as steering nurse. She serves all patients in that department. All nurses serve in all capacities throughout the Center in the special fields for which they are trained. All take turns in the weekly Health Department radio program. Negro doctors are invited to clinics to observe and to give treatment when necessary. There is a common waiting room for all patients who likewise wait their turns for service, and the staff is taught to think of each as a "ten-dollar patient" requiring the utmost consideration.[16]

In Charlotte, the city manager appointed a committee to conduct a survey of the City Health Department. This Committee invited the Charlotte Dental Society and the Negro Medical Society of the city to send representatives to be added to the committee.[17] Thus, qualified Negroes are sharing the privilege and responsibility of making recommendations for community health.

Where the public policy is not as well developed as it is in North

[15] North Carolina State Board of Health, *Health Bulletin*, September, 1943.
[16] Materials sent by N. C. Newbold.
[17] Charlotte, North Carolina, *News*, June 24, 1943.

Carolina, more enterprise and effort are required to make even a little progress. This should be borne in mind in connection with the following reports from some other southern states.

Tennessee

The State Supervisor of Negro Education reports that in Gibson County, the County Health Unit serves white and Negro schools alike, providing vaccinations, typhoid, and diphtheria immunizations and the like. It recently sponsored a dental clinic for Negro school children: the state, the local Rotary Club, and the Trenton Chamber of Commerce shared the expense of employing a Negro dentist to conduct the clinic.

In Williamson County all the health authorities, teachers, and other citizens of both races cooperate in both the county-wide health program and the hot lunch program for Negro school children. A colored nurse is also employed as tuberculosis inspector, with an office in the same building as the offices of the white nurses. "They sponsor programs for both white and colored audiences jointly, and members of the staff ride together in the same car whenever called upon to render service." White nurses accept all invitations from colored groups to give health lectures.

One Tennessee city, Memphis, has an excellent public health program which will be discussed in the section on Special Services.

Virginia

An educational program in nutrition for Virginia has been set up with the cooperation of the General Education Board. Negro and white workers are employed on the same footing and have adjoining offices in the Clinic Building of St. Phillips Hospital in Richmond.[18]

Georgia

The West Side Health Center, the first public health center for Negroes in the state of Georgia, was opened in Atlanta in September, 1944. The first emphasis of the center was to be on a venereal disease program. To organize and direct the work in its initial phases, a director has been loaned by the United States Public Health Service.[19]

[18] M. W. Cooper, letter, March 18, 1943.
[19] ANP release, September, 1944.

These better current southern practices in public health cannot rightly be called racial or even interracial practices. They are public health practices, born of the recognition that the health of the citizens is the public health, calling for public concern, public measures, and public support. Before this recognition and the common-sense determination to act on it, the ancient bogies of "race" fall back into the limbo of that past from which the living South is quietly but surely moving out into the main stream of American life.

SPECIAL SERVICES—WAR PROGRAMS

To meet the increased wartime demand for nurses, Congress established in 1943 the United States Cadet Corps of Nurses, to provide aid in training nurses for both military and civilian work, the girls to be paid while in training. A number of units of this corps were set up for Negroes, one of the first having been established at Freedmen's Hospital School of Nursing on August 3, 1943. For the two years previous to that time, the entire senior classes had already been members of the Student War Reserve Corps of the American Red Cross. Sixteen graduates of the school served in the Army Nurse Corps. Two of them were stationed in North Africa; the others in military duty in hospitals in this country.[20] At John A. Andrews Memorial Hospital in Tuskegee, the nurses' training school had a 1943 enrollment of one hundred, fully half of whom were cadets under this same act.[21]

Negroes participated in large numbers in the first aid and home nursing courses being given all over the country in connection with the Civilian Defense program. Both Negroes and whites were trained as instructors in first aid, sometimes meeting together in the same classes. In one Tennessee county, for instance, the course was given to 48 whites and six Negroes who met together at the white high school.[22] Similarly, in a North Carolina county, the 1942 summer course for first aid instructors was held at the white high school for all students without regard to race. Of the 65 persons who took the course, about one-third were Negroes. "Two classes, a morning and evening class, were formed. Although the morning class was primarily for Negroes, there were about as many whites as Negroes in the group. There was

[20] *National Negro Health News,* July-September, 1943, pp. 9-10.
[21] Dr. John A. Kenney, letter.
[22] W. E. Turner, letter.

only one Negro in the evening group. However, membership in either group was largely determined by the convenience of the time. In class discussion and in activities involving practice work in First Aid, the mixed group worked as a unit. Examination papers of whites were graded by Negroes, and the papers of Negroes were graded by whites. Everyone's attention seemed to be fixed upon learning First Aid, and as a result the feeling of being First Aiders rather than Negroes and whites seemed to be uppermost. At the close of the course all the members of the two classes and their guests attended a barbecue sponsored by both classes and held at a cabin on the shore of a lake, one of the beauty spots of the county. The cabin belonged to a prominent white man who was a member of the class. Most of the class members were teachers and civic leaders, and the atmosphere of the gathering was natural and friendly. Everyone felt that the experience of the class had been enlightening and had contributed to a better understanding of one another."[23]

In Birmingham, Alabama, at the suggestion of a Negro citizen, a special training course for Negro men to serve as volunteer orderlies in civilian hospitals was set up by the Red Cross to help meet the shortage of hospital workers. Twenty-three Negro men volunteered for the course, the first of its kind in the country. The course, an adaptation of that given to volunteer nurses' aides, called for 35 hours of class work and 45 hours of duty on hospital wards. Enrollees were from 18 to 50 years old, high school graduates, in good health and of acceptable personal character. The volunteers, chiefly men deferred from military service for various reasons, showed a fine spirit of patriotism and service.[24]

One interesting variant on general patterns is the appointment of two Negro nurses by the War Relocation Authority to serve in a relocation center hospital in Arizona. These young women, Civil Service appointees, live in the quarters provided for the regular nursing staff, and have been accepted by the other members of the hospital staff, some of whom were of Caucasian, others of Japanese descent.[25]

[23] Report of Mrs. Laura Jones in Newbold materials.
[24] Birmingham, Alabama, *News,* May 31 and June 1, 1943.
[25] Dr. J. H. Provinse, letter.

TUSKEGEE INSTITUTE INFANTILE PARALYSIS CENTER

Negro victims of infantile paralysis are served at this center, which is connected with the John A. Andrew Hospital in Tuskegee. Initiated by the interest of a Negro physician, the Center was established through the cooperation of the National Association for Infantile Paralysis and the Crippled Children's Service of Alabama.[26] Its patients come from every state in the union.

PSYCHIATRIC SERVICE FOR NEGROES

The field of psychiatric service for Negroes has until lately been largely overlooked. This is particularly tragic, for not only are Negroes subject to all the same threats to mental and emotional health as other Americans but they also suffer the constant nervous and emotional strain of living in an atmosphere of prejudice, frustration, and insecurity. At the same time, provisions for the abnormal or defective are less adequate in the case of Negroes. Some provision is made for them in the state hospitals for the insane in all southern states, but beyond this there is little help. This leaves more uncared-for cases at large in the population. Moreover, few Negroes have been able to afford the long, costly training needed for psychiatric work.

At last, however, a voice has been raised in behalf of these many sufferers. Dr. R. S. Lyman of the Department of Neuropsychiatry at Duke University has called attention to the problem; he is exploring a possible small-scale approach to it locally and suggests the need of further investigation and action. His action arose from facing an actual local situation.

"All the major clinical services at Duke University have space allocated to Negroes on wards except psychiatry. Medicine, surgery, obstetrics and gynecology, and pediatrics all have beds for Negroes. There are no neuropsychiatric beds for Negroes. I could not be satisfied to work anywhere in this country with such a gap in service to the community, or such a gap in my personal experience, and this is especially true for me in my work in the South. Accordingly, I have set out to fill the gap in another way; namely, by trying to build up some little Negro psychiatry which does not require hospitalization in a psychiatric ward."[27]

[26] Julius Rosenwald Fund Report, 1940-42, p. 10; Dr. John A. Kenney, letter.
[27] Dr. Lyman, letter and speech.

The man in the street may feel that in this highly technical field, important as it is, there is little that he can do. But any individual can find out whether, in his community, the same kind of provision for neuropsychiatric service, in clinics or hospitals, is made for Negroes as for whites; and any group or individual can work for the training and appointment of Negro psychiatrists and Negro case workers in hospitals or on services where they are needed. Texas, for instance, employs one Negro case worker at one of its mental hospitals.

Pitifully inadequate as these two examples are, they may serve as signposts pointing to a neglected area which in the next ten years may witness advances similar to those which have been made in the last decade in the fields of tuberculosis control and venereal disease control.

THE CONTROL OF VENEREAL DISEASE

Because venereal disease is particularly a problem of low income groups, its incidence is greatest in the South. It follows that since southern Negroes are a lower income group than whites the problem is greatest among Negroes. For that reason the federal program has centered on the South and on Negroes, although no part of the country is neglected.

On the whole, local response to the federal venereal disease program has been excellent, and on a community basis. Intelligent southern whites and southern Negroes have both welcomed the aid of the federal government and worked with its agents. "In general," reports the Assistant Surgeon General, "the treatment programs in Glynn County, Georgia; Tuskegee, Alabama; Memphis, Tennessee; Jacksonville, Florida; and Pike County, Mississippi, might be termed outstanding examples of cooperative effort." The account of the program in Memphis which follows may serve as an example of one of these cooperative programs.

Memphis Health Program

The control of venereal disease among Negroes in Memphis is part of a general city health program giving increasing recognition to needs of the Negro community and the use of Negro personnel in meeting these needs. To see it in its setting we need at least a brief story of this more general development. As early as 1910 the Memphis Health Department included a Negro nurse on its staff; in 1917 there were two, one of whom is still serving; by 1930 there were ten; today there are sixteen. About 1930 "a number of well-baby clinics for Negroes were established throughout the city, and through the participation of community agencies such as Parent-Teacher Association, child groups, etc., Negro physicians were invited to take part in these clinics. Many of them gave voluntary service at the invitation of some community lay organization. At these clinics the Health Department furnished all medical supplies, biologicals, and nursing service. It also, through its Director of Child Hygiene, gave short pediatric courses to the Negro clinicians who worked in the clinics.

"For several years the Health Department has encouraged Negro physicians, school teachers, ministers, etc., to take the lead in such activities as National Negro Health Week. The Health Department participated in the various programs at the school, church, or other sponsoring agency.

"In 1939 the present Venereal Disease Control Program was organized through the cooperation of federal, state, and local governments and the University of Tennessee Medical College. Clinicians, both white and colored, were employed on a per hour basis from among the private practioners in the city. Colored physicians provided the medical care in Negro clinics where Negro nurses from the Health Department provided the nursing care. The first Negro clerk was added to the department to do clinic work in these clinics in 1939.

"Through the cooperation of the Medical College of the University of Tennessee and the State Department of Public Health, an Institute for Negro physicians in the Division of Venereal Diseases was given to all who were interested in taking it. At the close of this Institute, clinicians were selected from the group who were employed for the medical service in the clinics.

"In 1940 the Wellington Health Center was opened. This Center provided various types of public health clinics for Negroes. The venereal disease clinics, however, are by far the largest. Clinics for the treatment of these diseases are conducted daily, and several sessions are held in the evening for patients who cannot attend day clinics. At the present time there are five Negro physicians, four Negro clinic nurses, and three clerical workers on the staff at this Center.

"In addition, there are sixteen public health Negro field nurses who do generalized nursing in their various districts.

"All of these programs have received the full cooperation of the leading Negro and white organizations of the city. We feel that the participation of the Negroes themselves in the program has made a definite contribution to the advancement of Negro health in Memphis.

"I am enclosing a few reports which will give some idea of the reduction in the Negro death rates from such causes as tuberculosis, diphtheria, and maternal and infant cases. It is also interesting to note that although the Negro death rate exceeded the Negro birth rate in Memphis each year previous to 1938, beginning with that year, the birth rate has run consistently higher than the death rate."[28]

This reduction in the Negro death rate is so great as to be worth noting in terms of three sets of specific figures. The general death rate for the resident population of Memphis, white and Negro, has been as follows:[29]

1930	White 10.1	Negro 22.5
1938	White 8.3	Negro 16.5
1942	White 9.1	Negro 13.4

Thus while the white rate has been reduced a little, the Negro death rate has been reduced so fast that from being over 200 per cent of the white rate in 1930, it was less than 150 per cent of the white rate by 1942. Deaths from tuberculosis have been reduced as follows:

| 1938 | White 42.0 | Negro 197.9 |
| 1942 | White 41.2 | Negro 142.0 |

The venereal disease picture is more complicated. Syphilis cases (not rates) reported.[30]

| 1938 | White 674 | Negro 3,654 |
| 1942 | White 1,030 | Negro 7,745 |

On the face of it this looks like an enormous increase in the number of syphilis cases. The death rates bear this out. They were:

| 1938 | White 3.9 | Negro 66.3 |
| 1942 | White 15.5 | Negro 47.9 |

[28] Dr. L. M. Graves, letter, February 22, 1944.
[29] Per 100,000 in population.
[30] Annual Reports 1939, 1941, 1943, Department of Public Health, Memphis.

The striking fact here is that despite the evident general increase of syphilis and the increasing white death rate, the Negro death rate has been markedly reduced. This can best be understood when we realize that in 1942 there were 859 white cases and 16,358 Negro cases of venereal disease under treatment in the health department clinic of Memphis. Evidently Negroes are reporting for examination and treatment in larger numbers than whites. This raises the apparent number of Negro cases, for only cases diagnosed can be reported; but it is also enabling Negroes to get the disease under control in their group so that the death rate which is rising among whites is falling among Negroes. This is eloquent testimony to what can be done in the Negro community with a well-planned attack on this scourge.

A program that deserves mention in this section is the educational program for better health now being carried on for the sixth year in fifty Negro colleges in the South. This program, which places special emphasis on syphilis, gonorrhea, and tuberculosis, has been jointly sponsored by Howard University, the National Tuberculosis Association, and the American Social Hygiene Association. These employ a director travelling among the colleges, while the colleges on their part cooperate in planning and executing the detailed programs on their own campuses.

THE CONTROL OF TUBERCULOSIS

Tuberculosis, too, is a disease of poverty and ignorance, worst in crowded city areas. Hence, it too, is a scourge to southern city dwellers, and especially to Negro Southerners. The Federal Government, the National Tuberculosis Association, and state and local authorities have all taken a hand in combatting it. Here again the recognition of community need and community responsibility is helping Americans to forget racial bogies in a common endeavor.

The National Tuberculosis Association carries on an active and extensive Negro program under the direction of Dr. C. St. Clair Guild. In developing and carrying out this program, an advisory board of four white and four Negro advisers and four members of the National Association staff has proved an invaluable aid to the director.

Essay contests among Negro college students have proved the

most effective of all methods in arousing interest and developing sound health attitudes and practices in the Negro community. Before these contests were launched, it is safe to say the sale of anti-tuberculosis seals among Negroes all over the United States did not amount to $10,000; last year in South Carolina alone it amounted to $20,000.

Matching grants to the states for special scholarships for workers in this field have also brought excellent results. Starting with a single scholarship in one state, the National Association has met with such good response from southern states, associations, and public health officials that there are now a considerable number of such scholarships, with some state sponsors voluntarily assuming more than half the costs in order to get more workers trained.

Another feature of the program is a placement service for Negro physicians, nurses, and other qualified workers through which a number of new positions have been opened up for Negro physicians. Indeed, so rapidly is the South coming to recognize that the group which suffers most from tuberculosis has the greatest need for training and employment in its control that, with the war shortage of doctors and nurses, the demand for Negro doctors and nurses outran the supply.[31]

At least twelve new Negro health workers were employed by state and local anti-tuberculosis associations in 1943. Two of these, in Texas and Arkansas, were with state associations. Eight were with local associations in Houston, Texas, in Atlanta and Savannah, Georgia, in Louisville, Kentucky, in New Orleans, Louisiana, in Tulsa, Oklahoma, and in Miami, Florida. At the present time several associations are seeking qualified health workers.

The National Association also operates a very vital program of postgraduate institutes for Negro doctors, covering tuberculosis, syphilis, pediatrics, and obstetrics. In this it works cooperatively with state and local associations as well as interested health agencies. "In the past year or two these Institutes have brought two to four days of worthwhile postgraduate instruction to something like 20 per cent of all Negro doctors outside of New York and Chicago. Such institutes have been held in Texas, Missouri, Florida, Tennessee, Kentucky, South Carolina, and other states."

[31] Dr. C. St. Clair Guild, statements in conference with M. C. McCulloch, April, 1944.

Dr. Guild goes on to say: "I should say that of the southern states, North Carolina and Maryland come closest to giving equal and adequate service to both whites and Negroes. . . . Locally, I think that Waverly Hills Sanitarium at Louisville, Kentucky, would rate rather high. They have an excellent colored division in charge of a well-qualified Negro physician. Arkansas also has a state sanitarium for Negroes." From other field reports this list is confirmed and increased. A second reporter refers also to the Alexandria Sanitarium in Arkansas, a modern, well-equipped state institution for Negro tuberculosis patients, in charge of a Negro physician who does much of the chest surgery. He refers also to the sanitarium in North Carolina already mentioned and to the Waverly Sanitarium in Louisville, Kentucky, adding that it has a modern, well-equipped Negro unit. "Dr. Ballard, a Negro physician, takes a large part of the responsibility of the institution as well as assisting with chest surgery and treatment."

In Maryland in Henryton Sanitarium and the Druid Health Center, and in the health center in Birmingham, Alabama, there are also excellent set-ups. Special demonstrations have been put on in a number of southern cities, notably St. Louis, which put on a four-year health demonstration with special emphasis on tuberculosis control in one of the most congested Negro areas. Houston's Anti-Tuberculosis League has a special program for Negro physicians; special courses are offered in tuberculosis, and any Negro physician successfully completing these is given a certificate and made an associate staff member of the chest clinics; he then conducts clinics weekly.[32] In Louisville, which keeps cropping up on the honor roll in this field, the Louisville and National Tuberculosis Associations jointly offer fellowships in health education to Negro nurses, teachers, and health education workers of the city and county for study at the University of Michigan summer session.[33]

In Baltimore, largely on the initiative of the Baltimore Urban League, the city officials a few years ago began the employment of sixteen Negro nurses in the colored tuberculosis ward at the General Hospital.[34] Doubtless, if the entire country were surveyed, this list could be indefinitely extended.

[32] C. Franklin, letter.   [33] Louisville *Courier-Journal*, March 18, 1943.
[34] *Urban League Secretariat*, July, 1940.

Atlanta, Georgia

Atlanta's chapter has generously reported its program in detail, so that we may follow it here.[35] The Atlanta Tuberculosis Association saw the need of developing work among Negroes long ago. Organized in 1907, it placed in its by-laws provision for a Negro branch and began to look about for Negro leadership. From that beginning, it has continuously "operated tuberculosis clinics and a tuberculosis home nursing service. In 1935, Negro doctors were added to the medical staff and have rendered effective service since that time. There are at present four Negro doctors on the medical staff. Joint medical staff meetings of white and Negro doctors are held, and there has been a fine spirit of working together evidenced by the two groups. Negro nurses have, since a very early day in the Clinic's history, been a part of the regular staff. We now have five Negro nurses and four white nurses. Sporadic attempts to have other full-time Negro workers have been made, but because of the financial limitations of the Association, we were not able to go on with this program until early in 1943.

"At that time, we added a Negro educational worker who was well prepared both by education and experience to do an effective job and we also added a Negro stenographer.

"This was done in order to accomplish more work in the Negro group, and the services rendered by these two workers supplement the usual service to Negroes of white staff members. For instance, the rehabilitation secretary, who is white, handles all of the rehabilitation work regardless of whether the clients are Negroes or white persons. Also, the white educational secretary and the executive secretary work in Negro groups in various ways.

"The Negro Board of Directors meet each month except in July and August and are very active in participitating in program activities.

"There are six Negro colleges in this area, and all of these colleges heve been very active in promoting not only better health for the student body but for the whole Negro community. The tuberculosis Association has for a number of years done case-finding surveys among the college students at the request of the college, and this program seems now to be on rather firm foundations. All of the colleges

[35] Mrs. Milton W. Bell, executive secretary, letter, October 1, 1943.

participated in this project in 1942 and in 1943; and since the service is directly available from the Division of Tuberculosis, State Board of Health, we anticipate that our part in it will be largely educational from this point on.

"An unusually fine Essay Writing Project on tuberculosis, sponsored by the National Tuberculosis Association, has been conducted for a great many years in the Negro high schools and colleges. In 1943 over 5,800 essays were written, and the quality of the essays is attested to by the great number of national and state awards made to the Atlanta area. During the past two years we have not accepted essays except from students enrolled in classes where the Tuberculosis Teaching Unit was used.

"The Atlanta School of Social Work sends students to us each semester for field work experience in community organization. Many of these students are now holding very fine positions in communities throughout the nation. The Annual Meeting of the Atlanta Tuberculosis Association and the Negro Branch of the Atlanta Tuberculosis Association is held jointly.

"It would be difficult to list all of the groups and agencies which contribute in some way to the total tuberculosis program, but we do not know of any groups with whom we should be working or who should be working with us who do not in some way fit into the picture. Just to mention a few, we might list the Atlanta Social Planning Council, the Atlanta Community Fund, the Atlanta Urban League, Housing Projects, State Vocational Rehabilitation Service, State Division of Tuberculosis, Department of Public Welfare, Child Welfare Association, Family Welfare Association, etc.

"Since the Atlanta Tuberculosis Association operated throughout DeKalb and Fulton Counties and the city of Atlanta covers part of the two counties, we have three school administrations with which to work. All of these have given the fullest support to our educational activities in the Negro schools.

"All of the work of the Association, both Negro and white, emanates from the state location. We own two large two-story buildings which house the offices and clinics of the Association.

"Excellent publicity is given to the work done among Negroes by the *Atlanta Daily World* and the Negro news editors of the *Atlanta Constitution* and *Atlanta Journal*.

"We have a provision for membership in this association providing that those who give $2.00 or more annually in the Christmas Seal sale, who make their request in writing, will be enrolled as members. We now have a total membership of about 3,100 and 189 of these members are Negroes. The Negro group raised something over $2,500 in the 1943 Christmas Seal sale. Our total budget is $57,883."

LOOKING IT OVER

As we look over the really remarkable progress that has been made in a single decade, it becomes clear that the field of health is one in which the South has increasingly recognized that a common problem calls for a common effort by all groups. It has worked to extend health education, toward equalizing the opportunities for medical and nursing care, and for employment in professional capacities; and Negro citizens are being increasingly taken into the administration and the planning of these services and programs. Disease and ill health are dangers which everyone understands and which we are increasingly learning how to control. It is not surprising that in this field a degree of cooperation has been developed which may indicate what can later be done with reference to dangers which are less generally recognized and whose control is not so well understood.

CHAPTER X

RELIGION: THE CHRISTIAN CHURCHES

No ONE CAN measure the influence of Jesus Christ in terms of the organized and official actions of religious bodies. Deep into the hearts and minds of men penetrate the underlying elements of our faith, and many a man or woman reared in a Christian church is truer to the faith nurtured in him there than is that very same formal and organized institution called a "church" which reared him. Therefore the weaknesses and failures of formal organized church bodies in this whole area of race, however tragic, must not lead us to ignore or underestimate the role of the Christian faith in American life. It is one of the foundations upon which even our secular democracy itself has been built. It lies behind most of our philanthropic foundations, our welfare activities, our societies for civil justice, our race relations committees, our quest for a decent and human solution of the relations of all our people one with another. Thus to a certain extent almost every good practice and every advance described is a testimony to the active presence of Christian faith.

The second major thing that can be said for the Christian church is that white churches, largely in the North, but somewhat also in the South, have contributed very generously in the past to Negro education, and still maintain to a large extent some of the colleges and schools for Negro southern institutions, the loss of which would be a tragic blow to Negro leadership.

In the churches, however, where the demonstration of Christian brotherhood should be most vital, the unity of the Christian family most unmistakable, the members have shown little evidence of Christianity. For the most part we do not have Christian churches, but white men's churches and Negroes' churches, where fellow Christians are not welcome unless they can qualify on a skin and hair test. Christians of the same denomination will openly object and even refuse to break bread together around the common communion table of their Lord, yet venturing to expect that he will be present with them, while they exclude their fellow Christians. In deed, the churches have commonly reversed the command of Jesus and have conformed to the world instead of transforming it; in practice, they sometimes remain among the stubborn strongholds of racialism. Even where gifts are made, they are not infrequently accompanied by a denial of Christian fellowship that renders them degrading alike to giver and receiver.

Over against this general state of affairs, we shall try to set those evidences that have come to us that the Christian church is beginning to awaken to a genuine concern over its own spiritual state and to revise its practices. Yet it must honestly be confessed at the outset, that so few and so feeble are these changes that when over three hundred letters of inquiry were first sent out to people from one end of the South to the other asking for instances of particularly good practices in race relations, less than a dozen replies referred to any known instance of organized church action. So little does the Christian church exemplify any practice better than that of the world to which it conforms.

The instances that have been compiled then have been gathered in almost all cases by inquiries directed specifically to organized Christian bodies as to what they could say for their churches, or from printed reports of these bodies. The existence of excellent published materials readily available on Roman Catholic activities and some Episcopalian activities and the extraordinary pains and precision with which Methodists and Congregationalists troubled to reply, may have placed these bodies in an unduly high light in the accounts that follow. The very fact that they did so concern themselves beyond others would seem to point to some greater awareness and readiness to act. Materials collected in this manner do not give us as much of the local detail and human interest as on-the-spot field reports, but they are indicative. Where reports are lacking we do not assume that there are no good facts to report; we can only say we do not have records of them and hope that when this book reaches our readers we shall be besieged with accounts of good practices that should have been included.

THE CATHOLIC CHURCH

The Roman Catholic Church is, of course, essentially a world church of all races. Nevertheless, due largely to historical factors, its ministry to Negroes in the United States had been somewhat neglected prior to 1929. At that time Father John Gillard made a national survey of colored Catholics and the work of the Catholic Church for them in the United States. Twelve years later, repeating his studies, he was able to report: "Since the publication of that work, however, it is no exaggeration to state that Catholic interest in the welfare of America's millions of Negroes has increased at least a hundred fold. Catholic newspapers are giving increased space to news of the Negro; Catholic periodicals are willing, even anxious to feature him; and several Catholic authors have published books and pamphlets on matters pertaining to him and his problems. Catholic clubs discuss the topic, lecturers on it are in demand; classrooms espouse his cause."

Pope Pius XII has roundly condemned racialism as anti-Christian, and expresses a special solicitude for "the Negro people dwelling among you," urging especial care for their religious and educational well-being.

In terms of membership, this aroused concern has borne fruit in the present roll of some 296,968 colored Catholics in the United States. Of these, 189,423—or nearly 64 per cent—claim membership in churches of all Negro members, the other 107,575 belong to predominantly white or mixed churches. "Naturally," says Father Gillard, "the greatest number of those attending colored churches live in the South where large centers of Negro population make separate churches feasible and social circumstances make them advisable." Yet even in the South many congregations are mixed and any Catholic, white or colored, may attend any Catholic church anywhere. Although over 24,000 colored Southern Catholics migrated North from January 1, 1928, to January 1, 1940, there was a gain over 23,000 in the southern Negro Catholic population, showing the tremendous activity of the Catholic Church among Negroes in that area during the twelve-year period.

Negro priests are being trained in small numbers. The first Negro priest, a Josephite, was ordained in 1891. Since then, seven have reached the priesthood after passing through St. Joseph's Seminary or Ephiphany Apostolic College. Both of these were Catholic, non-segregating colleges of the Josephites. But in 1920, despite Negro opposition, the church decided to establish a seminary for Negroes. This was done and the Sacred Heart Seminary was started in Greenville, Mississippi; it was moved in 1923 to Bay St. Louis, and renamed St. Augustine's. It now has seven seminarians in major and forty-five in minor departments.

Teaching missions are the backbone of colored missions; 1,670 sisters, belonging to 72 different communities of nuns, are working exclusively in colored missions. Four hundred and fifty-four of these are colored sisters. There are 237 grammar grade schools for Negroes, chiefly in the South, and 48 high schools, as against 28 twelve years ago. Vocational and industrial schools are beginning, and the church maintains one university for Negroes, Xavier in New Orleans.[1]

Specific interracial work of the Catholic Church in the United States was at first launched in New York state. Father John LaFarge, S.J., published in 1937 a book *Interracial Justice,* republished in 1943 as *The Race Question and the Negro; a Study of the Catholic Doctrine on Interracial Justice.* The book develops the theme that justice and charity both flow from Christian doctrine and imply not only equality of rights and opportunities and absence of compulsory segregation, but go beyond this to require positive charity towards one another. Not "justice or charity" is needed, but justice *and* charity. It is a well-developed, logical work, based on essential Christian doctrine, and widely read in both Catholic and Protestant circles. For some years, Father LaFarge has also edited the *Interracial Review,* a Catholic publication, and presided over the Catholic Interracial Committee of New York.

But this interracial work no longer stands alone. Catholic Interracial committees have recently been formed in Detroit, Syracuse, Los Angeles, San Antonio, Chicago and other cities, and in the South the demand of Catholics—especially of Catholic students—for more light on the whole issue is growing.

Moreover, the Catholic Church in the South is becoming increasingly aware of the problems of the relation of Christianity to social

[1] John Gillard, *Colored Catholics in the United States.*

issues. The Catholic Committee of the South recently held in Richmond, Virginia, a significant two-day conference on industrial problems. Among the subjects considered were such matters as post-war planning, wages and prices, labor relations, and the Negro's place in the post-war South. Among the distinguished speakers were both whites and Negroes; Virginius Dabney, editor of the *Richmond Times Dispatch,* P. B. Young, editor of the *Norfolk Journal and Guide,* William Green, president of the A. F. of L., James B. Carey, secretary of the C. I. O., Gordon B. Hancock, of Virginia Union University.[2]

Southern Catholics are also concerning themselves with projects to improve the health, housing, and economic status of Negroes. For instance, the Sisters of Charity of Nazareth, Kentucky, an order of white Sisters, have worked among Negroes for seventy-three years, conducting at St. Joseph, Kentucky, a 40-bed hospital annex for Negroes. More recently, they have interested themselves in health facilities for Negroes in Ensley, Alabama. As there was no hospital in Ensley open to Negroes, the Sisters opened a clinic in 1941 and began visiting the sick. Recently, with financial assistance secured through the Mother General of the congregation, they bought "three old shacks." Repairing and joining them together, they have established a 20-bed hospital. Now they are planning for a 50-bed hospital in which they hope in time to provide training for Negro nurses and interneships for Negro doctors.[3]

A Catholic priest in a Negro parish in St. Louis has initiated a number of successful projects which have contributed to the economic well-being of his parishioners. The first of these was a coal cooperative, to enable the residents of a low-income district to obtain the smokeless fuel required by city ordinance at a price they could pay. This priest, Father George Andrews, S.J., secured the cooperation of the Mayor in launching this project, and was able to arrange for leasing vacant lots from the city for a dollar a year to serve as coal yards. In their second year, the cooperatives, operated entirely by Negroes, sold more than 3,000 tons of coal. The board of directors is interracial. Through the redemption of purchase certificates in stock, the cooperatives will eventually be owned by the consumers.

---

[2] *Christian Century,* February, 1944, p. 182.
[3] Sister Berenice Greenwell, letter, February 24, 1944.

The next problem tackled by Father Andrews was the meat shortage and the high price of chickens in the winter of 1943. His parishioners, having gained confidence from the success of their coal venture, needed very little help in organizing a successful chicken cooperative. In the spring and summer of 1943, more than twenty-five thousand chickens were raised and marketed; at a time when the market price of chickens was fifty-six cents a pound, the cooperative was charging stockholders eighteen, and its general buying public twenty cents. It is entirely a Negro enterprise, receiving expert advice on the care and feeding of the chickens from one of its women directors who is a graduate of Tennessee Agricultural and Industrial State College.

Father Andrews was also active in the organization of a citizens' interracial committee in St. Louis, which was later given official standing by the Mayor as the St. Louis Race Relations Commission. At the priest's suggestion, the Commission has been able to have converted into small parks with playground equipment a number of vacant lots in the crowded areas where Negroes are living. For these and other services to St. Louis Negroes, Father Andrews was recently awarded a citation by a civic group for leadership in interracial matters.[4]

Father Andrews is not the only Catholic priest in St. Louis who has given evidence of the sincerity of his Christian teachings in his attitude toward Negroes. In April, 1944, St. Louis University, a Catholic institution, opened its doors to Negro students for the first time.[5] This action was taken at about the same time that the Reverend C. H. Heithaus, a teacher at the University, pronounced a scathing denunciation of race discrimination at a student Mass. The force of his eloquence "brought 500 students to their feet in a prayer that they might 'never again have any part' in the wrongs against Negroes."[6]

PROTESTANT CHURCHES

In almost every large Protestant denomination there are members of both races. In some, like the Episcopal Church, these are all members of one national church; in others, like the Methodist, all are members of the same national church, but in separate jurisdictions;

[4] Summarized from an article in *Survey Graphic*, May, 1944, p. 250.
[5] *Monthly Summary of Events and Trends in Race Relations*, June, 1944.
[6] *Ibid.*, April, 1944, p. 13.

in still others, such as the Baptist, there are many separate national churches, some all white and some all Negro. In almost all denominations, the actual congregations in the South, and frequently in the North too, are generally composed wholly of one racial group.

In those churches which have separate national churches or separate jurisdictions, it is easier to distinguish characteristically southern practices and trends. This is not wholly possible in the case of the truly national churches, such as the Episcopal Church, or the smaller but rapidly growing Seventh Day Adventists. The fact that in creed, ritual, and organization these churches are supra-sectional and supra-racial will be seen to be a force which constantly draws these congregations toward a truer Christian brotherhood.

Baptist

It is one of the most significant and hopeful signs in Baptist life that several years ago the northern, southern, and Negro Baptist Conventions appointed a Committee on Ministerial Education and Race Relations which meets each year. Dr. Ryland Knight, pastor of the Ponce de Leon Baptist Church, a white church in Atlanta, is chairman of the Committee. The Committee has met at Washington, Atlanta, Richmond, Louisville, and Nashville in a Christian fellowship unbroken by segregation. The purpose of the Committee has been to promote understanding of the problem of Negro ministerial education in all these conventions, and a spirit of cooperation in seeking its solution. The Southern Baptist Convention pays the salary of a teacher of Bible and Religion in each of eighteen Negro colleges. Each of these professors is also leading in holding Institutes for Negro ministers in his locality. Appropriation by the National Baptist Convention and the Southern Baptist Convention to the American Baptist Theological Seminary has also been increased.[7] The Southern Baptist Home Mission Board, meeting in Atlanta in December, set up a budget of $765,000 of which $285,000 was for missionary work among Indians, foreigners, and language groups in the South, and $41,000 for missionary work among Negroes.[8] Meantime, the Southern Baptist

[7] R. C. Barbour, letter, March 17, 1943; Ryland Knight, letter, April 6, 1943.
[8] Associated Negro Press, December, 1943.

Theological Seminary in Louisville, Kentucky, and the Southeastern
Theological Seminary at Fort Worth, Texas, are offering evening
courses for Negroes.[9]

In Atlanta in 1938 there was held a meeting of the World Baptist
Alliance. Baptists of all America attended, including several thousand
Negro Americans. The president of the Alliance announced that
there would be no segregation during the session, and white southern
Baptists accepted this decision along with the rest.[10] Occasionally,
local groups of white southern Baptists join in special projects. For
instance, in the summer of 1942, the missionary societies of the white
Baptist and Methodist churches of Obion County, Tennessee, together
paid the expenses and tuition of some Negroes to go to Lane College
for a short training course to prepare to teach in a Bible Vacation
School.[11] These Daily Vacation Bible Schools, some for white children,
some for Negro, are among the projects frequently sponsored or aided
by white southern Baptists. They gather together groups of children
often from underprivileged homes for daily schooling, generally for
a two-week period during the summer holiday. The children have
a common worship service and are then separated into groups for
special study and project work. The teachers are volunteers, and are
generally trained in preliminary short courses.

Younger Baptists are beginning, also, to take initiative in race relations, especially through the Baptist student movement. For instance,
white students of Louisiana Tech. in Ruston, Louisiana, recently
visited Grambling Normal College and helped its students organize
a Baptist Student Union among the 550 Negro Baptist students there.
The Union is reported to be doing splendid work. Similarly, a large
group of students from Mercer University (white), recently visited
Fort Valley State College, Georgia (Negro), and helped set up a Baptist Student Union there. They enjoyed their visit heartily and came
back greatly pleased with the response they had met.[12]

Here and there, too, small groups are meeting in southern cities
across the barriers of racial proscriptions to work together on common
problems as Christians. The account of one such meeting in a south-

[9] R. C. Barbour, letter, March 17, 1943.   [10] *Ibid.*
[11] Board of Education of Northern Baptist Convention, *Whom Do We Represent?*
[12] Claude U. Broach, letter, March 16, 1943.

ern city is the only one given us in any detail. Several "incidents," as we euphemistically term our acts of inexcusable violence, had recently occurred in this city, giving evidence of rising racial tensions. While other efforts were going on on a city-wide scale to meet the situation, two Negro Baptist ministers decided to work at the matter within their own church. They called on one of the influential white Baptist pastors of the city to discuss the matter with him. He showed immediate interest and in turn called on other white pastors whose response was also prompt. The president of the white Baptist ministers' conference was so interested that he invited the two Negro pastors in to discuss the matter. Out of these two conferences came the suggestion to call six persons from the Negro group and six from the white group who could find a common basis for discussing the problem sympathetically and frankly, and who would be willing to accept the kind of leadership needed for this situation. The suggestion was accepted and the twelve pastors met at the Y.M.C.A. the next day. The members got to know each other and agreed that in acting upon any suggestions which might grow out of their thinking together, they would move only as fast as they could go with the consent of the entire group. Their ultimate aim is to include all of the Protestant forces of the city, not necessarily in this specific organization, but by a combined process of gradual growth of the interracial group and of suggestions reaching an ever wider group of church leaders of the city. The group has been organized and functioning for about a year.[13] At a public interracial gathering not long after its inception, one of the elder white Baptist pastors, who had been part of the group, stated that it had been an awakening and revealing experience to him; he confessed he had gone along all his life in great ignorance of the whole matter of Negro life and race relations problems, though he lived in the midst of these, but having once been awakened, he was determined to learn and to do what he could towards a more just and Christian situation.[14]

A significant item is reported from North Carolina. Early in 1944, white and Negro Baptist ministers of Durham met to form a Ministerial Union. "There were present fifteen white ministers and twelve

[13] Jesse J. McNeil, letter, April 9, 1943.
[14] M. C. McCulloch, Field Report.

Negro ministers. The pastor of the leading white Baptist Church got up and made the motion that the moderator be the pastor of a Negro Bapist Church and without any division or question, the vote was carried. . . . This would have been unthinkable a few years ago."[15]

Episcopal

The Episcopal Church is one of the distinctly national churches. Although most of its congregations are all white or all Negro, it is not divided into northern or southern, Negro or white branches. This unity of the church is probably its primary contribution to race relations. The church trains Negro clergy, and employs them to minister to Negro congregations. They may be trained either at the unsegregated General Theological Seminary in New York City, or at Bishop Payne Divinity School, Petersburg, Virginia. The basis of qualification, ordination, and service is one for all the clergy, irrespective of race. The organization of the church is by provinces, subdivided into dioceses. Each diocese is under a bishop to whom all clergy and their parishes and missions within the diocese are subject. Up to now, all the bishops have been white, with the exception of one Negro bishop without a diocese, who has had special but rather anomalous responsibility for the work with Negroes. This arrangement is the church's major concession to racialism, since a Negro bishop with a diocese would automatically have jurisdiction over both Negro and white clergy in his diocese. Diocesan conferences of the clergy are frequently unsegregated, regardless of the part of the country in which they are held; and at these meetings, meals are often eaten in the same dining room, although sometimes at segregated tables. Meetings of the Women's Auxiliary to the Board of Missions are often unsegregated even in the South. Upon special occasions, such as the consecration of a bishop or the ordination of a clergyman, white and Negro clergy often officiate together, South as well as North, and congregations at these services are mixed and unsegregated. While the usual parish or mission congregation is composed of members of one race, it is not uncommon in the South for a few whites to visit Negro churches as worshippers or for Negroes to visit white churches and

[15] From a speech delivered by Dr. James E. Shepard, president of North Carolina College for Negroes, to the annual conference of the N. C. Interracial Commission, April 20, 1944.

be received without discrimination. There are, of course, many exceptions to this pattern; some churches remain racially exclusive. But the general position of the church is the catholic one, that every church member is a member of the whole church and may worship in any congregation.

It is interesting to note that these church practices are sufficiently taken for granted within the church that no one thought to report them as instances of unusually good practices in race relations. The editor might not have learned of them had not one of the field reporters chanced to know of them at first hand, having repeatedly attended Episcopal services in southern cities where a few Negroes were present in white churches or whites in Negro churches in a normal and unnoticed manner.

A second major service of the Episcopal Church to race relations is the American Church Institute for Negroes, a division directed to the maintenance of a group of excellent southern church schools for Negroes. During 1941-42 there were some 3,100 students in attendance at these schools.[16] The total budget of the schools and the institute together was $419,000 of which $61,600 was contributed in the South by dioceses, individuals and organizations, and $133,000 by students for board and tuition. In addition to the full-time students, the schools ministered through extension services, special instruction to farmers' conferences and other group meetings at the schools and in the communities to about 11,000 other young people and adults.[17]

Because the Episcopal Church is primarily organized on a church rather than a race basis, it has not had occasion for formal interracial committees as such, and it has no department of race relations, although a secretary for colored work, a southern Negro, has charge of stimulating and aiding the work among Negroes through parishes and missions.

Recently, however, recognizing that anti-Christian prejudice does

[16] American Church Institute schools are: St. Augustine's College, Raleigh, N. C.; St. Paul Normal and Industrial School, Lawrenceville, Va.; Bishop Payne Divinity School, Petersburg, Va.; Ft. Valley College Center, Fort Valley, Ga.; Voorhees Normal and Industrial School, Denmark, S. C.; Gailor Industrial School, Mason, Tenn.; Okolona Industrial School, Okolona, Miss.; St. Mark's Normal and Industrial School, Birmingham, Ala.; Gaudet Normal and Industrial School, New Orleans, La.

[17] *Education in Wartime*, 1940-42 report of American Church Institute for Negroes.

exist and is practiced by individuals and even by organized groups within the church, an effort is being made to tackle this problem through various channels. The study of race relations has been urged as part of the program of Forward in Service, the social action department of the Episcopal Church. Recent issues of *Forward,* a daily devotional booklet used throughout the church, contain numerous passages and prayers seeking deliverance from race prejudice and the denials of Christian brotherhood into which it leads us; and the *Churchman,* a liberal church paper, has carried some very challenging articles on Christianity and race.

On November 29, 1944, the *Christian Century* reported that "steps leading to interracial understanding were recommended at the meeting of leaders in social relations from the eleven dioceses in the Seventh Episcopal Province held in Amarillo, Texas. Delegates agreed to recommend to their respective bishops and councils that efforts be made to guarantee constitutional rights and privileges to members of all races, to assure the extension of equal educational rights to all, to establish specific projects in interracial relations in local communities, to counteract propaganda directed against the ability or integrity of the members of any race, and to promote the observance of Race Relations Sunday and the use in study and action groups of the national council pamphlet *Interracial Understanding."*

The Girls' Friendly Society, a women's and girls' organization of the Episcopal Church, has adopted as a national organization a statement of policy in race relations calling for "the active furtherance of interracial fellowship within the society, the recognition of the contributions of all races to our common life, and the establishment of justice and equal opportunity for all racial groups in America." This society encourages the establishment of branches in Negro parishes, the inclusion in white branches of Negroes or members of any other race and their participation in all activities such as summer conferences, holiday houses, diocesan, provincial, and national meetings. It also encourages work by members of the society in the community for the correction of injustices to racial groups, and has urged "the study of the question of segregation to see what it implies for the building of a future society.[18]

[18] Mrs. Helen Gibson Hogue, executive secretary, Girls' Friendly Society, letter, 1944.

These policies of national departments and publications are, of course, not always reflected in local practices. It is therefore reassuring to know, although it seems wise not to identify, at least one Episcopal minister to a Deep South parish who gives the major part of his time and thought to devising ways and means of improving the living conditions of the Negro population in his parish, of bringing together white and Negro leadership in the community, and of changing the attitudes of prejudiced parishioners and fellow-clergymen.

Adventist

A church of mixed membership, somewhere between the Baptists and the Episcopalians in its organization, is the Seventh Day Adventist Church. One of its leaders has described its practices in race relations as follows:[19]

"Members of the constituency of the Seventh Day Adventist denomination in all the world, regardless of race or color, work under the supervision of the General Conference. In all sections of the United States, except the South, members of white and colored churches meet together in conference sessions and church conventions on a basis of equality. In the southern states, the organization known as the Negro Department is not self-supporting but receives a large subsidy from the parent body to assist in the operation of evangelistic and educational programs. In the South, committees composed of white and colored meet together to discuss and vote on matters pertaining to various phases of the church program and to nominate officers for various departments of the Conference. Some colored boys and girls receive educational and medical training in white institutions of the denomination. The Theological Seminary, located in Washington, D. C., operated by the General Conference, opens its doors to its Negro clergy. White and colored leaders of the Seventh Day Adventists are friendly and helpful to each other in the South and in all other sections of the country. In 1877, white volunteer workers of the Seventh Day Adventist denomination began work among colored people in the South. They established colleges and mission schools. Many workers rendered their service as instructors on a self-supporting basis. In the South, as in the North, all church

[19] G. E. Peters, letter, 1943.

organizations of the colored race hold membership in the white local conference where they are located."

Methodist

The Methodist Church is today the largest single denomination of Protestant Christians in the United States, comprising about eight million members, but to make any sense of its variant practice in race relations one needs to know that the present Methodist Church is the result of the merger of three earlier Methodist churches, two southern white and one northern organization of both races, each of which had its own distinctive patterns of action before the merger. It also includes Mexicans, Japanese Americans, and other groups of distinctive cultures.

In any merger of such large groups and organizations much mutual adjustment is necessary. Despite the fact that the majority of Negro Methodists remain in all-Negro churches, the African Methodist Episcopal, African Methodist Episcopal Zion, and Colored Methodist Episcopal Church, the merger itself was a great step towards terminating sectionalism and racialism and bringing many Methodists together into one great church stream of all-American life. But the realignment of individual and group attitudes and practices in accord with this more Christian and inclusive organization will not be completed over night.

There was, for instance, the thorny problem of the relation of Negro Methodists to whites in the new set-up. Ideally the pattern of the Catholic churches, Roman Catholic and Episcopalian, seems the answer. Yet that pattern, as we have seen, is a mixed blessing to Negroes, for the independent and separate Negro denominations have their own clergy and their own bishops or others of corresponding rank, whereas from 1891 to 1941, only seven Negro priests had been ordained by the Catholic Church, and no bishops, and the Episcopal Church has done nothing more than the appointment of one Negro bishop without a diocese.

It was felt necessary at the time of the Methodist merger, to work out some sort of compromise between a practice of complete integration and one of complete segregation within the churches. The solution devised was to divide the whole United States into jurisdictions parallel to the provinces of the Episcopal Church, with an additional jurisdiction called the Central, which, geographically, overlaps a number of others and is composed of the Negro churches in that area. Negro churches in certain other areas remain within the jurisdiction where they are located.

The movement of Negroes into the main stream of American life is not in a single direct line, but meanders by many separate channels, circumventing many and peculiar obstacles; and the self-contradictory organization of Methodism is an interesting example. Although the merger of the different Methodist bodies left an entire segregated jurisdiction, it was, as a whole, a constructive move toward church unity. As a result of it, one now finds Negro staff members on the board and commissions through which the Church carries on its nation-wide enterprises and a considerable degree of Negro participation in the common work of the Church. There are two Negro members, for example, on the national staff of the Methodist Board of Education and Publishing House, working along with white staff members in the national office at Nashville, Tennessee.

One of the Negro staff members gives the following partial account of interracial activities of the Church:

"The Methodist Church functions in its benevolent enterprises through eleven Boards and Commissions. Our church is so organized that Negroes participate in the activities of all of these, so that to some extent all are interracial and engage in some form of interracial work. However, the Board of Missions and Church Extension, together with the Women's Division of Christian Service, have the largest interracial program. . . I shall confine myself to the activities of the Division of Educational Institutions of which this department (Educational Institutions for Negroes) is a part.

"In addition to the fifteen Negro schools and colleges related to the Board of Education, the Department of Educational Institutions promotes the annual observance of Race Relations Sunday. The Methodist Discipline of 1940 says: 'As a means of educating the church in regard to better race relations and the needs of Negro schools, Race Relations Sunday (second Sunday in February), shall be observed in all the congregations as the date when the interest of Christian education for Negro youth shall be presented.'

"The Department of Public Relations of the Board of Education cooperates with this Department in assembling data, in preparing articles for the church and secular press, and in making available helpful information bearing on the general subject of Race Relations to the pastors of Methodism. We usually send information to 25,000 pastors and material for 40,000 Methodist churches. Possibly 10,000 Methodist pastors observe Race Relations Sunday in one way or another.

"Last year, contributions from the observance of Race Relations Sunday amounted to $57,000. This amount was allocated to Methodist Negro colleges and schools in addition to regular annual appropriations.

"Many of the Methodist churches initiated community interracial projects.[20] One of the outstanding achievements in interracial work was a campaign conducted in the white Arkansas Methodist Conferences for Philander Smith College, a Negro Methodist institution. These two conferences observed July 18, 1943, as Philander Smith College Day, and raised approximately $5,000 for that institution. This was matched by the Chamber of Commerce of the city of Little Rock with a similar sum."[21]

Another Methodist staff member who works with youth groups writes:

"Naturally I have got to begin at home with the Student Department of the Board of Education of the Methodist Church. In this department, since unification, we have had no segregation of races in our meetings, conferences, and training schools. Obviously this has not been perfect, but it has been our general policy. Likewise the student department has organized on the state basis and does not recognize jurisdiction as does the general church, wherein the Central Jurisdiction, the Negro group is segregated. Furthermore, our publication *Motive* has had Negro members on its student editorial board together with the white group. . . . Then, too, our National Conference of the Methodist Youth Fellowship has constantly kept at this particular problem. . . . In the January issue of *Motive*, which

[20] Requests to the official compiling reports on these were not answered. It is hoped the church will soon issue its own report on them.

[21] M. S. Davage, letter, November 10, 1943.

will be devoted to race relations, we shall have two rather interesting articles dealing with the problem from this specific point of view."[22]

It is perhaps not without significance that the student youth of a church of eight million members should not accept segregated jurisdictions such as those set up by their elders, but should organize as Methodist youth without distinction of race, holding conferences together, listening to speakers of all races, and sharing in their church responsibilities.

Such developments, of course, do not just "happen." They call for patient, determined work and faith on the part of men and women and young people of both races, often against opposition and even abuse. For within the Methodist Church, as within other churches and within most American communities, there may be found all shades of thought and action, from the downright anti-Christian who will not work or worship with a fellow-Christian to the self-sacrificing and deeply religious individual who strives without respite to restore the Church to the ways of its Lord, in whom is neither Jew nor Gentile, Greek, nor barbarian, bond nor free.

In another chapter we have discussed the program and spirit of Scarritt College in Nashville, a Methodist training school for religious workers. A part of every student's experience is training to deal creatively with local situations involving interracial and intercultural contacts, and since the college "family" affords experience of fellowship with all groups but Negroes, students naturally seek this fellowship also through other channels, participating in intercollegiate group activities with students from the Negro colleges of Nashville, and in occasions of shared public worship when possible. Happily, Fisk University in Nashville also has students from many parts of the world, including Latin America and Africa, and its faculty is drawn from all over the world, so that an extraordinary degree of learning to live in a Christian student world-fellowship is possible to these students. In their contacts also with students of less liberal white colleges in the city, and in work with social agencies and churches, both faculty and students of Scarritt College are often able to make a contribution to interracial and intercultural understanding.[23]

[22] Harold Ehrensperger, letter, November 17, 1943.
[23] Louise Young, letter; M. C. McCulloch, Field Report.

The Methodist Department of Christian Social Relations serves hundreds of thousands of Methodist women, white and Negro, and many thousands of these share actively in its program. One of its major committees deals with minority groups and interracial co-operation. The present co-chairmen of this committee represent white and Negro women in the South. Like that of all other committees of the department, the membership includes both white and Negro women, and this committee includes also women representing Jewish, Mexican, and Indian groups. The principle of the department is "non-segregation and non-discrimination because of race, class, or creed." Such principles are not always in evidence in local practices in the South and elsewhere. However, reports indicate that women are taking the matter seriously and working toward the goals indicated.[24]

For instance, an all-southern conference of white Methodist women meeting in Atlanta in February, 1943, went on record as stating "that the denial of equal opportunity between the races in America, particularly in the South, is a denial of the Christian faith in the unity of all mankind. We believe white citizens should pledge themselves to a program working toward fair participation of Negroes in American life."[25]

Perhaps even more effective is the work done by Methodist women on the level of the local church and community, working as individuals or in groups on local projects that are small in themselves but impressive in their total results. Such activities include aiding the work of a local Bethlehem Center, cooperating with a committee of Negro women in securing much needed improvements in a city detention home for Negro children, cooperating with Negro and interracial organizations to bring about a reduction of police brutality and to improve the methods and personnel of the city police force.

The Bethlehem Centers, Methodist community settlements for Negroes, are in themselves a major avenue of service in race relations for the Methodist Church. There are at present Bethlehem Centers in twelve southern cities, one in Gary, Indiana, and one in process of organization in Atlanta. The whole initiation and development of these centers was southern. In 1912, a young southern white woman,

[24] Thelma Stevens, letter, November 11, 1943.
[25] *Southern Frontier*, March, 1943.

Mary de Bardeleben, educated for church work, offered herself to the Women's Missionary Society of the Southern Methodist Church (white) and was accepted as "a missionary to the Negroes of the South." She started her work in Augusta, Georgia, with an appropriation of $1,000, and there founded the first Bethlehem Center. Since then, the program has taken root in twelve southern cities. Here Negro children are now enjoying nursery schools, club and craft groups, reading rooms, supervised play, Boy and Girl Scouts, and other activities. Negro adults share in the program through sewing, home-making, and child-care groups, nutrition and first aid classes and so on. Generally, too, these centers contribute directly to better understanding and increased cooperation between the races. An account of one Center which is making an especially effective contribution in this field has been supplied by a former resident staff member. It does not attempt to state in detail all the Center's history and program, but to bring out its contribution to interracial understanding and cooperation.[26]

Nashville Bethlehem Center.—The Nashville Bethlehem Center was founded thirty years ago in answer to requests from the Negro community for kindergarten work for Negro children. It was sponsored by the Woman's Missionary Council of the Methodist Church, South, which at that time had only white members, but from the first it was a bi-racial project, and now it is supported, through its Board of Home Missions, by the United Methodist Church, which has many Negro members. Leaders in the Negro community were active in the planning and guiding of the work from the beginning, and soon a bi-racial Advisory Board was organized. As now constituted, this Board is composed of members from Scarritt College, Fisk University, and the Negro community, several denominations being represented. The Center is also used by the Sociology and Field Work Departments of these two institutions as a place for the training of students working for academic credit, and so the work done must be of a high caliber and must be properly supervised by a well-trained staff. This staff is also bi-racial, usually two white women workers from the Methodist Board of Missions, a Negro girls' worker and a Negro boys' worker from the Sociology Department at Fisk

[26] Account by Mrs. Olive Anderson, March, 1944.

University, or from some other college. Although up to this time the
head resident has been white, the greater part of the group work and
club work is under the leadership of the girls' and boys' workers, and
the supervision of the students from Fisk and Scarritt is their responsibility. The work is done on a basis of real cooperation and each
department head feels entirely free to make decisions and guide the
students as seems wise.

The Fisk students are nominated for the Center by the Sociology
Department, and are usually graduate students working for their
master's degrees. They live at the Center, receiving their board and
room for the group leadership work which they do under supervision. They are members of "The Center Family," sharing the third
floor of the Center with the resident staff. This gives a fine opportunity for group living, and is one of the richest sides of the interracial
association which the Center offers. Around the living-room lamp and
the dining-room table many of the problems of the individuals, the
Center, and the world are discussed in a spirit of real fellowship and
understanding. The Scarritt students miss a great deal of this "give
and take" of the home, for they come to the Center only for group
work, and for large staff meetings once a month. However, they get
enough to make the association very worth-while, and all who have
the privilege of being a part of this group, board members, faculty,
and students from the two institutions, and many friends, feel that
here the high point of comradeship is touched. On guest night, anni-
versaries, and the return of former members of the group, there is
mutual sharing of experiences, hopes, fears, and faith.

Besides the students, there are volunteer workers, Negro and white,
from the churches and homes of Nashville, and many of these make
their first real friends across racial lines at the Center. There is also
a group of young people from the churches and colleges of the city,
called the Junior Board. This group is bi-racial, and its purpose is to
study the needs of the Center groups and try to meet as many of
them as possible. During the war, it was hard to keep this group
functioning, but it should be preserved, for it has great possibilities
for interracial cooperation.

Many larger groups from both races feel a very real responsibility for the work of the Center, and a deep interest in it. The Women's Society of Christian Service of the Methodist Church has many local church groups which send gifts and supplies. The Mothers' Club of the Center has become one of the sponsoring organizations, and is very active in all kinds of service for the Center. In many unexpected places "friends of the Center" are to be found, who have some understanding of its great purpose and function, and who give of their time, money, and prayers to help carry on its service.

One of the great challenges of a community center in these days is to train its people in citizenship and open up for them lines of social action. Bethlehem Center has included in its activities cooperation with many of the Social Services and Community Organizations. A well-baby clinic, conducted by a popular Negro doctor and several Public Health nurses, is largely attended. Inoculations, vaccinations, physical examinations, a child-spacing clinic, and such health education are a part of this program. Under the Lanham Act, a nursery school was conducted for the children of working mothers, and they were given hot lunches. Under the Office of Price Administration and the Office of Civilian Defense, the Block Organization plan helped in the Food Rationing program, the Air Defense program, and many other phases of the citizens' service to the community in war time. Classes conducted by the Red Cross were sponsored by the Center, in sewing, knitting, home nursing, first aid, nutrition, and mass feeding. The Bethlehem Center Disaster Unit was the only Negro unit in Nashville trained and equipped to feed large groups whenever an emergency would arise. The gymnasium was opened to groups of Negro soldiers. All of these activities were interracial in the fullest sense, because they superseded racial lines, gave the Negro group a sense of being an integral part in the whole community war effort, and trained them to take their place and carry their part of the total work of the city and nation.

In the care of the unemployed, the aged, and the poor, the Center cooperates with the social agencies of the county and the city. The staff are members of the Council of Community Agencies. One of its real problems is that of juvenile delinquency, and its staff and leaders spend much time in efforts to meet this problem. One of the vacant lot playgrounds of the city is located at the Center, and the Nashville Boys' Club furnishes part-time workers in the craft room and the game room, and plans a banquet each year for the boys of the Center clubs. The Center owns its own camp, eighteen miles from Nashville, and tries to meet the vacation needs of its city-bound children by periods of camping in the country. The camp is supported by many gifts from churches and clubs of the community, both Negro and white, and the group of fine Negro and white counsellors make it one of the projects that offers splendid opportunities for the sharing of experiences and broadening of the bases of cooperation and understanding.

The third rich avenue of interracial cooperative action is found in the organizations, many of them interracial or supra-racial in their membership, that meet at the Center, or come there to observe and learn more of what is being done. First, of course, are the church groups, large and small, from both Negro and white churches, which come to the Center or which invite groups from the Center to meet with them. An interchange of speakers goes on, and groups of children or young people plan meetings together, when they can worship together, and share with each other experiences and aspirations. An annual meeting of the leaders of the Women's Society of Christian Service from all the Methodist Churches of both jurisdictions in the Nashville district has proved a time for closer fellowship in the work that is their common responsibility. A Twelfth-Night Service is held at the Center with choirs from white and Negro churches singing carols together; wise men of different races are asked to speak and bi-racial audiences share the challenge they bring.

The Center also cooperates with the Nashville Council on Community Relations, a group of citizens of both races, which is trying to find solutions for the problems that cause tensions in the community, such as friction growing out of segregation on buses and trains, inequalities in law enforcement, inadequacy of institutional care of delinquent and dependent children, and other issues. Several other organizations with interracial membership, working definitely for better relations, hold meetings at the Center, the chief ones being the N.A.A.C.P., the forerunner group of the F.O.R., and the labor locals of both the C.I.O., and A.F. of L. There are troops of both Boy and Girl Scouts which cooperate with other troops in the city. Through the local newspapers, both white and Negro, the Center tries to interpret one group to the other and to share information and points of view not readily available to the wider community. A fuller use of the press and of other printed materials would be a great help at this time, when many people have no contacts across racial lines, and so have no way of knowing even ordinary facts about the other groups. Groups of students from the white and Negro colleges and hospitals of the city come for observance of the group work and child-care being done by the Center, and these groups learn much about the inequality of opportunity in that section of the city, and the efforts being made to remedy some of the results. Many other visitors and guests of the Center share for a longer or shorter time the unique opportunities for natural human and social contacts across racial lines, and often express their conviction that only in such an atmosphere is real understanding possible.

Arkansas

In September, 1943, the Board of Home Missions of the Methodist Church initiated a new experimental program directed toward the improvement of race relations in the South. The laboratory was Little Rock, Arkansas.

With the help of an extension worker sent by the national board, a community-wide board was organized in Little Rock "to promote week-day activities, such as clubs, game rooms, week-day schools of religious education, community nights and the like" in five different neighborhoods throughout the city. The board at first consisted of the presidents of the Women's Societies of Christian Service and Christian Social Relations secretaries of the twelve white Methodist churches in Little Rock. The ministers were also invited to cooperate. Later the ministers and representatives from the women's groups of three Negro Methodist churches were added to the community board.

At present the basements of five churches (three Negro and two white) are being used for these activities. The goal is to build community interest and understanding of the project to the point where these five centers, which are non-denominational, can be taken over by a neighborhood council and a committee from the city-wide board. One of the existing neighborhood councils has representatives from every church in the neighborhood participating, and this council works with the board committee in discovering the needs and interests of the area and in providing the leadership for the activities of the center. Through this decentralized program there are already indications that the people of the community, with some assistance and leadership, are beginning to discover their own needs and to work out ways of dealing with their own problems.[27]

These activities by no means exhaust the race relations program of the Methodist Church, but they serve to show some of the main Methodist channels through which Negroes are moving out into the larger stream of life in the South.

Presbyterian

No comprehensive report on practices of the Presbyterian Church has been received, but an account has come to us of developments in the Presbyterian Church at Chapel Hill, North Carolina, which are at once so free from self-consciousness and yet so significant that the story bears telling in full:

"About two years ago a small group of students was meeting on Sunday morning for breakfast which was followed by a period of meditation and discussion. At one of these breakfasts the suggestion was made by one of the students that some Negro friends who were students in the North Carolina College for Negroes in Durham be invited to breakfast and to the morning worship. About five Negro students and one professor accepted the invitation of these students. Breakfast was served and they attended church without special seating arrangements. Friendships were formed between students in these institutions and these natural contacts were continued at intervals.

"January a year ago there was held an interdenominational worship service in which the ministers and members of the Baptist, Episcopal, Methodist, Presbyterian and Jewish religious (white) groups joined with the Negro churches of Chapel Hill. Seating of the worshippers at this service was handled by Negro and white ushers with no special seating arrangements for different groups. The preacher was Dr. Howard Thurman of Howard University.

[27] *Monthly Summary*, November, 1944, pp. 104-5.

"When the U. S. Navy Band came to Chapel Hill, it was recruited from young Negro students of North Carolina. Some of these band men had been members of Negro students' groups and had visited the Church as civilians. It was natural that they come to student meetings and on occasions attend Church worship services.

"Negroes have been in attendance on Church worship services not more than five times during the past two years. Negro attendance at student Friday evening meetings has been more often, probably at one-fourth the meetings."

It would be good if this account could be concluded here, if this acceptance of fellow worshippers in a Christian church could be recorded as having been unanimous and even unremarked. Truth requires the admission, however, that this report itself was written down as the result of a protest by a member of the Church. To do the congregation justice, this member was distinctly in the minority. The minister reported that "he had received little adverse criticism. No students had objected and they seemed to be helped by the experience. Three adults had expressed disapproval to him, only one of whom seemed to feel very deeply about the matter. He reported a number of people had expressed approval of this policy, but that he felt the vast majority had no deep feelings either way."

Because of the protests, the minister called a meeting of the Session to consider the question. After three discussion meetings, during which all points of view were thoroughly and carefully considered, the Session voted 5-2 to "entrust the matter to the conscience and judgment of the minister." This judgment may be inferred from a statement which he prepared as a basis for discussion at one of the meetings:

"It was the faith of Jesus Christ that all persons are the children of God and that God's love and concern extend to every person. In His fellowship Jesus transcended the barriers of race, color, creed or social position. The Christian Church, looking to Jesus for its faith and practice, should in like manner transcend these barriers.

"There is an honest difference of opinion among sincere Christians as to how to apply the teachings and spirit of Jesus in our day. But believing that the Christian church united in fellowship all who accept

Christ and His gospel, we declare it to be the policy of this Church to welcome any who wish to have a part in its life and program."[28]

Congregational-Christian Churches

The Congregational Church, now Congregational-Christian, has been historically a predominantly northern and white denomination. Scattered throughout the South, however, it does have both white and Negro churches, and through the American Missionary Association it has for a century rendered a major service to race relations in the South through its schools and colleges for Negroes. These schools have been throughout their history among the best staffed, equipped, and administered of the schools and colleges for Negroes and have played a large part in training the teachers, professional workers, and leaders of the Negro people. Gradually as the states have taken over in public schools the elementary and secondary education of Negroes, the American Missionary Association has closed out its work on those levels, concentrating on colleges and on experimental or demonstration centers of education for community life.[29] In 1943, it was still supporting to a considerable degree Talladega College, Alabama; LeMoyne College, Memphis; Tougaloo College, Mississippi; Dillard University,[30] New Orleans, Louisiana; Tillotson College, Austin, Texas; and Fisk University, Nashville, Tennessee. All of these colleges are now incorporated and directly responsible to their own boards of trustees on which the American Missionary Association is represented.

The American Missionary Association also maintains eight centers which were formerly elementary and high schools but which are now being developed along new lines of usefulness to the whole community.

Cooperative Centers.—The story of each of the old-line schools which the American Missionary Association, a division of the Board of Home Missions of the Congregational-Christian Churches, is either turning over to the state or converting into essentially southern cooperative centers is a fascinating one. The Association's Biennial

---

[28] *Ibid.*

[29] Fred L. Brownlee, *Work of the American Missionary Association,* 1943. Unpublished report is basis for the account of its activities.

[30] Jointly with the Methodists; also Flint Goodridge Hospital at Dillard.

Report for 1942-1944 lists ten of these schools with which it still maintains varying degrees of contact: Cotton Valley School, Cotton Valley, Alabama; Bricks Rural Life School, Bricks, North Carolina; Dorchester Community Center, Liberty County, Georgia; Lincoln Academy, King's Mountain, North Carolina; Lincoln School, Marion, Alabama; Trinity School, Athens, Alabama; Pleasant Hill Academy, Tennessee; Fessenden Academy, Florida; Ballard School in Macon, Georgia; and Avery Institute in Charleston, South Carolina.[31]

Of these ten, Pleasant Hill and Fessenden are still private AMA schools but are constantly seeking avenues for wider community service; Ballard and Lincoln Academy have made the transition from being private schools serving a few pupils and charging fees to being free public schools serving many students with better equipment and staff than before; Avery School in Charleston has been taken over by an Administrative Council of parents and patrons in Charleston, although the AMA still stands ready to advise and suggest; Lincoln and Trinity Schools in Alabama receive partial county support and are beginning cooperative activities; and Bricks, Dorchester, and Cotton Valley are unique experiments in community cooperation. A more detailed report on three of these centers will illustrate the ways in which the AMA is seeking to adapt the school programs to local needs and to stimulate the initiative and responsibility of the communities in solving their own problems.

Ballard School in Macon, Georgia, started as a missionary school for Negroes and came through the years to be a superior school for the more privileged, although its existence served as an excuse for not opening a public school in the area. Dissatisfied with this situation, the American Missionary Association saw a chance to correct it when a progressive superintendent and the Board of Education made an agreement under which the Board of Education undertook to operate Ballard as a free high school on a fully accredited basis and to build a modern well-located high school after the war. The AMA agreed to the use of its building and equipment, and further agreed to pay the salary of two teachers for one year, and of a principal for two years. These expenses have now been taken over by the Board of Education, although the AMA is providing a leader to help in

[31] Biennial Report of the American Missionary Association, 1942-44, *Seeking a Way.*

the development of plans whereby the Ballard building, after the new school is built, will serve as a people's center, providing facilities for clubs, forums, recreation and various lines of welfare service and adult education. Thus the cooperation of the AMA and the local authorities and residents will mean in the end not only that the minimum public educational services are available to Negro children but that these services will be supplemented by a wider and fuller program of service to the whole community.

Cotton Valley School in Alabama is supported jointly by the American Missionary Association and the county. The county pays as much as the law allows on the salaries of four teachers; the AMA makes up the difference necessary to give them a living wage and pays the whole salary of the principal. Of this program the Association's 1942-1944 report says: "We are particularly delighted with the progress that has been made and the fine way in which the County Board has cooperated with us. In an area where children start to work in the fields when they are scarcely tall enough to wield a hoe, we are showing them how to play. Where cotton had been planted to the back door, the school, through its garden and poultry raising projects, now teaches the folk how to provide food for their half-starved bodies. In a region which was bound by a sharecropping culture, parents here and there started several years ago to buy plots or a few acres at a time, as they were able. Now nearly half the community people own some land, and several have farms large enough to furnish a fair living. With food, and play, and a bit of economic security the Cotton Valley community has come alive. . . . The County Health Department took note of this awakening and agreed to give clinic service. The county doctor came over four times a month. Later the Children's Bureau in Washington set up a clinic for prospective mothers with a registered nurse specially trained for midwifery in charge. Cotton Valley asked for this service also and a full-time nurse was granted. Later, a second nurse was added. Within the classrooms of Cotton Valley School students and parents often may be found studying together about better housing, nutrition, clothing, and learning to read, write, and figure. They also concern themselves jointly about all kinds of social problems. The result is that more of the regular pupils are eager to go on to high school, while their parents are getting an entirely new vision of how to make a living and how to live." Such a program is a growing and living whole in which the church, public officials, teachers, and members of the community are working together on the total problem of improving community life.

At Lincoln Academy, King's Mountain, North Carolina, cooperation between the AMA and the county and state Departments of Education has been going on for at least twenty-five years. "We began with the County Board paying part of the salaries of a few teachers. We ended last year with all the teachers paid in full by the State Department of Education, save for one additional teacher paid by the Connecticut Congregational women."[32] Buses to bring the children to school are supplied through a cooperative plan. The boarding department remains in the hands of the Association, although the state pays part of the expenses of some students who come from areas where there are no schools for Negroes. A community worker, paid for by the AMA, is helping in the development of cooperative extension projects, including agricultural projects, a cooperative store, and a credit union.

Through these programs, Negroes are moving out from the status of wards of northern white churches in their educational life into partnership in cooperative ventures in which northern whites, southern whites, and southern Negroes are exploring together new possibilities of community life.

The southern Congregational Christian Churches are also responding to the challenge of a new day. Both Negro and white churches of this denomination are represented on its Southern Provincial Council. At its annual meeting in 1942 the Council created a Commission on Intercultural Relations, and it recommends that "under the framework of our democratic form of government our churches and schools be asked to explore certain points of contact in their several communities and endeavor to apply the teaching of Jesus in our daily problems. They should be asked to form study groups of good neighbors, to work for equal educational, employment, and recreational op-

[32] See AMA Report.

portunities for all people in their communities," to build confidence in each other and to build "bridges" between groups now separated.[33]

In accordance with this recommendation, the 1943 meeting of the Council at Raleigh, North Carolina, was jointly entertained by the United Church (white), and by the First Church (Negro). Special emphasis was placed on the need for better recruiting and training of Negro ministers for the denomination, and the churches were asked to provide scholarships to this end. The Council also recommended the development of a "Center of Christian Services at Franklinton, North Carolina, under a Director, this to be a center of retreats, short-courses, in-service institutes, and the like."[34]

In the fall of 1943, in line with this recommendation, a two-day retreat was held, thirty-five Congregational Christian ministers of both races taking part. All members participated freely in this meeting, without distinction of race, discussing, voting, worshipping, and eating together in one fellowship. So successful was this first meeting that the members voted unanimously to repeat the experience in 1944.[35]

Young people's conferences were also interested. A Negro minister spoke at the Vesper Service one evening at the North Carolina Young People's Camp and spent the night as a guest of the group. A Negro church extension worker visited the Virginia Young People's Camp for two days and spoke at the Vesper Service.

Congregational-Christian churches are few and scattered in the Central South, but Negro speakers were guests at the Texas Conference in 1940. A joint supper meeting of Congregational university students and Negro students from Tillotson College was held in 1942 at the home of a white clergyman in Austin, Texas. The meeting was marked by frank and friendly discussion and general satisfaction. In a Congregational Church in Oklahoma City, a group of high-school age white boys and girls invited a corresponding group from a Negro church to their Sunday night meeting, and all had a good time together.[36]

[33] Report of Southern Provincial Council, 1943; William T. Scott, letter, October 16, 1943.
[34] F. C. Lester, letter; report of the Council.
[35] H. Shelton Smith, letter, November 3, 1943.
[36] H. H. Lindeman, letter, October 8, 1943.

Even more interesting things are being done in the Southwest Conference, but they are beyond the scope of this volume.[37]

In 1942, recognizing that problems of race relations had reached a stage where something more than a program of schools and colleges was called for, the Congregational and Christian Churches took a new step. In their annual General Conference, representing all churches of the denomination, North and South, white and Negro, they declared unanimously that "The General Conference approves the action of the Board of Home Missions in appointing through the American Missionary Association Division, a representative to establish non-institutional ministries of reconciliation in communities of acute Negro-white tensions in the United States." Six months later the "non-institutional ministries of reconciliation" had taken shape in the form of a Race Relations Program headed by Charles S. Johnson, director of the Department of Social Sciences at Fisk University, and also associated in race relations with the Julius Rosenwald Fund. In announcing this appointment, the American Missionary Association said: "The primary purpose of the founders of the Association was to help remove the 'sins of caste' from American life. Progress here has been infinitely slower than in education. However, the circle of those who care intelligently about eliminating segregation as such is widening."[38]

Thus the denomination shifted its emphasis from a program of school and college operation directed from New York to one which still maintains what is valid of those services, but which also functions through a southern office, headed by a Negro Southerner, directed from Nashville towards the elimination of caste all over the United States. Into the new office flow many hundreds of letters from all over the South, containing reports on race relations, problems and progress, requests for materials and for help in planning programs of education and action. Out of it flow hundreds of answering letters, reading lists, program suggestions. Into it flow newspaper clippings, field reports, and magazine articles from all over the country; out of it comes the *Monthly Summary of Events and Trends in Race Relations,* a nation-wide service of information and interpretation to key

[37] Nelson C. Dreier, letter, October 11, 1943.
[38] Fred L. Brownlee, *Work of the American Missionary Association,* pp. 32-33.

individuals and groups.[39] Into it come requests for speakers, social surveys, and counsellors. Out of it go men and women, white and Negro, trained or in training as field secretaries and consultants. They have made surveys of tension areas in the North and West, as well as in such southern cities as Beaumont and Houston, Texas; Birmingham and Mobile, Alabama; and New Orleans, Louisiana.[40] They have collected the field information on better current Southern practices in race relations, and they have gone out on request, taking their knowledge and experience of the Southern scene, to give special services, and to make special studies in such western and northern cities as San Francisco, Detroit, and Chicago. In this southern center of activity, too, was held the first and second American Missionary Association Institute of Race Relations, the first of its kind to be held in the South. This Institute, held for three weeks in July, 1944 and 1945,[41] brought together more than a hundred and twenty white and Negro teachers, students, social workers and interested individuals from North and South, to hear all phases of the thorny problems of racial relations discussed by men and women of both races who have devoted their lives to the study of mankind and human problems.

[39] The Julius Rosenwald Fund.
[40] Findings summarized in *To Stem This Tide*, by Charles S. Johnson and Associates.
[41] And again in July, 1945.

CHAPTER XI

YOUTH, CHURCH, AND CHRISTIANITY

Of all the signs of promise in today's world, none is more heartening than the growing rebellion of youth against the un-Christian practices of their elders. It is a peaceful rebellion and surely an ironic one, for the rebellion consists in the determination of youth to do what their elders have taught them. More and more, all over the nation, there is arising from the youth of the Christian churches and fellowships the demand that the church either practice Christianity or stop preaching it. They are restless and, being restless, they are on the move.

Happily, Christian leaders in touch with Christian youth are aware of this and realize that organized Christian bodies face one of the supreme crises of their lives and that, unless they change, young people will be lost to them. Happily, too, young people want them to change so that they can stay with them and in them; and they balk only when the churches, colleges, Y.M.'s, Y.W.'s, and other such groups balk at letting them be Christian.

Leaders in both the Y.W.C.A. and the Y.M.C.A. have been frankly facing this crisis. Even while this section was being written, two booklets have appeared in heartening evidence of this. One is called *Interracial Practices of the Y.W.C.A.,* and the other, *Negro Youth in City Y.M.C.A.'s.* Both are the reports of thoroughgoing self-studies of the interracial practices of these organizations, with a definite challenge to the reshaping of practices into accord with the professed principles upon which the organizations were founded and for which, supposedly, they exist.

We can hardly ask that the practices of these organizations be transformed before the ink on the reports is dry. But we can point to changes already in evidence before the studies were made. A glance at earlier conditions is necessary to understand the element of forward movement involved.

THE Y.W.C.A. IN THE SOUTH

In 1907 there were a few Negro Y.W.C.A. centers, very feeble and all in the North, except for one in Washington, D. C. In that year Miss Grace Dodge called a conference of southern white women at Asheville, North Carolina, to consider promoting Y.W.C.A. work among colored girls and women. The white women at first refused to consider it, then agreed with some misgivings that the attempt might be made if it was entirely organized and supervised from national headquarters in New York City. Thus the work was begun and carried on for eight years, the white South absolutely abstaining. In 1915, however, the general secretary was able to report that "we have come to the point where these same southern women want to do something different," and in October, 1915, there was held at Louisville, Kentucky, the first southern interracial conference of the Y.W.C.A.[1]

Thirty years have passed since the first conference. Today there are in the South thirty-one Negro branches and centers of the Y.W.C.A. located in Alabama, Arkansas, Florida, Georgia, Kentucky, Louisiana, North Carolina, Oklahoma, South Carolina, Tennessee, Texas, Virginia, and the District of Columbia. Negro members are serving on the boards of directors or committees of management of twenty associations in the southern region. In 1943 there were the following "Y" groups and members among Negroes in this area: 423 younger girls' groups, 49 industrial, 80 business and professional, 35 home women, 472 in health education.[2]

The state of mind of the group who felt in 1907 that they could not touch "Y" work among Negroes is so much a thing of the past that it would scarcely be understandable to the southern white women who today are working with energy and devotion to expand this work and make it more effective. Each day now brings some new forward step. In November, 1943, the Juliette Derricote branch in Mobile, Alabama, one of the newest Negro branches in the South, had its formal opening. In Houston, Texas, the Y.W.C.A. Board of Directors recently called upon the Hogg Foundation to help

[1] J. LeFlore, Field Report, November 30, 1943.
[2] Juliet O. Bell and Helen J. Wilkins, *Interracial Practices on Community Y.W.C.A.'s* (New York: The Woman's Press, 1944), p. 63.

organize a six weeks' study course in race relations, with the emphasis on understanding of race and race prejudice. This intensive course, guided by faculty members from Houston educational institutions, included work-shop study by smaller groups during a part of each day.

The Washington, D. C., Y.W.C.A. had more than once taken the initiative in race relations programs; in June, 1943, it did so again. It had been impossible for Negroes employed in government offices to get service in downtown restaurants. So the Y.W.C.A. at Seventeenth and K Streets, N. W., opened its cafeteria to Negroes. A tea-room on the same floor continued to be restricted to whites, but both whites and Negroes use the cafeteria freely. Negroes do not seat themselves at the same tables with white patrons except on invitation, but there have been many instances of pleasant mixed gatherings.[3]

The Y.W.C.A. in Hot Springs, Arkansas, sends a report of two meetings under its auspices in which both Negro and white Girl Reserves participated, before mixed and unsegregated audiences; the November World Fellowship meeting, held at the First Methodist Church (white), and the annual Hanging of the Greens at the Y.W.C.A. club room, for which there was an audience of 150 persons, about a third of whom were Negroes. When the Y.W.C.A. recently brought Mrs. Grace Sloan Overton to Hot Springs for a series of meetings and discussions, the committee of white young people who were planning the young people's session voted unanimously to invite Negro young people to attend. At the afternoon session with Mrs. Overton there was a good representation of Negro youth. Since this visit, a small committee has been chosen to promote counselling of youth and parent education and to plan for other speakers and discussions; and this committee includes one Negro member, a home economics teacher.[4]

Something of the problems involved and the pattern of development of Y.W.C.A. work with Negroes in southern cities can be glimpsed in this first-hand report by a white faculty member of a Negro college who has been interested in the work in Memphis, Tennessee:[5]

[3] Wilmer Shields, letter, June 23, 1943.
[4] Mrs. J. H. Chesnut, letter, March 29, 1943.
[5] M. E. Bichnell, Field Report, April 3, 1944.

Race Relations Developments in the Memphis Y.W.C.A.

"Until about four years ago the Memphis Y.W.C.A. was entirely white; then an Interracial Committee was set up to study the possibility of opening a Branch. After six months' study, steps were taken to organize three Girl Reserve Units, and a training class for Negro leaders was given by the white Girl Reserve staff members at the Y. The work grew, and about two years ago the Community Fund granted a Y.W.C.A. request for an increase in their budget for the purpose of expanding the work to the Negro community. A full-time Negro staff member was employed and quarters were obtained near Foote Homes. Today a Business Girls' Club is flourishing; the number of Girl Reserve Units has increased to more than a dozen; and many other miscellaneous activities are being carried on.

"These developments are not particularly significant in themselves, since many southern cities have Negro branches older and larger than ours; the significance lies in the interracial relationships established as a part of the pattern of development during the preliminary study by the Interracial Committee. The 'purpose' of the national Y.W.C.A. as an inclusive Christian fellowship of women was adopted as the basis for the expansion, and it was agreed by the members of the Interracial Committee to make any growth only along these lines and to move only as fast as it was possible to do so along those lines. In the very beginning when this general definition of the relationships of the Branch and Central was accepted by the Board of Directors, four members who were not ready to accept it withdrew.

"One evidence of the carrying out of this policy appeared in the first training class for Girl Reserve leaders. The Girl Reserves' Department of the Central Association gave money for the necessary equipment for that training class and the white staff member gave the course. The second evidence was the way in which the Y.W.C.A. turned in its request for an increased budget to the Community Fund—not as a separate request for a special sum for the establishment of a Branch, but as a request for an over-all sum for the expansion of their work to include Negro women. Another evidence is that the Department Committee of the Employed Girls' Department, which is made up of women in the community serving as sponsors and advisers to the Employed Girls' Clubs, became interracial as soon as an employed girls' club at the Branch was planned for. They did not set up a Negro Committee for the Branch parallel to the white one for the Central, but enlarged the committee for the Employed Girls' Department to include Negro women. The whole committee meets together at the Central once a month.

"The Interracial Committee has been continued as a standing committee functioning under the Board and has been enlarged to give more people an opportunity for interracial experience.

"There are of course several ways in which the inclusive purpose of the Y.W.C.A. is not completely carried out. First, there are separate quarters; second, the electors of the Branch were not invited to the annual meeting to hear the annual reports and to participate in elections; they participate only in Branch elections. Third, the chairman of the Branch Committee should be, but is not, a member of the Board of Directors of the Central and Branch. Fourth, the groups themselves, such as Girl Reserve groups and Employed Girls' Clubs, are not interracial.

"It should be noted here that from the beginning the Branch Secretary who is a Negro is a regular part of the Y.W.C.A. staff and attends all the staff meetings at the Central building.

"The most interesting recent development is connected with the Community Fund's permission to the Y.W.C.A. to put on a drive for a $300,000 building fund. The Y.W.C.A. asked the Council of Social Agencies to conduct a survey to determine the basis for planning the expenditure of that money; for instance, how much of this should go into building and how much into other types of equipment; whether the old building should be enlarged and renovated or a new building erected, etc.

"The Council of Social Agencies undertook this survey and set up a Central Committee and three Subcommittees to conduct it and to make recommendations to the Y.W.C.A. The significant fact in all this for interracial cooperation is that every one of the four committees was interracial in make-up and that I was chosen to be the Technical Director of the entire survey so that the Negro members of the Y.W.C.A. and their future needs would not be overlooked in future planning. This has been a very comprehensive survey and is just now reaching completion. Parts of the recommendations relate to building and physical expansion, but parts of them are designed to correct the tendencies toward racial separation that I mentioned above.

"This is as brief a tale as I could write, but I am sure that the Memphis Y.W.C.A. has a goal of complete interracial cooperation and integration and that it definitely gives evidence that the Y.W.C.A. is a 'movement' rather than a crystallized institution."

New branches for Negroes in cities that have none, new groups formed, race relations courses conducted, opening of a white "Y" cafeteria to Negroes, unsegregated meetings of white and Negro youth, new patterns of relationship—all of these are evidences that there is life stirring. But they are not enough, and the Association does not think so; it is on the march towards a fully Christian association. At its sixteenth National Convention meeting in 1940, the National Convention passed a resolution offered by its National Student Council, asking for the study which is now just completed. That resolution is worth reporting in full:

"Whereas, the National Student Council of the Y.W.C.A. is and has been basically interracial in membership since its organization in 1932; and

"Whereas, there are forces in our nation and world which make for separation of those who differ, or are assumed to differ because of race, cultural, or historical backgrounds; and

"Whereas, the Y.W.C.A. has repeatedly affirmed a belief in cooperative relationships; therefore be it

"Resolved: That the Y.W.C.A.'s of the U.S.A. both nationally and locally endorse and commend the efforts of the student membership toward achieving in the student movement and in society those conditions which provide every individual, regardless of race, religion or nationality, opportunities to participate and share alike in all relationships of life, recognizing that such policy maintained consistently and progressively in practice requires the ultimate elimination of all segregation and discrimination."[6]

Something more of what young people in the Y.W.C.A. are doing

[6] Juliet O. Bell and Helen J. Wilkins, *Interracial Practices in Community Y.W.C.A.'s* (New York: The Woman's Press), 1944.

to achieve this ideal may be seen in reports from the Southern Area Council of the Business and Professional Women and from the Industrial Girls.

Among the business and professional women of the southern area, race relations had been discussed for some years at their annual conference. In 1934, it was decided to invite a Negro leader to the conference. Mrs. Grace Towns Hamilton was invited to come for a short time in the middle of the conference. She came and was so acceptable that she was reinvited for a longer period in 1935. The girls then decided they wanted to know also some "rank and file" Negro girls. For 1937 they invited one Negro leader and two Negro business girls, one from Louisville and one from Richmond. The leader led a study group on race and the two girls participated as delegates. In 1938 and 1939 there was one leader, and there were three girls. In 1939, however, the Negro led a dramatics group with no reference to race; and one of the girls, from New Orleans, was elected to the Southern Area Council to represent Negroes. The conference recommended to the National Council that the Southern Area be empowered to add a representative of the Negro Branches to its formal membership and the recommendation was accepted; the branches were asked to nominate; voting was slight, but a Negro girl from Richmond was elected. In 1941, the girls decided to go further. They therefore passed the following resolution:

"That whereas we recognize the need for the better understanding of relations with minority peoples, it is therefore recommended that representation from these groups be included in the conference leadership . . . (that) each Negro Branch in the southern area having an organized Business and Professional Club be given the opportunity to elect a delegate to the summer conference in 1942 and that the minority representative in the Area Council be included in that number." The resolution was passed, and so was a second, that hereafter the Council would meet only where it could be interracial. So old Jim Crow was quietly laid to rest without a funeral and nobody mourned his passing.[7]

The southern industrial girls have moved along, just a little behind the business and professional group, but on almost identical

[7] Miss Juliet O. Bell, letter, and mimeographed report, 1943.

lines. A few years ago they began inviting a few Negro branches to send representatives as guests. Gradually this invitation was extended to all Negro branches by 1943, but they were still guests. In 1943, some of the girls wanted to take the final step of admitting Negro girls on the same basis as whites, but the majority were not quite ready, so they passed the following half-way measure between the guest status and equal participation: "Whereas, we believe in true universal brotherhood of men, and feel we must have the courage to follow our true convictions, and whereas we believe that in order to build a democratic world there should be no discrimination, it is therefore resolved that the Southern Industrial Area Conference be opened to industrial departments of Negro branches in the South and to Negro Y.W.C.A. industrial groups organized in cities where there is no branch, on a basis of double the representation granted by the system adopted in 1943; that is, two Negro girls from each state or group of states used in the Area Council nominations would be eligible to attend the conference in addition to the representative of Southern Negro branches on the National Industrial Council." The resolution was adopted 28 to 17.[8]

THE Y.M.C.A.

The Y.M.C.A. program among Negroes in its early years had a similar history to the Y.W.C.A. However, the marked lag of its work among Negroes attracted the attention of Mr. Julius Rosenwald in 1912 and he offered to give $25,000 towards a Negro Y.M.C.A. building to any city association that would match this with $75,000. With this stimulus, twenty-five city associations built buildings for Negroes between 1912 and 1933, and these were more or less pace-setters for standards in other cities.[9] There are today Negro Y.M.C.A.'s in 19 cities of the South, including Oklahoma and Texas. Of these associations, 4 have independent local status in cities where other associations exist; the others have Branch status; 14 own their own buildings, 6 do not; the status of 3 in this respect is unknown. Total recorded

---

[8] *Ibid.* Also report of Miss Florence Teague to Industrial Girls' Committee, Nashville Y.W.C.A., 1943. It is interesting to note that one of the white girls most earnest in her plea for full participation by Negroes was member of a labor union comprising workers of both races.

[9] *Negro Youth in City Y.M.C.A.'s,* pp. 6-7.

Negro membership in the southern area is 15,342.[10] This surely is
no small growth. But the Association officers themselves recognized
as early as 1931 that all was not well. As in the Y.W.C.A., despite
progress, great discrepancies in the facilities available to whites and
to Negroes remained; plants, budgets, staff participation in the affairs
of the Associations were all still on a discriminatory basis; and
throughout the South segregation prevailed. A resolution was passed
at the twentieth World's Conference in Cleveland at the session of
North American delegates "That we go on record as urging all Associations to take definite steps towards the goal of making possible
full participation in the Association program without discrimination
as to race, color, or nationality." However, the record of steps to put
the resolution into effect is lacking. In 1942 and 1943, the National
Conference reiterated such principles and urgings; and it had under
way, through its research department, plans for the study of its own
practices. At about the same time, unknown to the Research Council,
the Quadrennial Conference of the Colored Work Department was
passing a resolution of strenuous protest: "It was the conviction of
the Conference that Negroes have arrived at a state of mind which
no longer permits them to accept the inferior and discriminatory
status assigned them within the framework of American Society in
general, and in the Young Men's Christian Association in particular. . . ." Since that time, the study has been made and the closing
paragraph of the findings contains this statement: "In its one hun-
dredth year of Christian character education, it would appear that
the Young Men's Christian Association faces in America perhaps
the sternest challenge of its honorable history." If no local stories of
changing southern practices have yet reached us, yet it is something
that members of such a nation-wide Christian body embracing
southern as well as northern youth of both races have studied their
own practices, weighed them in the balance, found them wanting,
and have faced, not evaded, the challenge.

Branching out of the Y.M.C.A.'s and Y.W.C.A.'s there are also
the Student Christian Associations of the colleges. The details of
their organizational relationships with the Y.M.C.A. and Y.W.C.A.
need not concern us, but the organic relationships enter to some extent

[10] Owen E. Pense, letter, October 13, 1943.

into an understanding of their activities. For instance, up to 1937 there were in the southern Y.M.C.A. area covering ten southern states, two completely separate councils, the white Southern Council and the Negro King's Mountain Southern Council. In 1937, there was a sort of coalition set up between these known as the Southeastern Field Council and operated with one full-time white secretary and one part-time Negro secretary. Their duties were to visit local campuses, counsel students, and set up intercollegiate meetings. They projected two annual summer conferences, one for Negroes at King's Mountain, one for whites at Blue Ridge. These conferences began to exchange fraternal delegates. They had got as far as parallel set-ups with a bridge across the top through the secretaries and between the students through exchange delegates. In 1938, however, the membership of King's Mountain took the initiative in a forward step. They voted their own conference out of existence, setting up instead with the aid of the secretaries an interracial conference to be held at Talladega, Alabama, with Negro students and any white students who would accept their invitation. The Blue Ridge conference for whites only was continued. In the following years through 1942, the Talladega conference was well attended, and those Blue Ridge conference members not yet ready for full fellowship invited some Negro leadership to their conferences. The war temporarily interrupted this development and in 1943 in place of the two conferences, a Leadership Training seminar for officers of both white and Negro Associations was held at Berea College in Kentucky. Opinion was divided as to its value and for 1944 the pattern of having one white and one interracial conference was resumed; but emphasis was placed on the interracial conference.

In recent years other instances of growing interracial fellowship have appeared. Leadership training institutes are being held in various parts of the South and are attended by members of both races; conferences of Negro and white faculty advisors are held jointly, two of them recently meeting "on so-called white territory"; and in 1943 the Student Christian Associations of two states, Tennessee and Kentucky, each held a single state-wide meeting of delegates from all the colleges, white and Negro, on an equal footing and unsegregated.

In Arkansas, Texas, Oklahoma, and Missouri, it is reported the situation is superior in many respects even to this reported from the Southeast, from the point of view of interracial integration and activity in the Student Christian Association Movement.[11]

Only one instance of this can be given:[12]

"At Hollister in the beautiful setting of the Ozark Mountains and the man-made Lake Taneycomo, students from Arkansas, Texas, Oklahoma, and Missouri come together for the Student Christian Association retreat. Of the two hundred students who attend the session, perhaps twenty-five are colored. The situation, however, is ideal; all those attending take part and share in all the activities which include boating, fishing, swimming, tennis, baseball, singing, and folk dancing, and, on the serious side, the morning devotions, quiet hour for meditation, class discussion groups, evening devotions, and lectures. Mixed dancing is taken as a matter of course, and during meal hours members are urged to rotate from table to table so as to become better acquainted with one another.

"There seems to be a tradition that the co-chairmen elected shall be one Negro and one white of opposite sex; meetings proceed as smoothly with one as with the other. . . .

"Transportation to and from the camps is most frequently by private car and buses; the buses stop at strategic points to pick up passengers.

"The townspeople are accustomed to the annual group meetings of whites and Negroes which have been held for the past ten years, and the very meager recreation within the town is available to all.

"Through such meetings as Hollister, suspicion and unfounded stereotypes disappear, mutual respect is gained, and lasting advantages won."

Now and then other organizations join hands with these student groups. For instance in Salisbury, North Carolina, in 1943 a young people's conference was held under the joint auspices of the American Friends Service Committee and the North Carolina Council of Churches to discuss various topics related to the building of a Christian world order. It was the fifth such annual conference to be held

[11] R. Edwin Espey, letter, November, 1943.
[12] Dr. R. C. Minor, letter.

in the South. Livingstone College, Negro, and Catawba College, white, cooperated as hosts, the meetings being held at Catawba. Delegates attended from 31 colleges, 8 Negro colleges and 23 white, and a similar conference is scheduled for the summer of 1944. Meetings were unsegregated and the young people of both races joined freely in all discussions, programs, and recreation. Two of the white girls from the Deep South reported an incident that occurred when they were making their way to Livingstone College. A local white resident of whom they inquired explained to them that Livingstone was a "nigger college" and that they wouldn't go there if they were from the South, they didn't know what they were getting into, and had better go back North where they come from. They told him they knew about Livingstone and that "where they came from" was Louisiana and Georgia.

The Southern Regional office of the Fellowship of Reconciliation also sponsors annual southwide conferences and frequent small gatherings to discuss various aspects of Christianizing the social order. Although inclusive of all ages, these conferences are generally located at or near colleges and attended by a considerable number of college-age young people, men and women, Negro and white. The Fellowship of Reconciliation has also conducted for several years past an interracial work camp each summer in Mississippi, where the work campers have helped to drain and clear a lake for a swimming pool, to build cabins, and to improve grounds for the only camp for colored children known to exist in the state. The Mississippi Federation of Colored Women's clubs has sponsored the undertaking and both white and Negro Mississippians from Jackson have taken a friendly interest in it. In 1943, the work-camp was moved to Nashville where the campers did an extensive painting job for a local community center for Negroes. For 1944, it was invited back to Mississippi for further work there, and accepted the invitation. In these work-camps, under the direction of an adult married couple with some experience in race relations work, young people of both races live and work together as one Christian family, and seek, through freely given manual labor and friendly contact in the communities where they serve, to develop and express their Christian faith in service and brotherhood.[13]

All these bare statements fail to give flesh and blood reality to the very vivid and moving thing that is actually taking place among southern youth. One has to see it, as a field reporter has done, to feel the full force of it—"to see a gay, headlong group of young people in paint-smeared overalls tumbling out of an old delivery truck which has brought them to their work, splashing around with their paint pots in the broiling August sun—when they might have been on vacation—with a dozen or so small Negro boys and girls trailing around behind them, now watching, now trying to help. One has to see them, after the washing up, sharing their home-made meal eaten on whatever tables or benches may be handy, eating with zest of hearty appetites and friendly gay hearts, then gathering around fire-place or piano for the closing sing—white Americans, Japanese Americans, Negro Americans—in happy and self-forgetful fellowship closing their day with worship of a common Father. One has to see two hundred of them, as I have seen them, seated about long tables in a banquet hall—students from fifteen nations and many races, students in the South and of the South, enjoying the fellowship of a common meal, listening to each other's music and exchange of formal greetings, hanging on the words of a Negro speaker challenging them with the problem of building a Christian world of all peoples out of the chaos of war, standing at the end of the evening, hands clasped in a long chain around each table, while a closing prayer is offered in turn by natives of eight different countries each in his own language. One has to see this, saying to himself, 'and these are southern youth, students in the South and of the South, bent on living out their Christianity,' before he can feel the full impact of the tide setting towards the free integration of all our peoples into American life and fellowship and beyond it into world life and fellowship."

COOPERATION ACROSS DENOMINATIONAL LINES

More and more, Christians are seeking to make real again the unity of the Christian family, to recover for the church that unity of spirit and life that characterized the early followers of Jesus. This

[13] Constance Rumbough, letter; M. C. McCulloch, Field Report, 1943-44.

goal has given rise in many countries to the Federation of Churches of different denominations, and beyond these to the vision and first steps toward a World Christian Council. In the United States this trend is reflected in a growing tendency of Christians of different denominational, racial, and cultural groups to seek occasions of fellowship in worship, study, and play, and to work together for those objectives which in spite of differences all good Christians must have in common.

Such a movement cannot be presented in narrow regional terms. But after viewing it in broad outline on a nation-wide scale, we can inquire how the South, white and Negro, is participating in it.

There are in the first place certain world, international, and national associations of Christians which transcend denominational, racial, political, and regional lines and in which Southerners of both races participate. The international organizations include the World Sunday School Association, the International Council of Religious Education, the Y.M.C.A. and Y.W.C.A., the Fellowship of Reconciliation. Among the national bodies are the Home Missions Council, the Foreign Missions Conference, the Missionary Education Movements, the United Council of Church Women, the United Stewardship Council, the Council of Church Boards of Education, the Federal Council of the Churches of Christ in America. With the exception of the Y.M.C.A., the Y.W.C.A. and the Fellowship of Reconciliation, these organizations are all federations, with a membership made of national church denominations rather than individuals. Besides these there are the inter-faith bodies such as the National Conference of Jews and Christians, reaching out to those of closely related faith and ideals.[14]

Membership in these organizations is not restricted by race, nor is participation theoretically limited by it. Their national and international conferences, generally speaking, include representatives of as many races as are in the membership, and are unsegregated. For example, the World Sunday School Association, meeting at Schwenkenfeld, Pennsylvania, May 14-16, 1943, included among its eighty delegates representatives of about twenty countries and of several

[14] The Bahai belong on the border between denominations and interfaith bodies, since their faith seeks to build on and draw together those of all religious faiths.

different races. Members from the southern states took part along with the others in all the meetings and other activities, in none of which there was any segregation. Among its actions, the Conference drew up a statement on Christian Education and Race Relations. This statement was based largely on papers submitted by preliminary local conferences, interracial and interdenominational, one of which was held in Nashville, Tennessee, in April, 1943. Both this preliminary conference and the Schwenkenfeld Conference stressed the necessity that the Christian Church rid itself of race discrimination and race prejudice if it would be fit to serve or even to survive in a shrinking world populated by all races.[15]

At its 1944 annual conference, the Home Missions Council of North America, representing many denominations and all parts of the country, elected as its national secretary for 1945 Mrs. Christine S. Smith of Detroit, a Negro.[16]

The Federal Council of the Churches of Christ in America, as long ago as 1920, expressed its sense of responsibility as a Christian interdenominational and interracial organization by the creation of a Department of Race Relations, headed by a Negro. This department provides materials and guidance for educational, social action, and social service programs in the field of race relations for various types of Church and community groups, promotes the annual observance of Race Relations Sunday and Brotherhood Month, and in other ways works for a solution of racial problems through the practice of a living Christianity. With the re-examination of our own democratic and Christian practices which recent years have brought, however, the Federal Council felt that even more fundamental action was necessary to bring the daily practices of the churches up to the level of their official pronouncements. They therefore created in 1944 a Commission on the Church and Minority Peoples, designed "to assist the churches to appraise themselves in relation to the Christian ideal of human brotherhood and race relations in the new world situation brought about by the war, also to make known concrete experiments of successful interracial adjustments and cooperation, and to overcome scientifically false and non-Christian theories of race."[17]

[15] Florence Teague, letter, 1943; conference reports.
[16] ANP release, January, 1945.
[17] *Interracial News Service,* November, 1943, p. 2.

The Commission has begun its work by a thoroughgoing study of the actual present practices of our churches today, findings of which are not yet complete.

A recent American interdenominational development of a different type is the movement of the Christian Ashrams. They appear to combine aspects suggested by Gandhi's Ashrams in India with the Protestant version of a spiritual "retreat" and something of American conference and camp patterns. In 1940 the first of these Ashrams was held at Blue Ridge in the heart of the Western North Carolina Mountains. It was "more than a religious conference, more than a summer vacation camp for tired Christian workers. Its chief aim was to have a heterogeneous company of followers of Christ live together for two weeks as if the ideas of Jesus were practicable in everyday life. Negroes and whites, Chinese and Japanese, Germans and Japanese representing all classes and callings, have actually lived together in love and with mutual helpfulness and understanding, in spite of their great differences in racial, national, and cultural backgrounds."[18]

WITHIN THE SOUTH

Interdenominationalism was at first rather slow to take hold in the South, and the Federal Council of Churches was widely viewed more or less askance. In the twenties the Department of Race Relations of the Federal Council informally restricted its activities more or less to the northern and western states, leaving to the Commission on Interracial Cooperation in Atlanta the development of a program of race relations activities among church people in the southern area. Today, all this is changed. The published materials of the Department go to many hundreds of southern churches, and its annual conferences on race relations are held unsegregated in southern cities. Race Relations Sunday, sponsored by the Federal Council, is observed by churches throughout the South and was proclaimed in 1944 by two southern governors. The words of these two proclamations bear repeating.

Governor Robert S. Kerr of Oklahoma said, " . . . America has been built through the unified contributions, efforts, and labors of all her citizens, regardless of race, color, political party, or beliefs. . . .

[18] *Interracial News Service,* October, 1941.

Now, therefore, I, Robert S. Kerr, Governor of Oklahoma, do hereby designate February 13, 1944, as Race Relations Sunday and the days immediately thereafter for a period of development of more free interracial and intercultural contacts."

Governor Forrest C. Donnell of Missouri said, " . . . the attainment and maintenance of friendly race relationships is a goal worthy of conscientious endeavor on the part of each member of the respective races which comprise our citizenship . . . I, therefore, proclaim Sunday, February 13, 1944, Race Relations Sunday in Missouri, and the period of thirty days, February 13—March 13, Brotherhood Month in Missouri, and respectfully suggest that the people of our state join in appropriate observance of that Day and period in their respective communities."[19]

Such pronouncements, in the face of current practices, sometimes strike the ear with a curiously hollow ring. Yet they need not therefore be despised as mere hypocrisy. They follow the curious but not unusual pattern in accordance with which we not infrequently announce to the world a great ideal and urge its acceptance upon others, and then later, sometimes a long time later, wake up with a start to the realization that if we really believe what we have been saying we shall have to make some drastic changes in our own practice.

Some such awakening is now taking place in many of our Christian churches, North and South. We can still smile at those who are caught napping, as when we read that "the white ministers of Richmond, Virginia, speaking through their Alliance, recently declared that voting privileges should carry no element of discrimination because of race." They went on to recommend that Negroes serve freely on juries, and be represented on the school board, and serve as policemen.[20] There is some irony in this pronouncement by an alliance of white ministers only. Yet these men are not hypocrites and in time the implications of their own words will dawn on them and refuse to be silenced.

In some parts of the South, the implications have already been perceived and acted upon. A state-wide Ministers' Convocation in Missouri in 1942, attended by ministers from every denomination and

[19] *Interracial News Service*, March, 1944.
[20] *Crisis*, June, 1943, p. 167.

based on the theme "Building Together a Righteous State," included Negro ministers for the first time. Really "building together," the assembled ministers voted to make all future convocations interracial in scope, and elected one of the Negro ministers, who had talked on the program, a member of the Executive Committee.[21]

North Carolina's clergy are also practicing what they preach. At Greensboro on September 23, 1943, the North Carolina Council of Churches voted unanimously to invite Negro denominations of the state to participate in the Council on an equal basis with white churches. "The retiring President of the Council, Bishop Edwin A. Penick, in welcoming the action, pointed out that no change was necessary in the constitution of the Council since from its beginning the Council had existed for the benefit of any church body 'choosing to use it as a channel of counsel and joint Christian expression.' The vote to welcome Negro denominations to this right and privilege, the Bishop said, merely makes it clear that we want the fellowship and cooperation of Negro churches . . . the motion was made on recommendation of the Council's Executive Committee which previous to the Annual Meeting had canvassed the question in consultation with outstanding Negro church leaders of the state." Several white members of the Council spoke strongly for the action, including Dr. H. Shelton Smith of the Duke University School of Religion and Dr. J. B. Cunningham, president of Davidson College.[22] The Charlotte, North Carolina, *News* hailed the action as "a glowing sign of the coming day."[23]

The city-wide federation of churches in Washington, D. C., recently added a Negro to its full-time staff as associate director of Christian Education, the first city federation of churches in the country to take such a step. The appointee, Mrs. Kyles, is a graduate of Oberlin College and has had graduate work at Oberlin Theological Seminary and Columbia University. She was formerly national director of social education and action for the African Methodist Episcopal Zion Church, a large independent Negro denomination.

Back of these large scale developments, there are numberless re-

[21] *Interracial News Service*, May, 1942, p. 2.
[22] Federal Council *Bulletin*, November, 1943, p. 14.
[23] Charlotte, North Carolina, *News*, September 23, 1943.

ports of small occasions of fellowship across denominational and racial lines. From Sullivan County and Williamson County, Tennessee; from Holiday's Cove, West Virginia; from Norfolk, Virginia; from Baltimore, Washington, Nashville, Charleston and other cities come reports of pulpit exchanges, special interracial services, women's group meetings and projects, and young people's exchanges. We can touch on only a few.

In Charleston, South Carolina, cooperation of the churches was sought by the Interracial Committee in the face of rising tensions. On Race Relations Sunday at an interracial interdenominational meeting of church women's groups, an address was given on "The Basis for Enduring Peace," followed by three nights of seminars on the same theme. Both races shared in the open discussion. As one result of this, the Woman's Auxiliary of St. Michael's Protestant Episcopal Church conducted a survey of facilities for Negroes in Charleston, and after the findings were in, sent resolutions to the City Board of Education, the mayor, the county delegation, a senator, and to other churches and church organizations, suggesting lines of action. New members have joined the interracial committee, including a good many young people; an Inter-Faith Group of Roman Catholics, Jews, Unitarians, and Protestants is being formed to study social problems vital to all races and to all creeds; and a joint meeting of the Ministers' Unions of the city was held on "The Mission of the Church to the Post-War World."[24]

In Wilmington, North Carolina, there is an interracial ministerial alliance which meets monthly, alternately in white and Negro churches.[25]

In Nashville, Tennessee, more than 160 white and Negro members of the Nashville Council of Church Women met in November, 1943, at a local Episcopal Church to adopt a constitution and to discuss the price of world peace. The discussion was led by one of the women and an address given by a local minister. As the Council was only formed in March, 1943, this was a remarkable response of the community.[26]

[24] C. S. Ledbetter, letter, April 14, 1943.
[25] *Christian Century*, December 15, 1943.
[26] *Nashville Tennessean*, November 12, 1943.

On a far larger scale and more dramatic was the 1944 Race Relations Sunday meeting at Asbury Methodist Church (Negro) in Washington, D. C. More than 2,000 white, Negro, and Chinese worshippers crowded the church. Several hundred had to stand and scores were turned away. "Marching down the aisles were persons of all ages from white and Negro churches from the Chinese Community Church, Howard and American Universities, and the Central Y.W.C.A." This was the climax of a long series of steps taken cooperatively by the Citizens Committee on Race Relations and the Washington Federation of Churches.[27]

In Baltimore, inspired by Fellowship House in Philadelphia, a group decided in 1942 to start holding an inter-faith, interracial service on Sunday afternoon once a month. This service has been going on for many months now, and other activities and steps towards organization have been added. Regular meetings are now held the first Wednesday in each month at 8:00 P.M. at a Friends' Meeting place, and a series of lectures and discussions on the races of mankind, called "Units for Unity," has just been launched, with an interracial group of 47 Negroes and 75 whites in attendance, coming from four colleges, a high school, and a nurses' training school. A committee is at work to find a permanent site so that the organizations may be placed on a more enduring footing.[28]

A similar project has been sponsored in St. Louis, Missouri, by the Fellowship of Reconciliation with the assistance of the Metropolitan Church Federation. This is an interracial Vesper Service, the first meeting of which was held at the Third Baptist Church on September 24, 1944, with a congregation of 175 Negro, Japanese-American and white Christians.[29]

The Fellowship of Southern Churchmen, an organization of southern Negro and white ministers with headquarters at Chapel Hill, North Carolina, recently made public a statement signed by more than one hundred leading figures in Southern religious and educational life. This statement advocated complete social, political, and

---

[27] *Interracial News Service,* March, 1944.

[28] Florence Kite, Marjorie Penney, and Dan Atwood, letters, February 14, and March 15, 1944.

[29] ANP release, October, 1944.

economic emancipation for the Negro in a world that is seeking true democracy, and declared that "so long as we perpetuate an attitude of race superiority in this country, we crucify man everywhere for a sane and decent world. The hard-won rights of labor are insecure as long as the Negro is excluded from its ranks. The defense of the liberties of this nation is seriously hampered so long as the Negro is not given a just and equitable share in the defense of the freedoms for which we now struggle. . . . We cannot with clean hearts struggle for the Four Freedoms unless we begin practice of them in our land now."[30]

[30] Statement of Fellowship of Southern Churchmen.

INDEX

AAA, 98
Academic work, on race relations, 168
Academy of Medicine of New York, 254
ACIPCO, 261
Adventist Theological Seminary, 293
Adventists, 293-94
Advisory board of libraries, Negroes serving on, 188
A. F. of L. *See* American Federation of Labor
African Methodist Episcopal Zion Church, 330
"Afternoon of Talent, An," 208
Agricultural and Canning Workers, 117
Agricultural Extension Service, in Arkansas, 91-92; mentioned, 90
Agricultural and Industrial College for Negroes, 147
Agricultural and Mechanical State College, 149, 150
Agricultural programs, state, 96 ff.
Agriculture, Department of, 90-92, 96-97; mentioned, 90 ff.
Air Defense, 301
Alabama, A. F. of L. in, 127; church hospitals, 285; FSA Negro borrowers, 95; hospital facilities for Negroes, 234; in Southern Regional Council, 7; Negro branch libraries, 188; Negro Girl Scouts, 192; Negro Health Week, 255; Negro physicians, 256; Negro YWCA, 314; recent welfare programs in, 60; State A and M College, 85; State Committee of the Commission on Interracial Cooperation, 15-16; state health department, 256-62; study of race relations, 154-55; training program for demonstration agents, 91; UMW in, 124; venereal disease, 272; mentioned, 54, 63, 85, 97, 99, 104, 117, 178, 207
Alabama College, study of race relations, 154-55

Alabama Dry Dock Shipbuilding Company, 47
Alabama State Department of Health, 252, 262
Alabama State Prison, 59
Alabama Tuberculosis Association, 260
Alderman, Dr. Edwin A., 143
Allen, Dr. Laurie, 254
Allen-White, 180
Alpha Kappa Alpha Sorority, 16
Amalgamated Clothing Workers, 122
A. M. and N. College for Negroes, 139
Amarillo, Episcopalian meeting, 291
Amendment, Fifteenth, 41
American Association Institute of Race Relations, 27
American Association of Pathologists, 255
American Association of University Women, 89
American Baptist Theological Seminary, 287
American Board of Surgery for District of Columbia, 254
American Cast Iron and Pipe Company, 260, 261
American Church Institute for Negroes, 291
American College of Surgeons, 238, 249
"American Community, The," 162
American Federation of Labor, in Richmond, 126; and Negroes, 124 ff; mentioned, 88, 115, 122, 220
American Friends Service Committee, 323
American Journal of Public Health and the Nation's Health, 264
American Library Association, 186-87
American Mission Association, 20, 100, 101, 173, 175, 219, 222, 258, 306 ff.
American Missionary Association Institute of Race Relations, 312
"American Negro and the War, The," 177
American Nurses Association, 251